MW00627783

The Nexus of Naval Modernization in India and China

THE OXFORD INTERNATIONAL RELATIONS
IN SOUTH ASIA (IRSA)

SERIES EDITORS
Sumit Ganguly and E. Sridharan

After a long period of relative isolation during the Cold War years, contemporary South Asia has grown immensely in its significance in the global political and economic order. This ascendancy has two key dimensions. First, the emergence of India as a potential economic and political power that follows its acquisition of nuclear weapons and its fitful embrace of economic liberalization. Second, the persistent instability along India's borders continues to undermine any attempts at achieving political harmony in the region: fellow nuclear-armed state Pakistan is beset with chronic domestic political upheavals; Afghanistan is paralysed and trapped with internecine warfare and weak political institutions; Sri Lanka is confronted by an uncertain future with a disenchanted Tamil minority; Nepal is caught in a vortex of political and legal uncertainty as it forges a new constitution; and Bangladesh is overwhelmed by a tumultuous political climate.

India's rising position as an important player in global economic and political affairs warrants extra-regional and international attention. The rapidly evolving strategic role and importance of South Asia in the world demands focused analyses of foreign and security policies within and towards the region. The present series addresses these concerns. It consists of original, theoretically grounded, empirically rich, timely, and topical volumes oriented towards contemporary and future developments in one of the most populous and diverse corners of the world.

Sumit Ganguly is professor of political science and Rabindranath Tagore Chair in Indian Cultures and Civilizations, Indiana University, Bloomington, USA.

E. Sridharan is academic director, University of Pennsylvania Institute for the Advanced Study of India, New Delhi.

The Nexus of Naval Modernization in India and China

Strategic Rivalry and the Evolution of Maritime Power

CHRISTOPHER K. COLLEY

Assistant Professor of Security Studies at the National Defense College of the United Arab Emirates. The opinions expressed in this book are those of the author and do not reflect the views of the National Defense College, or the United Arab Emirates government.

OXFORD
UNIVERSITY PRESS

Great Clarendon Street, Oxford, ox2 6dp,
United Kingdom

Oxford University Press is a department of the University of Oxford.
It furthers the University's objective of excellence in research, scholarship,
and education by publishing worldwide. Oxford is a registered trade mark of
Oxford University Press in the UK and in certain other countries

© Oxford University Press 2022

The moral rights of the author have been asserted

First Edition published in 2022

Published in the United States of America by Oxford University Press
198 Madison Avenue, New York, NY 10016, United States of America

British Library Cataloguing in Publication Data

Data available

Library of Congress Control Number: 2022939657

ISBN 978-0-19-286559-5

DOI: 10.1093/oso/9780192865595.001.0001

This book is dedicated to my parents David and Mary Liz Colley and my wife Zhaoya Colley. All three have constantly been there for me and have always encouraged me to strive for excellence. Their never-ending love and support was crucial in the writing and researching of this book.

Contents

Acknowledgements

This book has its origins in my Master's thesis on the Chinese navy that I wrote while a graduate student at Renmin University of China from 2006 to 2008. I then further pursued the study of maritime security for my doctoral dissertation at Indiana University Bloomington. Over the years I have benefitted enormously from interactions and friendships with both scholarly and military professionals in China, India, and the U.S. In particular I would like to thank my dissertation Chair, Professor Sumit Ganguly, for his considerable interest, time, and support over the years. The advice of other faculty including David Fidler, William Thompson, and Adam Liff, as well as Dr Andrew Scobell was extremely helpful. Their time and dedication to reading the full manuscript and providing suggestions and guidance was essential to the entire process. I deeply appreciate their commitment. I am indebted to the dozens of people whose names I cannot acknowledge, but who gave me their time and agreed to be interviewed for this project. Their knowledge and experience strengthened this book. I would also like to thank the Observer Research Foundation in New Delhi for providing me with a base during the summer of 2016. Furthermore, I would like to acknowledge the support of my classmates at IU. Finally, I am grateful for the support of my family. My wife Zhaoya who was with me for all of the ups and downs during my studies in China, India, and the U.S. was always there to hear my frustrations as well as celebrate the high points. My parents, David and Mary Liz Colley who always encouraged me and have also always been there for me. They read different versions of the manuscript and provided invaluable advice. While I have benefitted enormously from the help of others any errors in the text are my own.

Christopher K. Colley
Abu Dhabi
March 2022

Introduction

The Puzzle and Introduction

In December 2015, the Chinese government announced construction of its first overseas naval base in the African country of Djibouti, breaking with the long-time Chinese practice of avoiding overseas military activities that it previously derided as examples of colonialism and hegemonic behaviour. Concurrently, the Indian navy (IN) was testing its newest aircraft carrier in the Indian Ocean, while also building its own nuclear-powered submarines. These activities were taking place while other naval powers were actively downsizing their fleets (Farmer 2016). While European powers see less of a need for strong navies, China and India are pursuing naval modernization and are deliberately acquiring and building blue water navies. Both states have been traditional land powers for nearly their entire modern history as nation-states. These developments raise the question of why rising great powers decide to undertake sustained naval modernization?

The process of building a robust navy is an enormous undertaking. States that decide to make the transition from coastal 'brown water' or 'green water' navies to modern 'blue water' navies, with the ability to project seapower on the open oceans, are making a massive economic, political, and security commitment.[1] The ability to project naval power thousands of miles from one's homeports is not common. Few states in the international system have the financial means to project that power, and even fewer, who have the economic ability, follow through with military strategies that call for power projection beyond a few token ships that can show the flag in distant ports. Arguments for naval modernization

---

[1] A brown water fleet is often composed of small littoral craft, and is not designed to venture beyond a state's immediate coastal waters. A green water naval is also a coastal navy, but has limited ability to venture beyond the coast. A blue water fleet is made up of large ocean-going warships that are designed to project power on the high seas thousands of miles from their home bases.

The Nexus of Naval Modernization in India and China. Christopher K. Colley, Oxford University Press. © Oxford University Press 2022. DOI: 10.1093/oso/9780192865595.003.0001

that are based on bureaucratic politics models, nationalism, the security dilemma, or force replenishment, while having some validity on their own, are not sufficient. This book seeks to explain the driving causes of naval modernization over the past 30 years. In particular, it examines the case studies of two traditional land powers, China and India, and poses the crucial question as to why these two states have embarked on naval modernization? The core argument of this book is that strategic rivalry is the most important driver of this phenomenon and counter-arguments are only partial explanations. In the absence of a strategic rivalry, states do not feel compelled to develop powerful navies.

As a strategic rivalry evolves and starts to take on maritime dimensions, and is maintained through periods of escalation, decision makers' threat perceptions also increase. This leads to naval modernization, especially when a state bolsters its naval presence in its rival's backyard. Crucial to this argument are the periods of intense escalation or critical junctures within a rivalry. These junctures act as political shocks that have an enormous impact on decision makers and are extremely influential to understanding fluctuation in a rivalry (Mansour and Thompson 2020). While all rivalries experience periods of relative stability, the intense periods of escalation are vital to understanding why states pursue naval power. In other words, naval modernization is driven by increasing threat perceptions emanating from a rival's naval power.

Strategic rivalry in the maritime domain, which leads to naval modernization in one state, also has the ability to drive naval modernization in other states. It has been established that many rivalries are interconnected. As a state builds naval power to counter one rival, other rivals may feel threatened and embark on their own naval modernization programmes (Thompson 1999).

As Model I.1 indicates, critical junctures in the form of rivalry escalation at sea play a crucial role in increasing threat perceptions. This book utilizes the punctuated equilibrium model of rivalry maintenance and escalation. Key to this model is the idea that once a rivalry is initiated it enters a 'lock-in stage' that experiences periods of stability, as well as episodes of significant escalation (Diehl and Goertz 2000).[2] Critical junctures are a key factor in my model. In the punctuated equilibrium model,

---

[2] Please see the argument chapter for a detailed analysis of the punctuated equilibrium model.

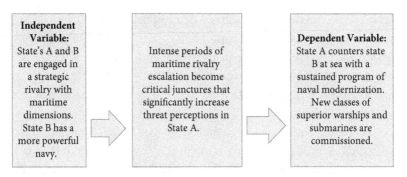

Model I.1   Main Causal Models. Strategic Rivalry as a Cause of Naval Modernization

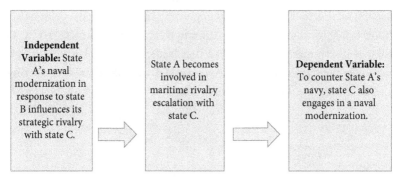

Model I.2   Linkages between Strategic Rivalries and Naval Modernization

not all episodes of escalation are equal. When escalation is intense it can significantly increase decision makers' threat perceptions. I classify these as critical junctures in the rivalry. These episodes stand out in the course of the rivalry's history and can lead to periods of force mobilization and actions just short of kinetic warfare. It is these critical junctures that play a prominent role in causing naval modernization and this book analyses them in the two cases under review.

Model I.2 demonstrates that the rivalry between states A and B is linked to state A's rivalry with state C, thus demonstrating the linkages between rivalries, and resulting in a drive for naval modernization among the various states. In Model I.2 the causal path is very similar to Model I.1. In Model I.2, as state A continues to develop a more robust navy, its increasing naval power raises threat perceptions in state C, which has a weaker navy. State C then embarks on its own naval modernization pro-gramme in order to defend against state A. Key to this process is the inter-connected nature of the strategic rivalries. The role of rivalry escalation and critical junctures repeats itself and produces another punctuated equilibrium model.[3]

Empirically, this book will demonstrate that China's strategic rivalry with the U.S. produces periods of intense rivalry escalation in the mari-time domain and these are critical junctures that cause naval moderniza-tion in China. China's rising naval power also causes a significant increase in maritime rivalry escalation in China's strategic rivalry with India. This causes threat perceptions in New Delhi to soar, leading to naval modern-ization in India. Thus, the Sino/U.S. and Sino/Indian strategic rivalries are linked together with each rivalry driving naval modernization. This book will show that Chinese decision makers have identified the U.S. as their primary maritime rival, and that leaders in India have identified China as their primary rival. Importantly, I will also demonstrate how Indian actions are linked to Chinese attempts to catch up with the U.S.

---

[3] This is not exactly the same as a rivalry triangle, which will be discussed in subsequent chapters.

1

Main Themes and
Competing Arguments

While the core argument advanced in this book was presented in the
introduction, the process of naval modernization and its drivers requires
both an examination of competing arguments, and a discussion of some
of the different types of modernization and how different strategies of
modernization play out. This chapter provides a discussion of the differ-
ences between spatial and positional rivalries, and why they matter. I also
include a discussion of two types of naval strategy, those consistent with
the writings of Julian Corbett that are centred on coastal and near seas
defence, and Alfred Mahan inspired navies that seek power projection.
In the second section, I point out that rivalry as a driver of naval modernization is frequently taken for granted and few explain what they mean by
'rivalry' when discussing maritime rivalries. In this section I also explain
how I know if my argument is correct, as well as discuss the importance
of critical junctures. The third part of the chapter deals with competing
drivers of naval modernization with attention paid to drivers based on
nationalism, bureaucratic politics models, and the security dilemma. The
fourth section discusses the research design of this book. The chapter
concludes with a literature review.

Mahan and Corbett

Naval modernization is also closely tied to the financial resources a state
has at its disposal. A state that is unable to counter its maritime rival
on the high seas is more likely to opt for a strategy of access denial, in
which a state utilizes its relatively limited resources to develop a navy that
can protect its interests out to roughly 100–200 miles. Such a strategy is

The Nexus of Naval Modernization in India and China. Christopher K. Colley, Oxford University Press. © Oxford
University Press 2022. DOI: 10.1093/oso/9780192865595.003.0002

consistent with the maritime strategy advocated by Julian Corbett. This approach differs from that advocated by Alfred Mahan, who advocated blue water capable battle fleets (Till 2013). If a maritime rivalry is maintained and has regular periods of escalation, and a state has the financial ability to buy or develop a blue water fleet, it will likely do so. Model 1.1 captures the stages of naval modernization, which are closely related to economic resources.

While details of Mahan's and Corbett's theories are found below, it is important to briefly explain their respective arguments. Mahan believed that a core mission of a navy was to establish command of the sea and deny its use by rival powers. In addition, a navy's purpose was to project power and to establish a form of regional hegemony. The ability to secure access to the ocean for commercial reasons was another key component for Mahan who also stressed the need for overseas bases as a way to further control the open oceans (Mahan 1987; Yoshihara and Holmes 2018). In contrast to Mahan, Corbett saw the limitations of naval power and although he viewed seapower as important, he did not believe it was essential to warfare. Perhaps the greatest area of disagreement between Mahan

Stage 1. Corbettian influence

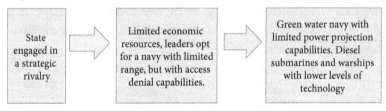

Stage 2. Mahanian influence

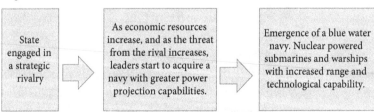

Model 1.1 Stages of Strategic Rivalry and the Evolution of Naval Modernization

and Corbett was in Corbett's belief in the utility of asymmetric warfare. While great powers might have the ability to pursue powerful blue ocean fleets, Corbett called for smaller, faster coastal fleets that could defend a state's coastal assets and deter a larger more powerful navy from attacking a weaker state. Key to his strategy was a state's relatively limited economic ability to build expensive warships. Corbett also did not call for foreign bases to exercise sea control in the open ocean (Corbett 1988; Till 2013).

This book does not take a monocausal approach to naval modernization and engages in theoretical competition. Other competing explanations do have some limited utility, but on their own they are insufficient to cause significant and sustained naval modernization. As will be discussed at length below, arguments based on bureaucratic politics, which stress that decisions by governments are the result of competition between various players and organizations which strive to have their narrow interests adopted by leaders, are not well supported by either the academic literature or the extensive fieldwork undertaken for this book. Explanations centred on nationalism, in which decisions are made as the result of the state or the leadership attempting to enact certain policies or build specific platforms for national prestige, do not hold up well to academic scrutiny. Strategic rivalries are the driving force that calls for naval modernization.[1] The alternative explanations are best understood as secondary causes.

Taking Rivalry for Granted

There has yet to be a compelling theoretically informed comparative study that addresses the puzzle of why these two states have opted for naval modernization. The vast majority of the work has been centred on policy analysis or it tends to view naval modernization in isolation and does not attempt to connect it with relevant theoretical literature.[2] This

---

[1] A core component of naval modernization is the acquisition of a more powerful and technologically sophisticated fleet. Evidence of this can be found in modern destroyers, frigates, and corvettes, as well as diesel-electric and nuclear-powered submarines. Please see the research design section of this chapter and Chapter 2 for a more detailed explanation for what constitutes naval modernization.

[2] Please see the literature review.

book seeks to fill this gap and argues that naval modernization does not happen by chance. For a state to devote the necessary resources to such an endeavour, it must perceive a clear and present danger from a rival state. In other words, understanding the dynamics of rivalries and the perceived threat environment is crucial to explaining naval modernization. While the argument that naval modernization is driven by rivalry may seem to be obvious, there has yet to be a detailed theoretical study that provides a granular analysis of the drivers. Too often scholars and policy analysts take rivalry for granted, and do not attempt to provide a rigorous examination of the actual links associated with rivalry and naval modernization. This book fills this void.

Strategic rivalry is measured primarily through episodes of rivalry maintenance and escalation and statements from leaders that reinforce perceptions of rivalry. Crucially, variations in rivalry intensity are directly related to naval modernization. Critical junctures have a much greater causal effect on naval modernization than do events that are considered regular rivalry maintenance. I have constructed two datasets on the rivalries that are the subject of this work and utilize the 'punctuated equilibrium model' of rivalry maintenance and escalation. In particular, I have combed through various sources for the period from 1991 to 2020 in order to ascertain what constitutes maintenance and escalation. If an event is perceived as threatening to one state this can take the form of maintenance or escalation. For events that are relatively mundane, I consider these to be general maintenance of the rivalry. In other words, they sustain the rivalry, but they do not result in any major diplomatic or military response. For events to be considered an episode of escalation, they must increase decision makers' threat perceptions to the point that they may cause a major diplomatic crisis, or even military mobilization. I classify the most severe points of escalation as critical junctures. I derive this classification from both documents that examine these episodes and my interviews in which experts were asked to comment on the severity of specific points of escalation. By speaking with experts and examining documents, I have been able to find compelling evidence that strategic rivalries have been a main driver of naval modernization. Previous studies have mentioned the role of rivalry in naval modernization, however, they have taken the role of rivalry for granted, or have not specified what they mean by 'rivalry'. These studies have also failed to examine any variation in rivalry and how this manifests itself in terms of threat perceptions and subsequent acquisition of naval assets.

Spatial and Positional Rivalries

As mentioned in the introduction, developing a powerful navy is a rare event. Many states are engaged in strategic rivalries, but few of these rivalries cause naval modernization. In addition, most rivalries are not global. The two rivalries under review in this book (Sino/U.S. and Sino/Indian) have evolved from spatial rivalries to both spatial and positional rivalries. In a spatial rivalry, states tend to contest the control of various pieces of territory, while positional rivals compete for influence and prestige within a system or subsystem (Colaresi et al. 2007). While both rivalries examined here are still concerned with spatial aspects, they are increasingly contesting influence and prestige within a subsystem in Asia.[3] I argue that as both of these rivalries have experienced points of significant escalation, and as the states involved have become more powerful, the rivalries have increasingly taken on maritime dimensions, especially with the Sino/U.S. rivalry spilling over into the Sino/Indian rivalry. Crucially, higher levels of GDP have enabled the states to purchase and construct more powerful navies that increasingly engage in rivalry maintenance and escalation with the state's strategic rivals.

A major contribution of this book is to demonstrate through qualitative methods how the rivalries under review shifted to the maritime domain. Through a granular qualitative approach, I am able to show why critical junctures in the rivalries produced calls for naval modernization that were designed to counter a strategic rival at sea.

How Would We Know if Rivalry Is Not the Cause?

An essential aspect of this book is whether my argument based on strategic rivalry is correct? How do I know that my argument is the best explanation, and of equal importance, if it is false, how do I know others

---

[3] Although the Sino/U.S. rivalry is evolving into a more global rivalry.

are correct? There are several approaches I take to ascertain the drivers behind naval modernization in this study.

One way to determine if my argument is without merit would be if we witnessed a sustainable increase in tensions in the rivalry, while at the same time there was a prolonged decrease in naval modernization. In other words, the cause was not leading to the supposed effect. Another challenge could be a situation in reverse where a sustained decrease in tensions in the rivalry was matched with a sustained increase in naval modernization. What we see over the period under review is a sustained rivalry with significant periods of escalation that is matched with a constant increase in naval modernization. This modernization cannot be mistaken for force replenishment as larger, more powerful, and much more lethal platforms and submarines are taking to the seas in both cases. Even when controlling for nationalism and bureaucratic politics, there is still a rivalry and naval modernization. I control for each of these by examining specific periods of the rivalry and analysing the multiple drivers. For example, in the China case I focus on the drivers of the nuclear submarine programme in the 1990s and dig into the evidence that supports or refutes each competing driver.

In addition, I critically examine the most compelling counterarguments to the drivers of naval modernization in my two cases through close readings of open-source official government publications and other materials both in English and, in the case of China, Mandarin. Evidence supporting each counterargument is carefully scrutinized for its logic and the context of the period in which it was written or spoken as in a formal policy speech. Second, I review articles and publications from scholars and analysts whose expertise is maritime security and, in particular, naval modernization. While reviewing these sources I weigh the evidence for and against each possible driver. In each case I found informed writings from the resident in-country experts who enjoy greater access to centres of decision-making. Third, I analyse what international scholars and other experts (for example, defence officials) say and write about the topic.

Finally, my in-depth interviews with experts in the field (China, India, the U.S., and Australia) provided enormous insight into primary and secondary drivers of naval modernization. On the crucial question of knowing the veracity of my argument, I specifically look for counterarguments and competing explanations that would discredit strategic rivalry. For example, if I find evidence that nationalism is the primary driver, I not only look for supporting documents and other forms of evidence, but I also ask my sources to directly comment on this. If the evidence is greater for this explanation, then my argument based on strategic rivalry loses explanatory power. As will be elaborated on in the case study chapters, nationalism does have some utility in the case of aircraft carriers.

Crucially, this project does not claim that the process of naval modernization is strictly monocausal. The competing drivers listed above do have explanatory power, but on their own, they do not fully explain naval modernization in the cases examined. However, when combined with strategic rivalry, they provide a more robust explanation for naval modernization. Importantly, I argue that strategic rivalry is the *best explanation* and a necessary condition, but is not the only explanation. As will be demonstrated, the evidence gathered for this project points to strategic rivalry as the strongest explanation. On their own, the other potential drivers do not offer convincing explanations.

I confine this study to the period from 1991 until 2020. This period witnessed the strategic rivalries between China and the U. S., and India and China, and progresses through various episodes of escalation and maintenance. Of equal importance, it also witnessed the Sino/U.S. strategic rivalry spill into the Sino/Indian strategic rivalry, as Chinese naval modernization directly influenced Indian decisions to develop naval power. The variation in the rivalries produced different stages and periods of naval modernization. The process of naval asset acquisition is also heavily influenced by the economic resources available to the state; this is measured through GDP. When a state has low levels of GDP, and is involved in a rivalry, it is more likely to pursue a naval modernization programme based on access denial. When it has higher levels of GDP, it is more inclined to invest in hardware that is capable of projecting power and achieving regional hegemony. This is not to suggest that wealthy states automatically seek regional hegemony, but if they are involved in a strategic rivalry that has maritime dimensions, they are more likely to develop powerful navies that have the ability to project power.

Importance of Critical Junctures

I demonstrate the outcome of these rivalries empirically through naval modernization. This is best measured both quantitatively and qualitatively. For rivalry escalation and maintenance, I chart disputes and points of conflict over the period under review. Through qualitative research, I explain which episodes constitute major points of escalation and critical junctures and which ones were less intense. Critical junctures are important in helping to establish causality by focusing on key events that mark turning points in history. They also help to overcome the challenge of where to start a point of analysis, otherwise researchers may be forced to go back in time for alternate causes that explain specific events or outcomes (Mahoney 2001). Capoccia and Kelemen define critical junctures as 'relatively short periods of time during which there is a substantial heightened probability that an agent's choices will affect the outcome of interest' (Capoccia and Kelemen 2007. P 348). While Mahoney defines them as 'choice points when a particular option is adopted from among two or more alternatives ... once adopted it becomes progressively more difficult to return to the initial point when multiple alternates were still available' (Mahoney 2001. P 113). These junctures are critical because they force various institutional arrangements on particular paths that are very difficult to alter once they are set in motion and constitute the origins of many path-dependent processes (Pierson 2004). Importantly, choices that are the product of critical junctures frequently eliminate alternative options and can create groups and institutions that generate a self-reinforcing and path-dependent process (Capoccia and Kelemen 2007). As will be demonstrated in this book, there are several points in the time frame under review that constitute critical junctures and that played critical roles in determining naval modernization.

Contribution

This study contributes to the field in several ways. In the strategic rivalry literature, scholars have demonstrated that rivals may increase defence spending to counter a rival. The punctuated equilibrium model of rivalry maintenance provides a solid understanding on how maintenance and escalation can occur. This study reinforces this theoretical argument with two new empirical cases: contemporary China and India. These cases are significant as both states are rising powers and there is an acute lack of scholarship on what is directly driving both states naval modernization. My main contribution is that I add to the knowledge of rivalry escalation and maintenance and demonstrate that rivalry is a key driver of naval modernization. I also demonstrate that the interconnected nature of the Sino/U.S. and Sino/Indian strategic rivalries is crucial to naval modernization in India. While the rapid development of the People's Liberation Army Navy (PLAN) is aimed at the U.S., it is also the main driver of India's naval modernization. On naval modernization, I show how it varies with threat perception and how it can transform from a force centred on green water forces, to one that seeks regional hegemony through the pursuit of naval power projection. Furthermore, I also show how the Sino/Indian rivalry evolved from a spatial to a positional rivalry as India shifted towards a more regional/ Indian Ocean Region (IOR) focus that required a much stronger navy that is capable of providing a credible deterrent to the PLAN.[4] I also contribute to the policy and area studies fields by providing a fine-grained analysis on Chinese and Indian security. This book also makes a substantial contribution to security and policy studies by explaining what is driving the naval development of two rising great powers.

Policy Contribution

While this book is not directly focused on policy, it does carry significant implications for policymakers. Understanding what drives naval modernization in China and India is of crucial importance in international security. The policy community may not be as interested in the theoretical contributions of this research, but the empirical findings and the critical junctures of each case will likely be very important. This book can provide policymakers in multiple states with a stake in both East and

---

[4] The Sino-Indian rivalry has always had elements of a positional rivalry, but it is only in the last 25 years that both states have had the economic and maritime capability to significantly extend the rivalry into the IOR (please see Garver 2001).

South Asian security, with a theoretically informed way of understanding naval modernization. Many of the explanations and competing explanations are of value and may challenge previously held ideas about each states' navy.[5] The major policy contribution is found in the Conclusion of the book.

What Should We Be Looking For?

Specifically, we should be looking for empirical evidence that connects rivalry maintenance and escalation to naval modernization. How have critical junctures derived from rival escalation influenced this process? What kind of evidence is available to support the argument that rivalry escalation drives naval modernization? What types of platforms were commissioned by each respective state to defend against a strategic rival? Are these vessels sufficient to dissuade the rival from encroaching in the state's backyard, or are modernization efforts not successful in this regard? In terms of rivalry linkages, we should examine evidence that China's naval modernization has caused India to signal China out as a main driver of Indian naval modernization. We should also search for evidence that shows a more modern PLAN encroaching into India's sphere of influence and engaging in rivalry escalation. The two cases provide us with rich data and a period that allows for an in-depth examination of naval modernization taking place in the context of a strategic rivalry.

Organization of Book

This book is organized into five chapters. In this first chapter, I lay out the puzzle and discuss some of the major competing arguments for naval modernization. This chapter also presents the research design of the project. The chapter concludes with a literature review, which provides an analysis of naval modernization as well as an overview of what leading

---

[5] While the majority of individuals interviewed for this project were in the academic and think-tank fields, those who worked in government expressed to this author that the projects findings are very important to various agencies that deal with naval modernization.

scholars have contributed to our knowledge of the two cases under review. Chapter 2 focuses on the main argument of the book: strategic rivalry as the best explanation for naval modernization. This section details the causal argument of naval modernization and explains why strategic rivalry is the best way to understand this phenomenon. In addition, the interconnected nature of the rivalries and how this contributes to naval modernization is discussed. This chapter also examines the rivalry research programme. The last two chapters are empirical case studies of China and India. Chapter 3 is devoted to Indian naval modernization and covers the period under review. Chapter 4 focuses on Chinese naval modernization. Because the Chinese case makes use of more data, I break it into two sections. The first section examines the years from 1991 until 2005, when the Chinese navy (PLAN) had more of a Corbettian approach to modernization. The second part focuses on the PLAN from 2006 until 2020, when the PLAN started to exhibit more Mahanian characteristics. Chapter 5 is the conclusion and has several policy recommendations for the states involved in the rivalries.

Competing Explanations

The following rival explanations for naval modernization are examined throughout the book and specific attention was devoted to them during interviews. These explanations do have various degrees of utility when either combined or embedded in a rivalry. However, on their own they have significant limitations in their explanatory power.

The Security Dilemma Argument

The security dilemma results from the inherent uncertainty about an adversary's intentions, which leads leaders to conclude the worst possible outcome if a state fails to build up one's own military power. Adversaries often perceive another state's actions as threatening and this is compounded by the fact that most weapons systems can be used for both offensive and defensive operations (Jervis 1978). Key to this process is that a threatened state will respond to an arms build-up with its own arms build-up. These measures are then perceived as threatening to the state that initiated the build-up, thus causing that state to continue military modernization in an action-reaction cycle. In practice, the theory can have different levels of intensity depending on whether the military technology is advantageous to offense or defence (Schweller 2010). At the centre of this dilemma is the idea that actions states take to increase their security often induce a counter response from an adversary that results in a decrease in security and an arms competition between the two sides (Levy and Thompson 2010; Jervis 1978; Liff and Ikenberry 2014). While this definition is straightforward, the security dilemma is frequently loosely defined or stretched, twisted, and misused. Tang argues that it is often misguided and incorrectly applied (Tang 2009).

The two cases under review cannot be explained by the security dilemma that dictates that if state A arms, then state B will arm to counter state A. State A will then continue to arm against state B as a reaction to B's arming against state A and this process will continue in an action-reaction cycle. In the case of India's naval modernization, I argue that it is primarily driven by Chinese naval developments. Crucially, I argue that China's naval modernization is driven, not by India, but by the American navy. For the security dilemma to be effective, China would have to arm against India and not the U.S. In other words, India is arming against China, which is arming against the U.S. In the security dilemma one finds uncertainty in the other side's intentions. In a rivalry, one already identifies the other side as an enemy and therefore believes its intentions to be inherently and unambiguously hostile; this is a major difference between the two explanations. Scholars who view Chinese and Indian naval modernization as a case of the security dilemma do not clearly demonstrate that *both sides* are arming in response to the other. While the Chinese and Indians are engaged in a strategic rivalry, the causal arrow of naval modernization points one way, and not both ways as the security dilemma would predict. The Chinese may be very wary of the Indian navy in the IOR, as well as its increasing forays into the South China Sea and Pacific Oceans, however the rivalry between Beijing and Washington is the primary driver of Chinese naval modernization. The Chinese are attempting to develop a navy that is capable of inflicting severe damage on the American navy, this would also be sufficient to damage the Indian navy.

While not the main focus of this book, it is important to note that there is limited evidence that Washington was actively arming against China during the period under review. From 2001 to 2015, the U.S. was engaged in the War on Terror and while China may have been deemed a 'strategic competitor' by the George W. Bush administration (Baum 2001), with the exception of a few systems that have yet to become fully operational, there is little hard evidence that specific American naval platforms were being devised with China in mind. Most of the new platforms are for general purposes that would also be sufficient for deterring China. O'Rourke has pointed out that new systems on the Gerald Ford class aircraft carriers and Virginia class nuclear attack submarines may be partially intended to counter Chinese anti-access warfare, but these are modifications on previously ordered platforms that have been in the development stages for years, if not decades. These warships would have been commissioned regardless of a perceived threat from China (O'Rourke 2016). James Holmes of the U.S. Naval War College agrees that while Beijing is building platforms and capabilities to counter the American navy, Washington is not deliberately building China-specific platforms. He has argued that 'Successive U.S. administrations ... have deliberately avoided wholeheartedly competing with China' (Holmes 2012. P 137). With this said, since 2001 Washington has increasingly directed its attention towards the Asia-Pacific. With direct access to former senior George W. Bush and Obama administration figures, including former Defense Secretary Rumsfeld's personal archive, Nina Silove has demonstrated that Washington was strategically tilting towards Asia, and China in particular, since 2001. However, this 'pivot before the pivot' consisted of relocating strategic resources to the Pacific, and *not* building specific naval platforms to counter Chinese platforms, as would be consistent in a security dilemma scenario (Silove 2016).[6] The China chapter will explore in depth the small number of platforms that may be influenced by China and will discuss the role of the Trump administration in this process.

---

[6] Multiple active duty and retired military personnel support the argument that most of the American military's new weapon systems are not designed solely for China. Some of the weapons systems, for example the new SSNs, would certainly be useful in any China contingency, but they are not built specifically to counter China. Author's interviews. Beijing 2016–2017.

Nationalism/Rising Power Argument

Nationalism is a powerful tool for mobilizing both resources and people. If a state seeks prestige in the international system, it may embark on a naval modernization programme to demonstrate its power to rival states, while at the same time showing its own people that it can defend the nation's interest. Crucial to this argument is the ability to both measure and identify what nationalism is and how it influences a state. The ability to conceptualize nationalism is difficult because embedded in the concept is the rising power argument. Rising powers recognize the status and prestige that is commensurate with a strong navy that is capable of projecting power at great distances. In order to demonstrate power projection to their neighbours and other potential rivals, they embark on a naval modernization programme that will provide them with the ability to project force to distant lands and to protect their political, economic, and strategic interests on the high seas. The main deficiency with this argument is the fact that nationalism is very difficult not only to conceptualize, but also to operationalize and measure.

Nationalism can play a contributing cause of rivalry, although on its own, it is insufficient to cause rivalry onset. The process of 'othering' a specific state as an 'out-group' can be a contributing factor in rivalry and can play a role in rivalry maintenance. For example, the strong anti-China and racially tinged rhetoric from the Trump administration has exacerbated the Sino-U.S. rivalry and have caused a significant increase in negative perceptions of China amongst the American public (Silver et al. 2020).

Robert Ross has argued that naval nationalism has frequently driven continental powers to develop strong surface fleets. In states as diverse as Napoleon's France, Germany at the end of the 19th century, Russia in the late 19th and early 20th centuries, as well as the USSR in the 1970s, and Imperial Japan in the early 20th century, naval nationalism according to Ross, was the driving force. In the contemporary period, he argues it is the driver behind China's naval modernization. He views this form of nationalism as generating prestige projects as well as a force that pressures elites to modernize the navy (Ross 2009). Ross' explanation has come under attack by those who believe he underplays China's strategic environment and does not pay sufficient attention to China's changing threat environment. Glosny and Saunders argue that his explanation is 'unconvincing' and that the causal role is underdeveloped. In addition, they point out that he lacks a definition of nationalism (Glosny and Saunders 2010). The IR literature also casts doubt on the nationalism argument that public opinion forces elites to build powerful navies. Public opinion may have the ability to constrain the options available to leaders, but it does not dictate or drive strategic decisions (Baum and Potter 2008). Interestingly, Till has argued that the navy needs public support, and it is the government that lobbies the public to support naval modernization. In this argument, the public needs to be convinced that a stronger navy provides value in preserving security and prosperity (Till 2013). Zhao Suisheng has argued that China currently fosters a 'pragmatic nationalism' where the state promotes political and social stability as well as guiding the process of identity formation through forms of 'invented histories and traditions' (Zhao 2004. P 29). How this causes naval modernization is not easily demonstrated.

Scholars who have studied nationalism in China and India have tended to focus on religious, ethnic, and linguistic nationalism in India (Jaffrelot 2011; Jaffrelot 2007; Varshney 2003) and the states' attempts to foster and control nationalism in China (Gries 2004; Wang 2014; Zhao 2004). Fundamentally, for nationalism to be transformed into a direct cause of naval modernization, one would have to measure it and demonstrate that it places enormous pressure on the state to dedicate tens of billions of dollars towards developing a navy. Some scholars have attempted to measure nationalism in China, but their results have not increased support for a form of naval nationalism. Tang and Darr have argued that China has the highest levels of nationalism in the world, but they do not explain how this influences security policy (Tang and Darr 2012).

The common narrative of 'rising nationalism' in China has been refuted by Johnston, who demonstrates through a time-series survey dataset, that at least in Beijing, nationalism is not rising and has been declining over the past two decades. In fact, negative feelings towards the U.S. and Japan actually declined from 1998 to 2009, and then levelled off. If nationalism is in fact deceasing, it is difficult to argue that it is putting pressure on leaders to build up their navies (Johnston 2016/2017).[7]

---

[7] For a greater discussion please see the section on China's aircraft carrier in Chapter 4.

Weiss has argued that the authorities in Beijing are able to control and prevent various forms of nationalist protest. For example, there has never been a nationalist protest over the highly sensitive Taiwan issue. Weiss writes that nationalist protests are used by the government in diplomatic manoeuvrings with foreign states (Weiss 2014). Weiss' argument that nationalism can be controlled by the government was supported by nearly every expert interviewed for this book. It is difficult to prove that a state that is capable of preventing nationalist protest over an issue with such a high saliency level as Taiwan would then succumb to nationalist pressure to spend hundreds of billions of dollars on a navy.

Despite the methodological liabilities associated with nationalism as an explanation for naval modernization, it is not entirely without merit. Experts interviewed for this book disagreed with nationalism as the primary cause of naval modernization in India and China. However, many did argue that for prestige platforms such as aircraft carriers, nationalism and perceived great power status were partial explanations.[8] While nationalism on its own, may fail to explain the two cases under review, when combined with a strategic rivalry it does offer a partial explanation.

Bureaucratic Politics Argument

Bureaucratic turf battles are common in all states. The bureaucratic politics model views the actions of government as political resultants that emerge from a competitive game, in which multiple players, holding different policy preferences, struggle, compete, and bargain over the substance and conduct of policy. The policy positions taken by the decision makers are determined largely by their organizational roles and can be simplified in the statement 'where you stand depends on where you sit'. The final decision is not the product of a single rational choice where a unified body of decision makers pursue a coherent set of national objectives, but rather politics is the mechanism of choice (Allison and Zelikow 1999). The role of diverse personalities in various bureaucracies as well as strong personal networks that have existed for years also complicates

---

[8] Please see chapters 3 and 4.

decision-making. Hudson sums up the challenges presented in bureaucratic politics in the quote:

> Bureaucratic politics produce the most intriguing soap operas to be found in government. While the game of international relations may be played according to national interest, there is also a second game being played within each government, a game of personal and/or organizational interests and ambitions, which may in fact be more determinative of a nation's foreign policy than the game of national interest. (Hudson 2014. P 101)

For it to have explanatory power, the bureaucratic politics model relies on certain attributes. First, one must be able to identify the relevant stakeholders whose expertise, roles, and bureaucratic territory allow them to influence a specific political outcome. This is crucial as one's organizational affiliation frequently decides the strategy in a bureaucratic setting. Second, one must examine the 'resultants', that is the political decisions and ascertain how much of the decision was the result of bureaucratic infighting. Finally, and of direct relevance for this project and for the strategic rivalry literature, one must identify the levers of manipulations. How situations and phenomena are presented and framed is key to this approach. Framing allows groups and individuals to understand a situation and to persuade others that a situation is important or not for various reasons (Hudson 2014). If a state is viewed as a strategic rival or is perceived as trying to contain one's own state, the frame will resonate much more strongly with the intended bureaucratic audience. In addition, if a frame is easily understood and is advocated by an individual or a group that is perceived to possess specialized knowledge (like the intelligence community or the military) it has a much greater chance to gain traction and be effectively used in bureaucratic politics (Beasley 1998).

This model has some explanatory power for this book. When certain groups in a state rise to the top decision-making levels they can advocate a more robust maritime military strategy. Groups that advocate a strong navy may see this as a way to safeguard the state's security as well as its overseas interests. If this pro-navy faction is successful, a state will embark on power projection strategies. The scholarly community is divided in their approach to bureaucratic politics and the two cases under review here. Both Scott (2007–8) and Ladwig (2012) discredit the bureaucratic politics model for the Indian case, but in interviews many experts stated that the model does have some explanatory power. As will be elaborated in the Indian case study, they argue that when viewed in the context of a strategic rivalry, the model is deeply embedded and therefore does help us understand part of the driving process of Indian naval modernization.[9] In the Chinese case, there is strong evidence that various bureaucratic organizations were unable to push through their interests in promoting naval modernization (Cole 2013; Erickson and Wilson 2007; Ross 2009). However, as in the Indian case, many experts interviewed for this project pointed out that bureaucratic politics is present in the modernization of the PLAN, but it is not the primary driver.

In both cases under review, bureaucratic factors are present as they are already embedded in the strategic rivalry. As the rivalry literature has demonstrated, bureaucracies are important to arms acquisitions and defence planning as they adopt long-term strategies that are based on the perpetuation of the rivalry (Rider et al. 2011). Within a bureaucracy, belief systems also harden over time, thus making changes in perceptions difficult over time (McGinnis and Williams 2001). As will be explained in the empirical chapters, bureaucratic politics exists at both the ministry, and sub-ministry levels. For example, one finds support for the argument of inter-service rivalry and bureaucratic politics in both the Indian and Chinese ministries of defence. It is important to note that the bureaucratic rivalries that push for naval modernization either would not exist or would be significantly reduced in the absence of a strategic rivalry that is perceived to threaten a state.[10]

Research Design

My chief argument is that when a strategic rivalry experiences critical junctures in the form of rivalry escalation, leaders' threat perceptions also increase. When the rivalry takes on a maritime dimension, decision makers increase their calls for naval modernization, especially when a

---

[9] Author's interviews in New Delhi, 2016.
[10] This is according to those interviewed for this book in Beijing and Shanghai.

state expands its naval presence in its rival's backyard. This project specifically seeks to ascertain why rivalry matters and constructs data sets to measure and demonstrate rivalry maintenance and escalation. I also show how different explanations contribute to answering the puzzle of the drivers of naval modernization. The competing arguments are fully analysed and taken into account throughout the book.

Naval modernization, and specifically variation in modernization over the period under review, is heavily centred on specific types of ships. As will be demonstrated in the argument chapter, the process of naval modernization is an evolutionally process. I argue that states originally develop a more Corbettian influenced naval strategy and this gradually evolves into a Mahanian navy with greater ability to project power and a shifting in force structure to larger platforms more geared to high seas operations. For example, the force structure of a Corbettian navy makes greater use of corvettes and littoral combat craft, while a Mahanian inspired navy employs larger vessels, destroyers, frigates, and even aircraft carriers. For this task the following warships are of paramount importance and are classified by the International Institute for Strategic Studies (IISS) as 'principal surface combatants', aircraft carriers, destroyers, frigates, and depending on the year corvettes are also included. IISS does not classify submarines as principal surface combatants, but I include both nuclear powered ballistic missile submarines (SSBNs), nuclear powered attack submarines (SSNs), and diesel electric attack submarines (SSKs). While other platforms are important and perform roles consistent with naval modernization, they are not as strategic as those listed above. (For example littoral combat craft are very useful to a navy, but are not as strategic as larger vessels.) One variable that helps differentiate modern from obsolete combatants are guided missile systems. These weapons, if properly deployed, are an enormous upgrade in naval development. The ability to target and destroy an enemy from afar with missiles is an important element of naval modernization (Till 2013; Modelski and Thompson 1988). The different types of platforms commissioned over the years demonstrate variation in naval modernization. The actual force structure of each navy changes over the decades as the rivalry is maintained and experiences periods of escalation.

In terms of naval modernization, quantitatively I provide data on missiles (for the India case), number of seamen, where possible specific budget allocations, and most important, principal surface combatants and submarines.[11] I employ these four measures to guard against error. For example, naval budgets suffer from significant flaws because payroll costs, and the expenses of shipbuilding often vary from one country to another. In addition, different levels of technology can have an enormous impact on the lethality of missiles (Modelski and Thompson 1988). Ascertaining a state's military expenditure can be a difficult task. During the Cold War, serious questions were posed about the reliability of data on Soviet military spending coming from the CIA. Holzman argued that comparisons between the USSR and the Americans were difficult because of the higher quality of American personnel and the better quality of American equipment. In addition, the paucity of information supporting CIA estimates was a significant concern as well as potential biases within the CIA (Holzman 1980). Qualitatively, I examine the perceived effectiveness of the platforms through extensive interviews in over one year of fieldwork in China, with interviews taking place in Beijing and Shanghai. Interviews were also carried out in New Delhi, Washington D.C. and Australia, as well as phone interviews with various experts. These interviews have helped to illuminate why different platforms have been chosen over others. For example, why has China opted for various nuclear submarines when their Yuan class diesel electric submarine is considered very quiet and effective. Through in-depth interviews with experts, I was able to shed light on why these choices were made. Subjects ranged from academics, to current and retired government employees, journalists with in-depth knowledge of the subject matter, and analysts in the think-tank community.[12] This interview section also directly addressed a gap in the empirical literature; no scholar has attempted to explain the key decisions in the history of the rivalry where specific platforms were selected.[13]

Data on rivalry escalation and maintenance came from multiple sources that were utilized to build the two data sets constructed for this

---

[11] For the definition of 'principle surface combatants', I use the International Institute for Strategic Studies' measure of aircraft carriers, destroyers, frigates, and for some years corvettes. Submarines include both nuclear and conventionally powered boats.

[12] Please see the appendix and interview section for a description of those interviewed.

[13] It is important to note that this author did not have any access to classified materials. While naval modernization is a long drawn-out process, through extensive interviews, the timing of when certain platforms were decided on and how this relates to rivalry was examined.

book. During interviews, I discovered that many instances of rivalry escalation are either missing from the scholarly literature, or are not perceived to be critical junctures in the rivalry.

This book utilizes qualitative methodology. In particular, I examine open-source documents and statements from the Chinese, Indian, and American governments. Data on warships are derived primarily from the IISS and scholarly works published by the Naval Institute Press. Every year IISS publishes 'The Military Balance', which details defence-related data for many states including India and China. This data includes military budgets, number of service members in each branch, as well as warships and their missile systems. 'The Military Balance' is very helpful as it has consistent and updated data sheets for every year included in this book. This helps to limit challenges that can arise from different intelligence reports, as well as counting methods. Several sources including the U.S. Office of Naval Intelligence and the U.S. Department of Defense's annual reports on the People's Liberation Army are also referenced for data and analysis. I also examine various Chinese publications such as the Chinese ministry of Defense's White Papers and other Chinese language sources. Chinese language sources are cited in both Chinese characters and English translations.

The time period of the study is from 1991 until 2020 for both states. This period fits well as the Cold War was over and both states were involved in economic reforms. For India, significant and sustained economic reforms began in 1991, and it was also in the early 1990s that the Indian navy started to receive a much greater percentage of the military budget. For the Chinese case, the PLAN also started to experience greater importance as advocates of naval modernization started to gain influence in Beijing. The early 1990s also witnessed the renewal of the Sino/American rivalry.

Interviews

Naval modernization is a long-drawn-out process and it can be difficult to ascertain when and why specific platforms were ordered. A primary method utilized in this book was in-depth interviews with experts in the field. These individuals were drawn from a number of professions ranging from think tanks, the media, academics, to re-tired and active-duty military personnel. From 2016 through 2018, I conducted over 60 in-depth interviews with these experts. Please see the appendix for a description of interviewees. Unfortunately I am unable to name the people interviewed for this project. However, where possible, I provide a very rough background of the individual who was interviewed.

These interviews were important because many questions that I had are not adequately answered in the existing literature. I was able to interview many of the authors of noteworthy documents, ranging from government publications, to books and scholarly articles. I was also able to speak with retired military and diplomatic staff who had direct knowledge and experi-ence with my topic. While this book utilizes multiple forms of qualitative research, the interviews were crucial, and without them, many of the recent developments (post-2005) would have been more difficult to explain and understand. Certain sources also do not write about their area of expertise. These individuals have enormous knowledge that is not secret, but has not come to the attention of the public, thus the importance of my travels to various locations to interview them.

Interviews were focused and specific questions were asked that centred around drivers of naval modernization. In particular, I asked each indi-vidual what they saw as the primary driver/drivers of Chinese or Indian naval modernization. I also asked them to comment on competing ex-planations for naval modernization. Most interviews lasted over one hour and many went over 90 minutes. In some cases, snowball sampling was employed. This was especially the case in China where access is increas-ingly difficult and I had to rely on both my previous contacts in Beijing, but also the personal contacts with the people I was interviewing. None of the interviews were recorded, but I was able to take detailed notes during the process. Typically, an interviewee would comment on a specific as-pect and this would be followed up with more detailed questions. While a direct causal link was difficult to establish, there was wide agreement that strategic rivalry was the paramount driver of each states naval mod-ernization. Many experts noted that it was difficult to argue that a specific event directly caused decision makers to opt for a specific platform, but they did believe that overall rivalry dynamics were the cause. However, in the Chinese case, multiple experts believed, or had knowledge, that specific events caused certain platforms to be commissioned.[14] Questions were specific to naval modernization and I began with a general set of questions that became much more in-depth as the interview progressed.[15]

Literature Review

The study of naval modernization consists of many related, but distinct concepts and theories. Some scholars disagree with proper ways to measure modernization, while others concentrate on why navies feel compelled to develop new and more powerful platforms. There is a wide literature on how we should conceptualize seapower and the types of vessels states put to sea. Scholars, who are more concerned with empirics, tend to focus on the drivers of the process or concentrate on specific geographic regions or individual states. This section seeks to provide a solid review of this diverse literature and is broken into two distinct halves. The first part is divided into three sections and is primarily concerned with more abstract and theoretical aspects of naval modernization. In the first section, I examine different means scholars have devised to measure seapower. The second part reviews various concepts of seapower and breaks them down into different types. Closely related to the second part, the third section delves into some of the major theories that deal directly with the development of naval power. The second half of the review examines the literature that addresses the two case studies in this book and breaks them down according to drivers of naval modernization.

Part I: Measures, Concepts, and Theories of Seapower

The key concept of this project is naval modernization and as detailed above it will be measured in multiple ways. Scholars differ on ways to measure this phenomenon equally and they disagree on the purpose of naval modernization. For example, is naval modernization designed to

---

[14] Please see empirical chapters.
[15] Please see Appendix I for details on questions and locations.

establish a credible deterrent, to raid sea-lanes of communication, or to project power to dominate the open ocean? This section of the literature review focuses on some of the key works that address these important issues.

Measures

Modelski and Thompson's *Seapower in Global Politics, 1494–1993* directly addresses the process and operationalization of naval modernization. The authors argue that navies constitute a critical politico-strategic factor that, in combination with other factors, such as economic, cultural, and social, help to establish a foundation for global reach. They define seapower as a means to control the sea, and is considered the sin-qua-non of action in international politics. They argue it is a necessary, but not sufficient condition, for operations of a global scope. By developing seapower, a state creates greater mobility, as well as utilizing a higher order of technology. The authors are especially concerned with 'Long cycles', where world powers succeed each other roughly every 100 years. The key to long cycles is found in the establishment of seapower. Changes in the composition of world leadership are linked to shifts in the distribution of seapower. The role of the nuclear attack (SSN) and ballistic missile submarines (SSBN) is the key to the future of seapower, as the authors contend these have replaced the aircraft carrier as the current capital ship (Modelski and Thompson 1988).

Geoffrey Till has also devised a number of means to measure and operationalize seapower. He breaks naval power into five qualitative and quantitative measures. He first looks at force structure and focuses on the type, age, and the number of warships. Second, he examines the sustainability of a navy. Third, the function and capability are discussed. Fourth, the flexibility of the force is taken into account, which is the number of missions a navy can take on at the same time. A navy's access to technology is the last measure (Till 2009. Cited in Kirchberger 2011). Todd and Lindberg break naval power into two types, blue-water, and non-blue water navies. They devise four specific criteria for naval power. First, they ask what a naval fleet is designed for, second they examine the types of ships, third they ask what are the defining capabilities of a navy's ships, and finally they provide examples of various navies that meet their criteria for blue and non-blue water navies. A significant flaw with their method is that they categorize navies with only token blue water warships as blue water navies (Todd and Lindberg 1996). Employing their measures in 2011, Kirchberger finds that Pakistan and New Zealand are both blue water navies (Kirchberger 2011).

Kirchberger questions how one defines, measures, and compares naval power. While openly admitting that naval power is a fuzzy concept, she measures it primarily through economic variables. By quantifying military spending, the GDP share of defence spending, the size of a state's exclusive economic zone (EEZ), and a state's share of the percentage of world trade, she attempts to develop a better measure of naval power. While her measure of the percentage of world trade is in line with Mahanian theory, she does not pay adequate attention to actual platforms, and crucially, to levels of technological sophistication in various warships. In an unconvincing argument, she compares the navies of the 'BRIC' countries (Brazil, Russia, India, and China). She states BRIC countries are suitable for comparison because 'they have similar strategic aims of becoming less dependent on outside assistance and influence' (Kirchberger 2011. P 159).

Theories

The writings of Alfred Thayer Mahan are critical to understanding naval modernization. In his seminal work 'The Influence of Sea Power upon History 1660–1783', Mahan argues that seapower is founded on three pillars; production, merchant and naval shipping, and overseas markets and bases. His logic of seapower dictates gaining access to the ocean for commercial reasons, and securing access through large numbers of warships. For Mahan, command of the sea meant bringing overbearing power on the sea, which would drive away a state's enemies (Mahan 1987). In addition to this American case, Mahan's theory of seapower is alive and well in the 21st century. Various Western and Chinese scholars have looked to Mahan as a model for China's naval modernization (Yoshihara and Holmes 2010).

Powers that seek blue water navies, but do not have the economic means to develop them, are better understood through the framework put forth by Mahan's contemporary and rival naval theorist, Julian S Corbett. Corbett agreed with Mahan on the importance of maritime power to a nation and the need to keep SLOCSs (Sea Lanes of Communication) open. However, he argued for a more limited use of naval power. Corbett was also concerned with a navy's ability to project power ashore and differed with Mahan by viewing amphibious operations as important. Notably, Corbett had a strong sense of the limitations of seapower (Till 2013). He argued that command of the sea may be a paramount goal, but for weaker states, it did not have to be an immediate goal. Of direct relevance to this project was Corbett's advocacy of asymmetric warfare for a weaker state. An inferior navy could adopt a defensive strategy in order to overextend an enemy's logistical links and SLOCs. This would present dangers for a more Mahanian influenced rival that concentrated its forces and would prevent the larger navy from being able to secure command of the sea. At the core of Corbett's argument is the idea of a more nimble and resilient navy that is able to move with speed and outmanoeuvre a larger more powerful fleet obsessed with hegemony over the sea (Holmes and Yoshihara 2010).

States that focus on raiding an enemy's SLOCs do not always find success. The German 'wolf packs' of the Second World War lost an astounding 30,003 submariners, or 70 per cent of all who sailed during the war. These men died on 739 diesel submarines that were destroyed. In a major blow to the utility of a submarine focused naval strategy, only 272 allied ships (or 0.6 per cent) were destroyed by German U-boats (Herwig 2009). As will be elaborated on in detail in the empirical chapters, an anti-access/area denial strategy (A2/AD) is also closely associated with state's that have maritime security concerns and limited naval budgets.

Concepts

Noted naval scholar Geoffrey Till provides several different conceptualizations of seapower and how it can be understood. He argues that seapower 'can be seen as a tight and inseparable system in which naval power protects the maritime assets that are the ultimate source of its prosperity and military effectiveness' (Till 2013 P. 17). He also discusses the 'broad view' of seapower and points out that seapower can be viewed as an input where navies, coastguards, industries connected to maritime issues as well as relevant land and air forces come together. When viewed as an output, seapower can be viewed as the ability to influence the behaviour of others, in this perspective, it is defined in terms of its consequences (Till 2013).

Most of the theories that attempt to explain naval modernization and maritime strategy rely on various forms of 'access denial' and 'command of the sea'. Corbett certainly had access denial in mind when contemplating naval strategy, while Mahan was more concerned with controlling the high seas. The ability to control the sea is a controversial topic. It is very difficult for a navy to completely control the sea, and in the modern era, with submarines that can stay submerged indefinitely, as well as anti-ship and ballistic missiles, it is nearly impossible. Till breaks down various forms of sea control and lists three types that are helpful in understanding the various degrees of this concept.

1. Absolute control: allows a fleet total freedom of action with the ability to operate without any interruptions from enemy forces.
2. Working control: the ability to operate with a high level of freedom. The enemy is only able to conduct missions with high levels of risk.
3. Control in dispute: each side operates with a high level of risk. (Till 2013)

'Sea denial' is more of an attempt to prevent an enemy from entering a specific area. As will be demonstrated next, the concept of A2/AD is alive and well in both the scholarly literature and in official government publications. Tangredi devotes an entire book to the study of this phenomenon and defines A2/AD as 'strategies intended to prevent an attacker from being able to bring forces to bear at a defenders center of gravity' (Tangredi 2013. P 2). He specifically examines multiple historical cases of where A2/AD did and did not work.

Part II: Case Selection

Part A: Literature Review on the Drivers of Indian Naval Modernization

The literature that addresses the drivers of Indian naval modernization is heavily orientated towards the policy community and does not attempt to engage in theoretical explanations. Many of these works are also largely descriptive. However, this does not mean that they fail to explain the driving forces behind India's emerging blue water navy. The purpose of this section is to provide an overview of some of the leading works on Indian naval modernization, many of these books and journal articles do contribute to our understanding of some of the dynamics involved in this process. Most publications actively speak of the 'rivalry' as being a cause of modernization, but they all fail to specify what they mean by rivalry, nor do they attempt in any way to show how variation in rivalry produces variation in naval modernization. Perhaps most importantly, authors assume that rivalry is a cause, while failing to prove this assumption. It is this gaping hole in our knowledge that this project aims to fill.

Strategic Rivalry: The Role of China as a Driver

There is widespread agreement within the Indian scholarly and policy communities that China poses a threat to India and this threat extends to the maritime domain. This threat is increasingly articulated by those in power. Rajejwari Pillai Rajagopalan points out that concern about the PLAN in the IOR dates back to the early 1960s. In the aftermath of the 1962 war, a comprehensive government review saw China as a primary threat, which led to calls to increase the strength of the navy in the event the PLAN would make forays into the Bay of Bengal. Defense Minister Y.B. Chavan even spoke of Chinese capabilities and intentions in the Lok Sabha in 1963. He then clarified that the government agreed on the need for a submarine fleet. However, it needs to be pointed out, that at that point in the history of the rivalry, China did not have a strong enough navy to pose a serious threat (Rajagopalan 2016).

Several decades later the PLAN started to develop the assets to venture into the IOR and this was quickly noticed by the Indian government. David Scott writes that a 1998 internal naval document *The Strategic Defense Review: The Maritime Dimension—A Naval Vision* called for the Indian Navy to be able to deter a military challenge from a challenger and that primary challenger was China (Scott 2006). India's Naval chief Sureesh Mehta acknowledged the superiority of Chinese forces, but also added that India's strategy is to close the gap and 'counter the growing Chinese footprint in the Indian Ocean Region' (Mehta 2009).

Holmes and Yoshihara point out that the political leadership in India supported the Indian Maritime Doctrine in 2004, which called for a true blue water navy that is capable of sea-denial and sea-control in the IOR as well as the ability to control choke points that may be used as bargaining chips in the international power game (Holmes and Yoshihara 2009). This is code for the ability to prevent rival states (primarily China) from passing through areas such as the Malacca Strait. A group of respected Indian strategists wrote the report *Nonalignment 2.0: A Foreign and Strategic Policy for India in the Twenty First Century*, which argues for India to recognize the stalemate on its border disputes and take advantage of India's geographic location and counter its rivals in the IOR (cited in Rehman 2016).

The rise of the Chinese Navy (PLAN) plays the most prominent role in explanations of Indian naval modernization. In his book, *Samudra Manthan*, Raja Mohan argues that there is a security dilemma between India and China and that this is growing. According to Mohan, the increasing PLAN presence in the IOR is the chief preoccupation of Indian strategic planners. The fear of being 'encircled' by China is a great security concern for New Delhi. While arguing that this 'rivalry' is the driving force, Mohan does not provide a detailed conceptualization as to what he means by rivalry (Mohan 2012).

The international scholarly community has also contributed to the literature on the drivers of this phenomenon. Bernard Cole has argued that China tops the list of concerns in New Delhi. In terms of Indian strategic thinking, he states that Chinese naval modernization and incursions into the IOR dominate discussions (Cole 2013). Joshi and O'Donnell provide a thorough analysis of India's nuclear forces. These authors make it clear that India's emerging nuclear submarine force is designed to counter the

PLAN in the IOR as well as demonstrate New Delhi's resolve against the long-term Chinese challenge (Joshi and O'Donnell 2019).

Harsh Pant has argued in numerous papers that China is a threat to India and this is causing India to build a strong navy. He states that Chinese incursions in the IOR are 'driving Indian naval posture' and that China's SSBN programme has caused India to speed up its own SSBN programme (Pant 2009. P 294). In a separate chapter Pant argues that 'the emerging Chinese naval threat has largely underpinned India's current naval modernization plans, the IN will have to prioritize the procurement and development of necessary capabilities' (Pant 2012. P 12). Cordner speaks of a security dilemma taking place between China and India and how strategic competition is likely to play out at sea, but he does not fully demonstrate that a security dilemma is actually taking place (Cordner 2011). Finally, Singh (a former IN officer) argues that 'to a considerable degree, the impetus for the building up of maritime operations has been driven by China's aggressiveness in the South China Sea and the People's Liberation Army navy's (PLAN) increasing naval footprint in the Indian Ocean.' He further states that as a result of this India has decided to acquire its own strategic assets (Singh 2015. P 77).

Holmes and Yoshihara write of India's 'Monroe Doctrine' as a cause of naval modernization. According to this argument, this strategy seeks to prevent political and military intervention in the IOR from outside rivals (Holmes and Yoshihara 2008; Holmes and Yoshihara 2009). Kanwal of the Indian Institute for Defense Studies and Analyses is diplomatic in his approach by stating that India seeks to obtain blue water naval capability in order to 'effectively counter current and emerging threats' (Kanwal 2012. P 4.).

Rajat Ganguly acknowledges that India's naval expansion is driven by perceived threats and points to China, but he does not go in depth or provide extensive details on this claim (Ganguly 2015). The strategic threat is also cited by Pant and Joshi, who argue that China has caused the IN to rethink its role in maintaining the balance of power in the IOR (Pant and Joshi 2015).

In another article, David Scott directly addresses the impact the PLAN has on Indian naval modernization and planning strategy. He argues that India seeks to maintain clear military superiority over the PLAN in the IOR (Scott 2013). Gurpreet Khurana, a Captain in the Indian Navy, points out that China plays a major role in Indian naval planning. He mentions the fact that the Indian Maritime Strategy for 2015 does not mention China by name, but states that India's rivals cause the IN to focus on a continued state of preparedness (Khurana 2017).

Arguments Based on Bureaucratic Politics and Other Drivers

In the India case, various bureaucratic entities do push for certain maritime strategies. Holmes and Yoshihara provide evidence of current and former Indian naval chiefs imploring New Delhi to take the Chinese naval threat seriously and to provide the IN with more funding (Holmes and Yoshihara 2013). Pant and Joshi also view the IN as an interest group that has long articulated a more robust navy that is capable of power projection, especially in the forms of various official Naval Doctrines (Pant and Joshi 2015).

David Scott directly addresses the explanatory power of bureaucratic politics and argues that they are one reason for the push, but on their own, they are insufficient. He further states that the drive for a blue water navy has more to do with political factors (Scott 2007–2008). Cohen and Dasgupta discount the model in the navy by stating, 'the service lacks real political influence in New Delhi. There is no parliamentary lobby that pushes for naval construction and enhanced budgets, let alone for a rebalance of services'. They do however point out that the IN tries to maintain the rivalry in the minds of the Indian public and politicians by leaking stories about Chinese activities in the region, and especially about Chinese cooperation with Pakistan and Bangladesh (Cohen and Dasgupta. 2010. P 93–94).

Nationalism and great power status have very little utility as explanations for Indian naval modernization. While nationalism is a powerful unifying force, no scholarly work cites it as a primary driver. As will also be demonstrated for the China case next, nationalism does have an influence, although a lesser one. Scott has argued that national prestige is an important factor, especially when it comes to 'showing the flag' (Scott 2007–2008).

It is worth noting that the concept of the nested security dilemma is prominent in Gilboy and Heginbotham's work on Chinese and Indian strategic behaviour. This version of the dilemma is present across both geographic regions and between states. Unfortunately, they do not explain how this directly influences naval modernization. They just mention that this form of the security dilemma in South Asia could spark a response from India's rivals, such as China (Gilboy and Heginbotham 2012).

Indian Naval Modernization and Theoretical Frameworks

While most work has been either descriptive, policy-oriented, or both, a few scholars have attempted to place Indian naval modernization in a theoretical framework. Holmes and Yoshihara argue that India is exhibiting some Mahanian traits, while David Scott agrees and writes that India's grand strategy has 'Mahanian visions', and that India's emerging blue water navy aims to achieve 'Mahanist seapower' (Holmes and Yoshihara 2013; Scott 2007–2008). In contrast to these authors, Bernard Cole explains Indian naval strategy through Julian Corbett's theory of seapower, which emphasizes the limited use of naval power (Cole 2013).

Literature That Directly Addresses the Drivers

Few authors have directly addressed the specific drivers of Indian naval modernization, but two scholars have contributed to this emerging debate. As stated above Scott points to the PLAN as the primary driver for India, but he also discusses competing explanations. He rejects the bureaucratic politics argument because he believes that on its own it is not sufficient to explain the push towards a blue water fleet. While acknowledging that showing the flag is an important factor, he discounts the argument in favour of national prestige. Coming down squarely on China as the cause, he points out that competition with other states, such as Pakistan, only requires a 'brown water fleet', while arguing that the competition is China specific' (Scott 2007–2008). Ladwig shares Scott's scepticism with the bureaucratic politics argument, while downplaying the role of hostile foreign powers from dominating India as a driver.

A challenge with Ladwig's analysis is that he discounts hostile foreign powers as the drivers, but argues the driving force is the need to protect India's sea lanes from enemies. (Ladwig 2012). Overall, the vast majority of the literature on India's naval modernization is descriptive policy-centred writing. Very few have attempted to place this extremely important event into a theoretical framework. Most authors agree that the rivalry between China and India is either a contributing cause or the primary cause of this modernization. Unfortunately, no author has yet to explain what they mean by 'rivalry', and of equal importance, demonstrate precisely how this threat perception varies and how this variation leads to more modern naval platforms. This omission is of critical importance and represents a gaping hole in the literature. While empirical data exists on India's naval modernization, no study has yet to analyse the timing of India's naval modernization. Scholars and government officials have spoken about China as a driver and have stated that India will respond with a stronger navy, but no study has taken the time to discuss why India has opted for various pieces of hardware at a specific time. This project will directly address this lacuna.

Part B: Literature Review on Chinese Naval Modernization

Academic scholarship on China's naval modernization is more advanced than scholarship on India's navy. However, just like the case of India, the majority of writings on the PLAN are descriptive or policy-driven, or both. One area where scholars have distinguished themselves from their counterparts who research India is in their attempts to better explain the drivers of PLAN modernization. With this said, nearly all authors agree that China is involved in a rivalry with the U. S. and many argue that this rivalry is a significant factor in PLAN modernization. There is some level of disagreement among scholars on the top drivers of Chinese naval modernization, but no study provides a granular analysis that seeks to explain the drivers of this process, or to compare different explanations in any depth. Unfortunately, there has yet to be a study that utilizes the academic literature on rivalry as a cause of PLAN modernization. The research speaks of rivalry, takes rivalry for granted, and fails to show variation in rivalry over the years and never specifies what is meant by 'rivalry'. The past decade has witnessed an explosion of writings on the Chinese military and the PLAN in particular. This literature review will examine multiple perspectives on what is driving PLAN modernization and will also focus on works that attempt to place PLAN modernization in a more theoretical framework.

Strategic Rivalry: The Role of the U.S. as the Primary Driver

There is agreement in the scholarly and policy communities that the American military presence in East Asia is the driving force behind PLAN modernization. Many scholars assume this to be the reality and speak of 'rivalry' as a given and do not elaborate on it as a driver. Even though the PLAN has been modernizing since the 1980s, several events in the early and mid-1990s played crucial roles in the decision to pursue naval modernization. It should be noted that during this period China was a land-based power and many of its leaders were not inclined to pursue naval power (Shambaugh 2002).

The quick and efficient American victory in the 1991 Gulf War stunned many in the Chinese government and military. Chinese commentators believed the Americans would have a much more difficult time evicting the Iraqi military from Kuwait. In particular, this 'Revolution in Military Affairs' (RMA) demonstrated to the Chinese leadership that they would have to pursue rapid military modernization if they were to have a chance in a confrontation with the Americans (Shambaugh 2002; Cole 2013; Mahnken 2014). Erickson and Goldstein (2007) argue that the 1993 'Yinhe incident', where a Chinese cargo ship suspected of carrying arms to Iran was stopped by the American navy and forcibly searched on the high seas, played a major role in forcing Chinese leaders to begin naval modernization (Erickson and Goldstein 2007).

The 1995/96 Taiwan Crises that witnessed several American aircraft carrier battle groups sailing towards the coast of Taiwan as a warning to Beijing to not attack Taiwan, was a critical juncture for the modernization of the PLAN. Up until this point, the civilians in charge of naval procurement rejected Liu Huaqing's pleas for an aircraft carrier. After these series of incidents, Jiang Zemin, China's Communist Party Secretary General, reportedly gave approval for the development of a Chinese aircraft carrier (Ross 2009; Cole 2013; Erickson and Wilson 2007). China's defence White Papers also provide evidence that PLAN modernization is driven by the rivalry with Washington. While many of these documents are diplomatic in their treatment of the U.S., the 2000, 2002, and 2004 papers identify the U.S. or 'hegemonism' (meaning the U.S.) as China's most important challenge (Godwin 2007; China's National Defense 2000; 2002; 2004). The 2015 Defense White Paper calls for the PLAN to secure China's overseas interests and to carry out 'open seas protection'. Importantly, it mentions the American rebalancing strategy in Asia and speaks of external countries meddling in the affairs of the South China Sea (China's Military Strategy 2015; Blasko 2015).

The development of Chinese nuclear submarines and, in particular, Chinese SSBNs is believed to be driven by the rivalry with the U.S. The ability to pose a second strike capability and to keep the Americans from interfering in China's affairs are the main purposes of the SSBN programme (Godwin 2007; McVadon 2007). Erickson and Goldstein (2007) have also argued that the American missile defence programme would have great difficulty defending against SSBN launched ballistic missiles.

Overall, the scholarly community largely agrees that PLAN modernization is driven by China's rivalry with America. Although few focus on this particular issue or discuss rivalry in any depth, it is clear that the leadership in Beijing sees the American naval presence in East Asia as a danger to Chinese interests. In order to protect these interests from American dominance, the PLAN is increasingly developing naval platforms that can thwart the U.S. Navy in a potential shootout.

PLAN Modernization and Theoretical Frameworks

Yoshihara and Holmes have attempted to place PLAN modernization into a Mahanian framework. These authors argued that Chinese leaders are deeply concerned that the American navy will be deployed to deny China access to the commons, thus thwarting China's rise. They also utilize Mahan's theory to explain China's push towards securing its SLOCs from perceived American dominance. Implicit in their argument is the Sino/

U.S. strategic rivalry, however, the scholars do not go into detail about this rivalry, nor do they explain any variation over time (Yoshihara and Holmes 2010; 2018).

Robert Ross directly addresses the drivers of PLAN modernization and argues that nationalism is the primary cause. He links 'naval nationalism' with 'prestige strategies'. Like other scholars, Ross acknowledges the Sino/U.S. rivalry and points to the strategy of access denial employed by the PLAN to counter the American navy, but he does not describe in any detail what he means by rivalry (Ross 2009). A major liability with Ross' argument is the fact that he does not produce a compelling explanation for why nationalism has caused Chinese leaders to develop the PLAN, when in previous occasions it has not forced the leadership's hand. He also does not provide a concrete definition of what he means by nationalism (Glosny et al. 2010).

The Chinese Bureaucracy and PLAN Modernization

The role of the bureaucracy as a potential driver of China's naval modernization has been explored by several scholars. While acknowledging the rivalry between Beijing and Washington as influencing Sino-American security issues, Mahnken argues that this has limited influence on arms competition. He argues that bureaucratic politics, organizational culture, and government practices exert real influence (Mahnken 2014). Mahnken does not address the evidence that the Taiwan crisis caused Jiang Zemin to give approval to China's aircraft carrier programme. Nor does he point out that the PLAN and, most notably Politburo Standing Committee member Admiral Liu Huaqing, fiercely advocated for the acquisition of an aircraft carrier, but were regularly overruled until external factors (the USA) caused the leadership to reconsider (Ross 2009; Cole 2013; Erickson and Wilson 2007).

Glaser offers a slightly different analysis of the role of the military in procurement. She argues that the PLA advocated for certain platforms as a result of the 1995–1996 Taiwan crisis. Many of these weapons, including an aircraft carrier, have come to fruition. However, Glaser cautions that a causal relationship between the PLA and defence policy is difficult to demonstrate due to the non-transparent nature of the Chines political system (Glaser 2015). Tai Ming Cheung writes that Liu Huaqing tried on multiple occasions to push for more advanced platforms, but found that the timing in the late 1980s and early 1990s was not conducive to major upgrades. Events such as the 1991 Gulf War, the Taiwan crisis, and the 1999 bombing of the Chinese Embassy in Belgrade, caused the leadership to aggressively pursue modernization. In particular, Cheung argues that the U.S. was identified by Chinese leader Jiang Zemin as 'the enemy'. Jiang apparently ordered the military to intensify efforts to counter the U.S. in the form of 'assassin's mace' capabilities.[16] Many of these systems ended up in the PLAN. While Cheung does not provide a deep theoretical background to this modernization, he provides powerful evidence of the role the U.S. played as a driver in China's overall military modernization (Cheung 2015; Cheung 2009).

Yung directly addresses the question of a bureaucratic politics explanation in his examination of the PLAN lobby. His findings demonstrate that the PLAN does have influence, but that its influence is limited and it has been denied specific naval platforms in the past such as an aircraft carrier (Yung 2015). Addressing the issue of SSBN (ballistic missile submarines) acquisition, Erickson argues that these appear to be driven by organizational interests. However, he notes that these are designed to exploit missile defence systems. Overall, he writes that the protection of SLOCs is a major driver of PLAN modernization (Erickson 2014).

Protection of Sea Lanes of Communication and Other Drivers

The protection of SLOCs is in line with my argument that rivalry is the chief driver. Aircraft carriers and guided-missile destroyers are not necessary for Somali pirates. In fact, as mentioned above, the 1993 'Yinhe incident' where the Americans forcefully ordered the search of a Chinese flagged vessel was reportedly a major catalyst for naval modernization.

Bernard Cole pays attention to China's increasing demand for natural resources and expanding maritime trade links and argues that the

---

[16] Assassin's mace capabilities are asymmetric weapons such as mines and anti-ship missiles.

protection of these shipping lanes is a driver of PLAN modernization. According to Cole, the ability to secure 'vital national maritime interests' is of paramount concern to the Chinese leadership (Cole 2016. P. 52). Interestingly, Cole does not believe maritime theory is relevant to China's naval modernization attempts. He argues that China is attempting to bypass islands and therefore is not closely related to a Mahanian form of modernization (Cole 2016). In his excellent article, Yves-Heng Lim makes extensive use of Chinese language sources and argues for a 'grand strategic' hypothesis where the development of the PLAN is aligned with the need to secure Chinese SLOCs in the IOR. While Lim's article argues that the Chinese will be able to vie for 'sea control' in the IOR by 2030, he does not discuss the enormous challenges this would force the PLAN to overcome (Lim 2020).

Overall, scholarly writing on the drivers of PLAN modernization all tends to point towards a form of rivalry/competition with the U.S. However, no study actively explores the dynamics of this rivalry which has gone through various stages of escalation over the past quarter-century. While some scholars have pointed to the impact of specific events such as the 1995–1996 Taiwan crisis on weapons acquisition, no study has examined escalation and its impact on procurement over the same time period. Arguments about nationalism as a driving force fall short when critically examined. The bureaucratic politics argument may have some merit, but this too is often tied directly or indirectly to the Sino-U.S. strategic rivalry. Of equal importance, no study has yet to dem-onstrate the linkages between the Sino-U.S. rivalry and the Sino-Indian rivalries and how this drives naval modernization.

2

Theory and My Argument

This chapter is divided into two sections. The first provides a review of the rivalry research programme and demonstrates why it is useful for the study of security and conflict. In particular, I examine various approaches to rivalries and explain why the punctuated equilibrium model is helpful for understanding rivalry maintenance and escalation. The second part of the chapter details my argument and shows why it is the best explanation for the cases under review. This section does not argue that naval modernization in the selected cases is monocausal. The other approaches examined in the introductory chapter such as bureaucratic politics and, to a lesser extent, nationalism, are also helpful in understanding this phenomenon. However, as I will reveal, these approaches are frequently embedded in a rivalry and therefore are part of the explanation. However, on their own these approaches are not sufficient explanations for naval modernization in the two cases under review.

Overview of the Rivalry Research Programme

The study of rivalries is critical to our understanding of the causes of conflict and war. Through such a study, scholars can pinpoint many of the underlying variables that cause states to engage in belligerent behaviour. States that are engaged in a rivalry are much more inclined to fight each other than states that are not rivals. Specifically, this section will examine strategic rivalries and, after explaining the criteria for such rivalries, it will delve into how they are maintained and escalated.

A strategic rivalry is one where decision makers single out other states as enemies and competitors that represent a form of actual or potential military threat. This type of rivalry requires both competition and the perception of threat. Strategic rivalry frequently clouds the way decision

The Nexus of Naval Modernization in India and China. Christopher K. Colley, Oxford University Press. © Oxford University Press 2022. DOI: 10.1093/oso/9780192865595.003.0003

makers understand objective events and causes rivals to view events from the perspective of a worst-case scenario, thus causing rival powers to not trust each other (Colaresi et al. 2007). On the selection of rivals, three criteria must be met. First, actors must see themselves as competitors. Second, the rivals must view each other as a source of actual or latent threat that has the possibility to produce a militarized dispute. Third, the states must consider each other enemies. All three of these factors must be present in order to have a rivalry (Colaresi et al. 2007). The second criteria of viewing each other as a threat help to separate the strategic rivalry approach from the security dilemma. As discussed in the introductory chapter, ambiguity is a hallmark of the security dilemma. States partaking in this phenomenon are unsure of other states intentions. Crucially in a strategic rivalry, this ambiguity is absent as states believe the rival state is a clear threat.

It is worth noting that there are several ways of classifying rivals. One is the 'enduring rivalry' programme. Enduring rivals involve two states in a competition with the expectation of future conflict and they must have engaged in at least six militarized disputes that have taken place within a minimal interval of 20 years (Diehl and Goertz 2000). An obvious challenge to this rivalry set is that states that have not engaged in a militarized dispute in over 20 years are not considered rivals. It is for this reason that this book does not utilize the enduring rivalry approach. While both cases have witnessed significant periods of escalation over the past several decades, classifying these as 'militarized disputes' on at least six different occasions is not possible.

The study of strategic rivalry gives scholars an interesting insight into the dynamics of the causes of war. These rivalries have accounted for 77 per cent of all interstate wars since 1816. In the 20th century they accounted for 87 per cent of wars (41 of 27), and in the post-Second World War era, 91 per cent of interstate wars (21 of 23) (Colaresi et al. 2007). Within a strategic rivalry, domestic constituencies frequently develop that have a vested interest in lobbying for the continuation of the rivalry. These groups, often centred in various bureaucracies, can constrict a leader's room for manoeuvre, thus maintaining the rivalry (Colaresi et al. 2007).

Strategic rivalries can be divided into two groups: spatial and positional. As mentioned in Chapter 1 spatial rivalries are centred over the control of territory. Furthermore, states engaged in territorial disputes are more likely to go to war as this is frequently the first 'step' in the road to war (Sense and Vasquez 2008). Positional rivalries are contests waged over status and a state's relative influence either in the global system or at the regional level. Frequently these two types of rivalry mix, as will be seen in the case study section of this project (Colaresi et al. 2007). This project examines the process of escalation and maintenance in strategic rivalries. Several models and approaches have been developed to explain these phenomena. Specifically, I will examine the punctuated equilibrium approaches, while also demonstrating the linkages between the Sino/U.S. and the Sino/Indian rivalries.

The daisy chain rivalry configuration argues that rivalries can form complex 'daisy chain' linkages. Thompson argues that rivalries rarely take place in a total vacuum and that both sides may attempt to bring other actors into a dispute. Thompson also argues that rivalries are not always confined to a specific subsystem and what happens in one rivalry can have far-reaching implications in other rivalries (Thompson 1999). The issue of what drives states to acquire nuclear weapons was addressed by the daisy chain rivalry configuration. Reuveny and Thompson argue that nuclear proliferation has occurred along the lines of interstate rivalry. For example, the U.S. developed nuclear weapons out of fear that Nazi Germany might acquire them first. This then caused other states to develop nuclear weapons. If the U.S. had nuclear weapons, then the USSR also had to have a nuclear option, this in turn drove China, Britain, and France to develop their own nuclear capability. In the post-war environment, it appeared that the daisy chain had run its course, however, with nuclear proliferation in North Korea and Iran, it may still have a great deal of explanatory power (Reuveny and Thompson 2008). This book argues that rivalry linkages extend to the maritime domain and contends that China's increasingly powerful navy, itself the result of China's rivalry with the U.S., is the major driver of India's naval modernization.

The Punctuated Equilibrium Model

Why is it that certain rivalries tend to have short durations, while others can extend for decades? The punctuated equilibrium model seeks to answer this question. The model originated in the field of biology as a hypothesis to explain the evolutionary process that sees long periods of stability, interspersed with periods of extinction and the formation of new species. When applied to international relations, this model postulates that rivalries go through several different stages and the processes that occur demonstrate substantial variation over time. This model has a strong path dependency because much emphasis is placed on the initial disputes in a rivalry (Diehl and Goertz 2000). Importantly, theoretically, and for this book, the model stresses that during the initial stage of a rivalry, the rivals either quickly resolve their conflict, or patterns of mutual hostility are 'locked in' over the long-term. The first few interactions between rival states set the tone for the rest of the rivalry. After this 'lock in' stage, relations between rivals remain hostile with some regularity and consistency over the course of the rivalry. This model views rivalry maintenance as a consequence of a government's locking into a conflictual perception of its adversaries (Goertz et al. 2005). As will be demonstrated in the case study chapters, the model is very useful in explaining the process of rivalry maintenance and escalation.

Bureaucracies are also important in the punctuated equilibrium model as they tend to adopt long-term strategies that are predicated on the continuation of the rivalry. These strategies are often centred on arms acquisitions and defence planning, which are in direct response to perceptions of threat. Research has demonstrated that the probability of an arms race increases by more than 80 per cent when moving from a non-rivalry to a rivalry (Rider et al. 2011). McGinnis and Williams (2001) also argue that belief systems within bureaucracies also harden over time in a rivalry, thus making change or rivalry termination difficult. These authors also provide some empirical confirmation of the punctuated equilibrium model in explaining the US/USSR rivalry. It is important to note that leaders come to their decision to maintain the rivalry as a result of not just one instance of escalation, but of a series of them. In this case, the entire history of the rivalry to date serves as a driver of both maintenance and escalation. In short, this model represents the failure of effective conflict management as well as a failure of coercion (Goertz et al. 2005). The interaction between bureaucracies and the dynamics of strategic rivalries is a component of the cases presented in this book. As will be demonstrated in the empirical chapters and rivalry escalation datasets, the continuation and maintenance of a rivalry harden bureaucratic attitudes towards the other rival state.

Related to the punctuated equilibrium model is Hensel's evolutionary approach. This is based on the idea that rivalries are not inevitable or predetermined by structural conditions. Rivalries are dynamic processes that demonstrate variation over time. This approach shares with the punctuated equilibrium the idea that as two states build a history of conflict, a rivalry develops and tends to become 'locked in' with the result that future escalation and conflict are highly likely. It also shares the argument that once two states are in a rivalry, the national security policies tend to be heavily influenced by the rivalry (Hensel 1999).

Overall, the study of rivalry provides scholars with a powerful tool to understand the causes of war. States that are engaged in a strategic rivalry are much more likely to have conflictual relations with other states than those who are not engaged in a rivalry. The evolutionary approach and the punctuated equilibrium model greatly enhance our understanding of how rivalries are maintained as well as why they are prone to escalation. As is demonstrated in this project, the punctuated equilibrium model has great explanatory power for the rivalries under study.

My Argument

The puzzle of what drives naval modernization has received scholarly attention. Arguments centred on nationalism, bureaucratic politics, and the security dilemma, all contribute to our understanding of this process. However, they are at best only partial explanations and, at worst, they lack conceptual specificity and fail to explain this phenomenon. My central argument is that naval modernization is best explained through the study of strategic rivalry. Strategic rivalries, with their emphasis on threat perceptions, identification of enemy states, and lack of bilateral trust, offer a much more robust explanation. Naval modernization happens in the context of rivalry escalation in the maritime dimension where weaker states modernize in response to a rival's more powerful navy. Because many rivalries are interconnected, modernization in one state (China) is noticed by a third state (India), which reacts to its rival's modernization by building its own naval power. Importantly, the linkages between rivalries must not be ignored. As demonstrated in model 1 in the introduction, when strategic rivalries experience periods of significant maritime escalation (critical junctures) that dramatically increase threat perceptions within decision-making circles, they produce calls within various bureaucracies for naval warships designed to counter a rival's seapower. As Thompson has pointed out, rivalries do not occur in a vacuum, and a significant increase in naval power in one state engaged in a rivalry can lead to rivalry escalation in a different rivalry and cause naval modernization in a third state. As mentioned in Chapter 1 I argue that China's naval modernization is caused by rivalry escalation with Washington. A more powerful PLAN then greatly increases threat perceptions in India and also causes significant rivalry escalation (and critical junctures) in the Sino/Indian rivalry, thus driving Indian naval modernization as the Indian navy responds to a more powerful Chinese navy.

Viewing naval modernization through this perspective, one cannot disentangle bureaucratic politics from rivalry, and in particular, the punctuated equilibrium model of rivalry. When a rival state starts to project its naval power into another state's region, thus leading to significant rivalry escalation, the state will respond with its own naval programmes. Initially, if a state has low levels of economic resources, in line with the Corbettian approach, it will focus on access denial. As a state's economic resources increase, and the naval threat from its rival persists, it will start to develop the capability to dominate its maritime region and take on a more Mahanian dimension. Through close examination of the period under review, this project offers a granular account to establish causality between rivalry escalation and naval modernization.

Linkages with Other Explanations

The linkages between the various drivers were briefly discussed in the last chapter, but are elaborated here in Diagram 2.1. The overarching explanation is that strategic rivalry is the key driver of naval modernization, but this explanation also utilizes other theoretical approaches, specifically the bureaucratic politics model and, to a lesser extent, explanations based on nationalism. Crucial to the argument are the threat perceptions that emanate from major points in rivalry escalation (the critical junctures in the punctuated equilibrium), and these points of escalation are the key events that drive naval modernization.[1] In the Diagram 2.1, broken lines represent a more limited causal connection, while a solid line designates a stronger causal connection. The direction of the arrow shows the direction of influence. While the bureaucratic model is heavily influenced and embedded in the strategic rivalry, the rivalry is also influenced by the bureaucratic model. It should be noted in the cases presented here, that strategic rivalry is by far the main cause. In the absence of a strategic rivalry the other factors on their own are not sufficient to cause naval modernization. As will be demonstrated in the introduction of the empirical chapters, the initiation of the rivalry came before the respective bureaucracies started to identify the other state as a rival. The reason the arrow is pointed at the rivalry box is because in the absence of a rivalry bureaucracies do not have a strong justification for naval modernization. The rivalry is a necessary condition for this process. Bureaucratic politics are embedded in the process, in the absence of a strategic rivalry; various bureaucracies would not push for naval modernization. The causal connection of nationalism is present, but it does not exert nearly as much influence as the bureaucratic model. As will be elaborated in the empirical chapters, the nationalism argument is frequently platform specific. For the purpose of Diagram 2.1, the causal connection of nationalism is in the form of a broken line. This demonstrates influence, but it is not as strong as the other explanations. In both models, naval modernizations are based on a state's ability to fund naval modernization.

Most cases of naval modernization have occurred in the context of a strategic rivalry. Nations become seapowers, not because of cultural or historical ties, but because of geopolitical circumstances that reward certain defence strategies. In particular, naval modernization takes place between states that challenge each other on the sea (Ross 2009).

This section is divided into two main parts. First, I will explain naval modernization, and refine what I mean by this. Second, I will explain why strategic rivalry fits with my study. The data tables that chart rivalry maintenance and escalation as well as acquisitions of naval hardware can be found in the relevant empirical chapters.

---

[1] Please see the individual case chapters for a detailed breakdown on periods of escalation.

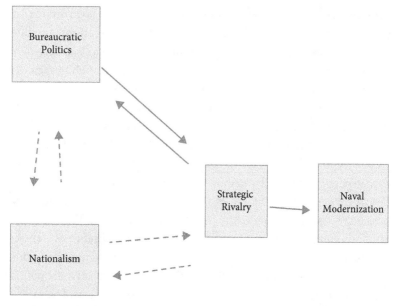

Diagram 2.1 Relationship of Various Drivers of Naval Modernization in the Context of a Strategic Rivalry

Naval Modernization: The Evolution of Maritime Power

Naval modernization demonstrates significant variation over the period under review. I argue that the best way to understand this process is through what I call the 'evolution of maritime power'. This process is best conceptualized as an evolution from a Corbettian to a Mahanian model of naval modernization.

The rivalries in this study originally did not have a naval dimension and were best understood as spatial rivalries centred on territorial disputes on land. Their transformation into positional rivalries is a more recent development. The maritime domain was not a major issue in the Sino/U.S. rivalry until the mid-1990s. As will be demonstrated in Chapter 4, rivalry escalation at sea caused Chinese leaders to push for a modern navy. China's rapidly increasing GDP also provided necessary funds for naval modernization. Beijing was also able to devote more resources to naval power after it no longer felt the threat of the USSR on its northern borders. For decades, India's rivalry with China centred on the northern Himalayan borders. As the Sino/U.S. maritime rivalry intensified causing PLAN modernization, Chinese warships started to visit the IOR on a consistent basis. New Delhi responded to increasing PLAN forays by modernizing its own navy. India was also helped by a rising GDP, which made available greater funds for the navy. In both of these cases, the naval dimension was the result of increasing threats emanating from the sea, and both India and China responded to the threats by building naval power. In short, both of the cases under review have evolved from spatial rivalries to both spatial and positional rivalries. Increases in power and wealth have seen rivalry escalation spread to the maritime domain, thus escalation is no longer found primarily along the Himalayan border for the Sino/Indian rivalry, or centred on Taiwan for the Sino/U.S. rivalry.

A state's inability to develop a large ocean-going fleet and instead concentrate on a smaller, but powerful fleet has a historic precedent. Perhaps the best example of this is the case of Imperial Germany's reaction to the Royal Navy (Yoshihara and Holmes 2010). Responding to the perceived threat of the British fleet at the end of the 19th century, Germany developed the 'risk fleet', which would be able to not only defend the German coast from its British rival, but also cause the British to pause when considering attacking Germany by sea. The key aim of this strategy was to build a fleet that would be strong enough to inflict significant damage on an enemy's navy, thus dissuading it from attacking the German navy (Kennedy 1984). Germany saw the 'risk fleet' not only as a way to challenge the British fleet but to avoid dependence upon London's political goodwill in global affairs. Furthermore, Germany believed the British would be less arrogant and would no longer constitute a threat to German overseas interests. Just as in the case where the U.S. navy ordered the boarding of a Chinese vessel (the Yinhe), Britain humiliated Germany in the maritime realm in 1900 when two German steamers were seized off Delagoa Bay during the Boer war. This led to popular support for the Second Navy Law of 1900, which would protect German commerce and halt British naval 'arrogance' (Herwig 2009). German Rear-Admiral Tirpitz hoped that a modernized navy would free Germany from an 'almost suffocating domination of the Royal Navy' (Kennedy 1984. P 135).

After achieving a certain level of naval modernization that is sufficient to protect a state's immediate geographic environment, a state's naval modernization can evolve and the number and sophistication of its platforms can expand. If a state's economy continues to increase, and if the rivalry persists and escalates, it is likely to follow a more blue water inspired naval modernization where power projection and some form of regional hegemony is the strategic goal.

Naval modernization is a long and very expensive undertaking. States engaged in a rivalry have to tailor their modernization programmes to accommodate these costs. In this regard, the economic health of a state is linked to its ability to develop a powerful and effective navy, and as such, it is an important component of an effective weapons programme. As seen in Graph 2.1, both China and India experienced substantial GDP growth during the period under review. It is important to note that the evolution form a green to a blue water style navy is not just a question of the financial resources of a state. Strategic goals are also a very important determinant. In both cases under review, greater revenues empowered leaders to build stronger navies, but the strategic goal of keeping their respective rivals at bay was also a critical aspect. In the India case, a major goal of New Delhi's naval

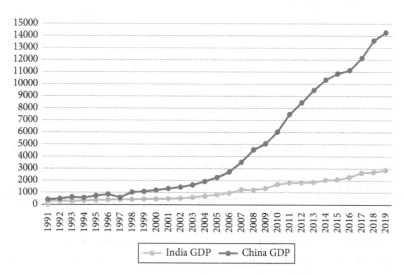

Graph 2.1 Indian and Chinese GDP from 1991 to 2019 in Tens of Billions of USD. (World Bank)

modernization has been to maintain and increase China's strategic vulnerability in the IOR (Brewster 2016). Both states have the financial ability to develop navies consistent with a Corbettian approach; however, they also have strategic ambitions that extend beyond their exclusive economic zones of 200 miles out to sea. China seeks the ability to keep outside rivals out of East Asian waters, and increasingly to protect its interests further afield. India has made it very clear that it does not want outside rivals in the IOR, and is building the platforms that are commensurate with these strategic goals.

The best way to empirically measure naval modernization is by examining naval platforms. This is both a quantitative and qualitative undertaking. It is quantitative in that I count several factors. First, I count the number of principal surface combatants and submarines, this consists primarily of aircraft carriers, destroyers, frigates, and corvettes. Submarines include both nuclear and conventionally powered boats. Second, I quantify the armaments in the form of missiles. For the China case, I take into account the percentage of warships that the American government constitutes as 'modern'.[2] Qualitatively and, perhaps of greater importance, I examine how these platforms fit into each state's naval strategy and how the navy views its role in a potential military confrontation. Third, I examine data for the number of seaman (for India), and fourth, where available, I look at the information on naval budgets. This qualitative section was a primary part of in country interviews. Significantly, both ways of measuring warships demonstrate wide variation in naval modernization, which corresponds to changes in the nature of the rivalry.

Note on Submarines

Submarines form an important role in the process of naval modernization. This is especially true when examining variation over time. There is an enormous difference between different types of diesel submarines. Many of the subs that were produced in the 1950s and 1960s were extremely noisy and were unable to travel far before being forced to snorkel

[2] Chinese ships that are considered 'modern', all have modern missile systems.

to charge their batteries. Most earlier submarines were not armed with missiles, and carried just a few torpedoes. The more modern diesel SSKs such as the Scorpene, the Kilo, and the Yuan classes are radically different machines. Many of these subs are equipped with Air Independent Propulsion (AIP), which allows them to stay submerged for extended periods of time and to venture out into the open ocean. Regarding lethality, these boats are clearly much more advanced than the older subs. Most of these modern SSKs can fire anti-ship cruise missiles as well as advanced torpedoes. They are also extremely quiet and have the ability to position themselves in close proximity to aircraft carrier battle groups. Crucially, SSKs are not just a simple upgrade to a slightly different type of sub, but instead constitute a clear attempt by leaders to modernize their navy.

Platforms and submarines change with policies and strategies that call for naval modernization. For example, the American Navy is not concerned with older Chinese Ming class SSKs, but there is a great deal of respect for Chinese Yuan and Kilo SSKs, which are considered some of the best SSKs in the world.[3] Overall, there is an enormous difference between SSKs. The types of weapons systems and technology in the latest versions are barely comparable with older classes. There is clearly a difference in decisions made by leaders who only seek basic cost-effective upgrades to their SSKs, and much more sustained modernization programmes of the sort one finds in China and India.

In terms of nuclear-powered submarines, I argue that the difference between SSKs and SSNs/SSBNs is also clearly about modernization. If a state with a fleet of SSKs wants to push out into the open ocean, it needs to modernize its fleet. They could use SSKs in the open ocean but this is not very helpful as these boats do not have the range and would need to regularly raise their snorkel, thus exposing them to potential enemies. In other words, a state cannot dramatically change its naval strategy without modernizing its fleet. If a state wants to develop an underwater nuclear deterrent, it needs SSBNs, while this may be their intended use, it is more about a conscious, and sustained effort to modernize a fleet. Acquiring nuclear-powered submarines is not about upgrades, it is about

---

[3] Author's discussions with American defence officials. Beijing. 2016–2017.

a structural shift in maritime strategy that must be met with a prolonged strategy of naval modernization.

The Concept of Naval Modernization

We know that a state is pursuing naval modernization when we see a sustained effort to develop a modern fleet. States that upgrade a few warships and do not actively pursue more powerful classes of warships and submarines, may not be fully engaged in naval modernization. Naval modernization requires a conscious effort by leaders who have visions of sustained and increased naval power. Empirically we can ascertain a state's naval modernization plans, or lack thereof, by examining their past, current, and future naval power. States that have developed new classes of ships (very important here is new classes of warships and not just upgraded combat systems to old warships) show a significant increase in the lethality of these ships as well as technological advances on new ships are engaged in modernization. What a state currently has in their shipbuilding docks, as well as what it may have ordered from abroad, also constitutes evidence of naval modernization. Of equal importance, various statements in the form of white papers, naval strategies made public, and official statements that are repeated over time that call for naval modernization, are very helpful in understanding this process. When official statements result in new warships and submarines taking to sea, this is when we are witnessing naval modernization. Naval modernization is not a common phenomenon.

On the subject of the move from brown/green to blue water navies, I argue this is about modernization. Leaders consciously pursue naval modernization to push into the open ocean. Modernization and the push into the blue water are so closely linked that in the modern era, states that lack blue water fleets must modernize their navies in order to achieve power projection. In the case of China, the PLAN had to first modernize its navy in order to develop a credible blue water force. Without modernization, the PLAN would not be able to achieve this. In the Indian case, India needs to first modernize its naval forces in order to have a reliable blue water force.

Time Lags in Naval Modernization

It is important to note that variation in modernization will take time to manifest itself. A significant time lag is expected between a specific event, or critical juncture, which may cause a change in military doctrine, and when an actual naval platform that was ordered as a result of a critical juncture takes to sea. For example, after the decision to develop an aircraft carrier was made, it may take five to ten years (or more) before the carrier starts sea trials. During the extensive interviews for this project, I was able to find evidence for the causal relationship between rivalry escalation and changes in naval modernization. As noted in the literature review, Modelski and Thompson have written extensively about the challenges associated with measuring warships, their advice is closely adhered to (Modelski and Thompson 1988). The time frame of this project was selected because it allows for the significant time lag of when a platform is ordered and the time it is either being constructed in the docks, or has been put to sea. A shorter time frame of perhaps 10 years would have a more difficult time demonstrating the link between rivalry and naval procurement.

Evolving modernization programmes that demonstrate considerable variation are present in the two cases under review. As a state increases its power, the state will develop a greater ability to project power to thwart what it perceives as its rival's attempt to contain it. China pursued a strategy around 2005 that maintained the economic growth strategy of the earlier period, while seeking to transform its navy from one that focused on denying the American navy access to China's periphery, to one that attempted to dominate the ocean several thousand miles from the Chinese coast. This strategy is designed to keep the American navy out of the region. On the Indian side, New Delhi's naval strategy evolved from a navy mostly based on a green water defence with limited power projection capabilities in the 1990s and early 2000s, to one that started to deliver power projection platforms from the late 2000s onward. The main aim of this new naval development was countering the PLAN in the IOR. Key manifestations of this modernization can be found in both weapons acquisitions and orders for future naval hardware. In addition, research from the policy and academic communities as well as official government reports such as the Chinese Ministry of Defense's White Papers and various editions of the Indian Navy's 'Indian Maritime Doctrine,' support the push towards naval modernization. In the chapters relating to both states, I provide charts that breakdown of naval assets for both China and India from 1991 to 2021. The best overall explanation for the driver of this phenomenon is found in strategic rivalries. My argument of rivalry as the driving force behind naval modernization has historical precedent.

Rivalry

China and India have been involved in a strategic rivalry since 1948, while the Chinese and Americans have gone through two different rivalry periods (Colaresi et al. 2007). For the purpose of this project, I will argue that the second Sino/American rivalry started between 1989 and 1991 and is still ongoing.[4] It also experienced an escalation in the last 10 years of the period under examination.[5] The Sino/Indian rivalry was originally spatial centred on disputed territory along both states' Himalayan border. As India's economy developed and India began to play a more prominent role in both Asia and the international community, the rivalry transformed into a positional one.[6] Key to this process was the spillover effect from the Sino/American rivalry. As the PLAN modernized and began to send warships beyond China's immediate neighbourhood and into the IOR, India responded with a naval modernization programme of its own. Thus, the Sino/Indian rivalry began to take on a significant maritime dimension.

---

[4] For the dataset of rivalry maintenance and escalation please see the relevant empirical chapters.

[5] The 4 June 1989 Tiananmen Square Massacre produced a critical juncture for Sino/American relations. Immediately after this event the Americans placed sanctions on China and Beijing learned that it could no longer trust Washington. This rivalry went through various stages of escalation. See Chart 1 (Mann 1999).

[6] It should be noted that India and China have competed for influence in the developing world since the 1950s, but their ability to carry out major projects was limited by economic factors and challenges associated with each state's state capacity. Please see Garver 2001, pp. 110–137.

A 'One-Sided Rivalry?'

It is worth noting that the Sino/Indian rivalry has been categorized as a 'one-sided rivalry'. Well-known China specialist Susan Shirk argues that China does not consider India to be an important enough geostrategic player to be regarded as a real rival. She notes that the Chinese response to the 1998 Indian nuclear test was 'limited' (Shirk 2004). While India may not occupy the same threat level as the U.S. in Chinese leaders' eyes, it is still a strategic rival. Other scholars disagree with Shirk's categorization of India. Veteran China scholar David Shambaugh argues that China clearly sees India as a threat, and that Beijing perceives New Delhi as seeking hegemony, wanting to control the Indian Ocean, developing as a major military power, and above all, manoeuvring to 'contain China' (Shambaugh 2002). John Garver also views the dyad in the context of a rivalry. Garver points out that the territorial dispute, which encompasses over 125,000 square kilometres, and the Chinese tacit opposition to India becoming a permanent member of the UN Security Council in the 1990s, is clear examples of hostility between the two states (Garver 2001). It should also be noted that the Indian state of Arunachal Pradesh (the Chinese refer to this as 'South Tibet') covers an area of roughly 90,000 square kilometres. This is nearly the same size as the Chinese province of Zhejiang. In addition, the Chinese played a crucial role in helping India's arch-rival Pakistan develop a nuclear weapon in the 1980s (Garver 2001). You Ji points out that the Chinese military has several plans for war with India, these are the 1.5 war scenarios that are elaborated on in the Chapter 3 (You 2018). Apart from downplaying the importance of the territorial dispute or the question of Tibet, Shirk does not fully specify what she means by a 'rivalry', nor does she argue against every major rivalry data set, which universally categorize China and India as rivals[7] (Colaresi et al. 2007).

As required in a strategic rivalry, China views the U.S. as a critical threat to its long-term rise and strategic interests. Official American government statements that are critical of China, arms sales to China's

---

[7] These rivalry sets include the following: Strategic rivalries, Enduring Rivalries I, Enduring rivalries II, Interstate rivalries I, Interstate rivalries II, and Enduring international rivalries (Colaresi et al. 2007).

neighbours (especially Taiwan), and the American military's presence in East Asia, contribute to both maintaining and escalating this rivalry. In Table 4.1 of Chapter 4, I list occurrences of escalation and conflictual events during the time period specified. Notably, this table demonstrates variation in the rivalry. A key task that this book illuminates is which events were considered minor and which events were crucial to PLAN modernization.

Leaders and policymakers in India regard China as a significant threat to India's aspirations to become a regional and global power. In addition to frequent border incursions in disputed regions, Chinese statements critical of India as well as the increasing Chinese naval presence in the IOR and expanding ties with India's neighbours (especially Pakistan) have all greatly increased India's threat perceptions regarding China. These perceptions stemming from PLAN incursions into the IOR have caused New Delhi to adopt a more muscular naval strategy that calls for a navy capable of projecting power into the IOR to defend against the perceived Chinese threat. Table 3.1 in Chapter 3 lists occurrences of escalation and conflictual events in Sino/Indian relations.

In regards to warship designs, rivals do not necessarily have to match each other in naval platforms. While my argument anticipates some form of naval modernization if a threat emanates from the sea, the type of combatant is determined by economic and strategic factors. The two cases under review as well as the experience of the Soviet Union demonstrate that naval modernization driven by a rivalry can evolve over-time. It is rare for states to match each other ship for ship, but as will be demonstrated, a rivalry predicts modernization of one's navy, but the types of platforms ordered can vary. One should also pay attention to the time lag of ship construction. This further complicates scholar's ability to pinpoint a possible tit-for-tat response to a rival state's naval development. For example, states with already existing highly industrialized shipyards can produce warships much faster than states with lower levels of industrialization and technological knowhow. In the Indian case, these structural impediments frequently cause platforms to be delayed for years.[8]

---

[8] Please see the India case study chapter.

A Strategic Triangle?

Of the two cases under review, India's rivalry with China does have some characteristics of a triangular rivalry. The key third party in this triangle is the U.S., which may be working with India to counter China. While it is tempting to categorize New Delhi's embrace of Washington as empirical evidence of a triangle, upon scrutiny, the evidence does not fully support the presence of a strategic triangle.

A strategic triangle is defined as a form of transactional game between three players. Lowell Dittmer develops various types of triangles and the one that would best suit the India/China/USA rivalry would be his 'stable marriage' triangle. Dittmer devised this during the Cold War to explain China's relations with the USSR in regards to the U.S. In the configuration from 1949 to 1960, one finds symmetrical amity between two players (China and the USSR) and enmity between these two and a third player (USA) (Dittmer 1981). A variation of this emerges from 1970 to 1978 when relations between Moscow and Washington warmed and those between Beijing and Moscow came dangerously close to war, while at the same time China's relations with the U.S. warmed. Dittmer classifies this case as a 'romantic triangle', defined as amity between one 'pivot' state and two 'wing' states, but hostility between the two wing states (Dittmer 1981).

A key question for this book is does the improvement of ties between Washington and New Delhi vis-a-vis China constitute a triangular rivalry? Based on the available evidence the answer is no. While there is an increase in political and security ties between India and the U.S., much of this has taken place in the last 10–15 years of the period under review and crucially there is no formal alliance between the two states. It is true that since 2005, bilateral ties have improved markedly, especially on the security front, but New Delhi is still cautious about fully embracing Washington as a partner in constraining China. In interviews, American military officials point out that India is still not nearly as forthcoming in areas such as maritime cooperation as they would like. Bureaucratic challenges also exist.[9] Perhaps a major challenge for Indian and American forces to prepare for a China contingency is New Delhi's 2012 decision to

---

[9] Author's interviews with American officials in New Delhi, 2016.

purchase 126 medium multi-role combat aircraft from France, and not the U.S. (Ganguly and Thompson 2017). Although parts of this deal have since fallen apart, this decision was as much political as it was strategic. Had New Delhi elected to go with the F-18, it would have signalled much greater integration with American forces and more dependence on the U.S. for strategic support.

The period prior to 2005 certainly was not a stable marriage triangle between the USA/India and China. The Americans placed sanctions on India in 1998, and Washington worked with Beijing on the Nuclear Comprehensive Test Ban Treaty in the mid-1990s, which directly threatened New Delhi's nuclear deterrent. In addition, during President Clinton's visit to China in 1998, he spoke of an internationalization of the Kashmir issue, which was perceived in New Delhi as interference in India's internal affairs. Overall, ties between India and the U.S. are strengthening, but the Indians still like to maintain control of their destiny. Over the next decade as China continues to make strategic inroads into the IOR, it is possible (and perhaps likely) that we will witness a much more concerted effort by New Delhi to reach out to Washington for some sort of alliance, or improved interoperability between militaries, and in particular, the maritime domain. However, until then, it is still too early to classify this as a rivalry triangle.

Rivalry as a Driver of Naval Modernization

Over the last century and a half, rivalry has played a major role in naval modernization. While scholars have identified rivalry as a major driver of arms races and military build ups (Rider et al. 2011), none have applied it to any in-depth historical or contemporary cases of naval modernization. This next section briefly touches on the role of rivalry in naval modernization.

Strategic relations between states in 19th-century Europe were dominated by rivalry. Hamilton argues that the rivalry between Great Britain and France in the 1860s drove the French to invest in naval modernization (Hamilton 1993). The link between access denial and military spending also has historical precedent. For example, in the 1870s Otto Von Bismarck and his naval high command realized that Germany did not have to waste enormous economic resources on the development of a blue-water navy. Bismarck's viewed France as Germany's chief rival and therefore the construction of a stronger navy would have to wait for the rivalry with Britain to escalate. During Bismarck's time, Germany elected to build smaller, less expensive vessels that could contend with the navies of smaller European nations and protect Germany's coastal interests. The concept of the 'risk fleet', elaborated on earlier in this chapter was not initiated until the late 1880s and early 1890s (Herwig 2009; Ross 2009; Kennedy 1984). In responding to Germany's British rival, Tirpitz called out Britain as Germany's 'most dangerous opponent at sea', and cleverly tried to tie naval expenditures to the projected rate of economic growth (Herwig 2009). By the end of the first decade of the 20th century, Britain sensing the growing naval competition with Germany, ended its rivalries with France and Russia initiated the *entente cordiale* in 1907 with these states. This led to an escalation in the rivalry with Germany and Berlin began to speak of British 'encirclement'. Rivalry with Germany caused the British in 1905 to launch the HMS Dreadnought, the most advanced warship of its time, complete with one-calibre, all-big-gun turrets. This development caused Germany naval planners to panic (Herwig 2009).

On the Asian front, Ross argues that nationalism drove the Japanese to pursue a naval buildup that was able to defeat the Russian military in the early 20th century. While Japan certainly did build up a powerful navy, this was more in response to their rivalry with Russia and less to do with nationalism (Ross 2009). From 1906 until 1941, in a Mahanian inspired modernization programme, Japan's growing rivalry with the U.S. led it to develop a navy that would be able to fight and deter the American navy (Cole 2013).

For three decades after the Second World War, the Soviet navy concentrated on building smaller ships and submarines to deny access to much larger American warships. The Soviet strategy of 'bastions' was designed for SSNs (hunter killer nuclear submarines) to form protective belts around Soviet SSBNs (Erickson and Wilson 2007). It was not until the 1970s that the USSR began to develop a more ocean going fleet, and only in the 1980s that its first aircraft carriers came online (Kolnogorov 2007).

Conclusion

Overall, naval modernization is a long-drawn-out process. Navies that simply upgrade a few ships with new missile systems and radars are not serious about modernizing their fleets. Multiple factors influence the decision to construct a powerful navy, a process that is extremely expensive and can take decades to manifest itself. Factors such as nationalism and bureaucratic influences do play a role, however on their own they are insufficient drivers. The presence of an ongoing strategic rivalry that is playing out in the maritime domain is the critical determinant of whether a state pursues naval modernization.

3

The Sino/Indian Rivalry and Indian Naval Modernization

Over the period examined, the Indian navy has gone from a force that was largely a green water navy in 1991, to one that is able to project significant power in not only the IOR, but also increasingly outside of the region in places as diverse as the South China Sea and north-east Asia. The IN has gone from a so-called Cinderella service, that was never a strategic priority in the late 1980s and early 1990s, to a force that in just over a quarter-century has made vast improvements in the sophistication and lethality of its platforms (Scott 2013). When one considers that in 1991 the IN had only 10 platforms that were equipped with missiles, and that the entire navy had only 91 total missile cells (not just for one class of warships), it is clear the IN has made substantial progress in its modernization (The Military Balance 1991). (In 2019, a single Kolkata class DDG had 48 missile cells.) By 2019, the IN had grown into a fleet that had moved well beyond the ability to deal with any Pakistani contingency, to a force where nearly all the major surface platforms were armed with increasingly sophisticated anti-ship missiles and surface-to-air missile systems (SAMS) (The Military Balance 2019). Many of these warships are equipped with dozens of missiles. The crucial task of this study is to explain what is driving this naval modernization? As noted in earlier chapters, India has been a land power since its independence in 1947. New Delhi's rivalries with Pakistan and China are alive and well and both share a common trait in that they represent land threats to India. While the rivalry with Pakistan may be more confined to India's northwestern borders, the rivalry with China has evolved since the 1990s into a rivalry that is both spatial and positional. This evolving rivalry with China is the most important driver of India's naval modernization. In particular, New Delhi's rivalry is connected to Beijing's rivalry with Washington.

The Nexus of Naval Modernization in India and China. Christopher K. Colley, Oxford University Press. © Oxford University Press 2022. DOI: 10.1093/oso/9780192865595.003.0004

As previously mentioned the dynamics of the Sino/U.S. rivalry are discussed in the next chapter, however, it is crucial to point out that China's naval modernization is driven by the American naval presence in East Asia. China's response has been to develop an increasingly powerful navy, which, causes rivalry escalation between China and India in the maritime domain, which subsequently drives Indian naval modernization. Diagram 3.1 below demonstrates the connection between China's naval modernization and India's naval modernization.

However, as will be discussed in detail, other explanations such as bureaucratic politics, nationalism, as well as natural force replenishment, will also be addressed. These counterarguments are not completely divorced from the rivalry explanations. Several of these, including bureaucratic politics, are firmly embedded in the strategic rivalry argument. This chapter does not make a mono-causal argument centred only on strategic rivalry, however; it does argue that rivalry is the best explanation.

Specifically, a major focus of this chapter will be the links between rivalry maintenance and escalation, and naval modernization. In particular, critical junctures are paramount in how they influence leaders' threat perceptions and subsequent decision-making. The following pages provide a granular account of the Sino/Indian strategic rivalry and trace how this is the major cause of Indian naval modernization. Importantly, readers should look for statements from leaders and those with direct

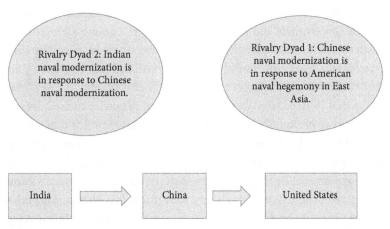

Diagram 3.1 The Interconnected Nature of the Sino/U.S. and Sino/Indian Strategic Rivalries

knowledge of decision-making, to ascertain Indian threat perceptions from China. Many of these individuals are on record calling China out as a threat and advocating naval modernization as a way of protecting India from the PLAN's increasing forays into the IOR. Scholars should also critically examine evidence of other causes of naval modernization and weigh this against the argument of strategic rivalry. Finally, the data presented in this chapter should measure what it is supposed to measure, and should support either directly or indirectly the main argument advocated in this book.

This chapter is divided into four main sections. In the first section, a brief background to the Sino/Indian rivalry will be provided. While the origins of the rivalry are not the subject of this book, the events prior to 1991 are extremely important to understanding how perceptions and misperceptions have been formed in various departments of the Indian Government, as well as society at large. (The focus of this chapter is mainly on Indian perceptions of the Sino/Indian strategic rivalry. When relevant, Chinese perceptions are also analysed, but the main argument is that India is responding to China and not the other way around.) The second part of the case study will examine the period from 1991 to 2004. This is done for practical reasons. The period under review is relatively long and in order to properly examine the case in a way that allows one to scrutinize specific time periods, it is best to organize the chapter in this manner. Importantly, even though the Sino/Indian strategic rivalry experienced escalation during the 1990s, the Indian Government did not have the ability to commence significant modernization until after the beginning of the new century. The third section focuses on the period from 2005 until 2020. It is in these years that sustained naval modernization becomes a reality and new platforms that were ordered in the 1990s started to take to the sea. During this 15-year period, the rivalry also experiences significant escalation in the form of PLAN warships visiting the IOR, as well as increasing Indian perceptions of being 'contained' by China. These PLAN incursions are critical in that they demonstrate the links between China's rivalry with the U.S. and its rivalry with India. It is also in this period that the Indian Government starts to have the financial ability to significantly modernize its navy. Empirical evidence of this is found in increasing naval budgets as well as new orders for modern warships. Many of these warships are currently undergoing sea trials, or are under construction. A rivalry maintenance and escalation data set is presented in this chapter to demonstrate variation in the rivalry in accordance with the punctuated equilibrium model. The final section of this chapter will discuss competing explanations of India's naval modernization. This part will not discredit each competing argument, but it will demonstrate the flaws of such approaches.

It is important to note that no two cases are identical. The Indian case has similarities with the China case that will be identified. However, because of India's smaller economy and subsequent smaller military budget, variations emerge in the exact type of platforms each state has decided to pursue. Indian naval modernization is less about quantity and more about quality. While the IN has grown in size, it has enormously increased its technological sophistication. New technologies allow the IN to undertake much longer tours. IN warships are equipped with better sensors, long-range weapons, as well as platforms that are interconnected through data-link (Menon 2012). India's new SSK submarines (many of which are now coming into service) are all equipped with advanced anti-ship missiles and are scheduled to be equipped with Air Independent Propulsion systems (AIP), which greatly increase the time they are able to stay submerged (Gady 2019). The India case is more of a rivalry evolution with periods of escalation that are important, but not as important as some of the critical junctures in the Sino/U.S. rivalry. In China's rivalry with the U.S., we find specific events that can be seen as major turning points in Chinese strategic thought. For example, the 1995/1996 Taiwan crisis was an escalation that involved the use of missiles and had the potential to escalate to war. While we do not have a similar kinetic example on the high seas between India and China, we still have a significant escalation in the maritime domain (as well as low-level kinetic events on land. See data set).

In contrast to China with its increasing fleets of SSNs, SSBNs, and other warships, India's modernization is not as impressive. However, as will be demonstrated in this and subsequent chapters, the IN may be a decade or more behind the PLAN in terms of modernization, but it is modernizing and the real or perceived threat of China is the primary driver.

Part I: The Origins and Rise of the Sino/Indian Strategic Rivalry

The origins of the modern Sino/Indian strategic rivalry can be traced to the late 1940s, when both China and India became modern nation states. India had historically viewed the Tibetan plateau and the Tibetan civilization as an extension of India's own cultural sphere of influence. While the details of the Sino/Indian dispute over Tibet are not the subject of this book, it is important to note that the Communist 'invasion/liberation' of Tibet deeply troubled Nehru and, in general, the Indian public. With the CCP in firm control of most of the plateau, New Delhi saw an Indian inspired culture and civilization threatened. Eager to preserve peace and to work with the newly founded People's Republic of China, Nehru agreed to Beijing's control and ownership of Tibet[1] (Garver 2001). In what would be vital for the long-term future of bilateral relations and for the current strategic rivalry, this agreement did not directly address the territorial dispute. Instead, this would be left for future discussions. Nehru insisted that the border must be based on the McMahon Line that was drawn up during the 1914 Simla Convention. This agreement was, and still is challenged by Beijing, as China does not recognize the validity of the borders.[2] Even though Nehru sought to keep relations with Mao on a cooperative and respectful basis, by the mid-1950s China started to build a road linking Hotan in Xinjiang province with Lhasa. This road was strategic in that it allowed the PLA to access Lhasa year round. The road also cut through territory in Aksai Chin that was claimed by India. In many ways, this road-building project initiated the rivalry between China and India that persists to this day (Garver 2001).

It is important to note that issues pertaining to Tibet were instrumental to the escalation of the rivalry and subsequent 1962 war, however even in the 1940s, Indian elites were sceptical of their northern neighbour and some were even concerned with China in the Indian Ocean.

---

[1] When writing on Tibet in this book, I am referring to what the Chinese government calls 'The Tibet Autonomous Region', as well as parts of Qinghai, Gansu, Sichuan, and Yunnan provinces. When discussing other parts of the Tibetan Plateau, I use the name of the specific place.

[2] For a detailed analysis of the territorial dispute between China and India please see John Garver's 'Protracted Contest', specifically chapter three, which is dedicated to the territorial dispute.

This was before China even had anything that could be realistically be called a modern navy (Scott 2006). Sardar Patel, who was nick named the 'iron man', took a much more hardline towards China than did Nehru and was more sceptical of Chinese intentions. For their part, the Chinese also held suspicions of India after New Delhi started to receive American aid. Mao also viewed Nehru's push for a non-aligned pan-Asianism as a potential challenge towards his ambitions to be the leading figure in Asia (Holslag 2010).

When the Indian army discovered the PLA road-building project in Aksai Chin, the Indian parliament demanded that the road be 'bombed out of existence' (Holslag 2010. P 39). In addition to the perceived infringement of Indian territory, in 1956 a rebellion broke out in the Tibetan areas of Western Sichuan province. The major cause of this revolt was the land reform policy initiated by the CCP, and what John Garver defines as the 'holocaust of Maoist misrule' (Garver 2001. P 56). By the late 1950s, the revolt had spread to Lhasa and the young Dali Lama fled Tibet for India where he has resided ever since. It is important to take into account Indian sympathy for Tibet during this period. This revolt was brutally put down, which further alienated the Indian public towards the CCPs stated mission of the 'liberation' of Tibet.

The revolt in Tibet did not cause the 1962 war, but it undoubtedly contributed towards negative feelings against Beijing. In order to make a statement and halt the Chinese construction project, in 1961 India launched the 'forward policy', designed to demonstrate to Beijing that New Delhi would not stand for what India perceived as a violation of Indian sovereignty (Fravel 2008). Relatively poorly equipped Indian troops marched into Chinese controlled territory in an attempt to demonstrate Indian resolve. By the fall of 1962, the forward policy had caused substantial alarm in Beijing. As China gradually saw its claim strength diminish in the disputed territory, it attacked Indian positions in October 1962. After pushing Indian troops back across the border and crossing the border, Chinese troops retreated into the previously held territory (Fravel 2008).

It is difficult to understate the strategic and psychological impact that the 1962 war had on the Indian public. From India's perspective, Chinese aggression had shattered the dream of a non-aligned pan-Asian movement that guaranteed peace and stability. From a strategic perspective,

New Delhi was ill-prepared to confront a modern, battle-hardened, mechanized People's Liberation Army that had less than a decade earlier fought the Americans to a stalemate on the Korean Peninsula. The legacy of the 1962 war lives on to this day. The belief that this can 'never happen again' is alive and well in India. Policymakers and scholars widely agree that the war still heavily influences India's relations with China.[3] (Interestingly, very few Chinese officials and scholars bring up the 1962 war, and many are unaware of how profound an experience it was for India.)[4] Even though the territorial dispute was the direct cause of the war, the rivalry between India and China extended beyond this. Nehru admitted in 1962 that the rivalry expanded to positional and hierarchical positions in Asia (Mohan 2012).

From a strict security standpoint, the 1962 war dramatically altered India's defence posture. In the following year, Nehru doubled India's defence budget, and from 1962 until 1965, India's political debate was heavily orientated towards China. During this period a comprehensive government review deemed China to be a primary threat, which led to calls to increase the strength of the IN in the event the PLAN would make forays into the Bay of Bengal. Defense Minister Y.B Chavan openly spoke of Chinese capabilities and intentions in the Lok Sabha in 1963. Specifically, he clarified that the government agreed on the need for a submarine fleet (Rajagopalan 2016). (It needs to be stated that during the 1960s neither China nor India had the ability to threaten each other in the maritime domain.)

China's 1964 nuclear weapons test further exacerbated Indian fears of the Chinese military (Cohen and Das 2010). The strategic rivalry between India and Beijing took on a new dimension in 1964 when China sided with Pakistan on the question of Kashmir and was further escalated in 1965 when China backed Pakistan in its war with India (Shankar 2018). This support for Pakistan is still significant today. PLA troops took up frontline positions along the Tibetan border, thus threatening New Delhi

---

[3] During the fieldwork stage of this book in New Delhi, nearly every single person interviewed by this author cited the 1962 war as a watershed moment for not only India's relations with China, but also for how India perceived the world. (Author's interviews with Indian experts in New Delhi. New Delhi, May/June 2016.)

[4] Many Chinese do not understand why this war was/is such a significant issue for India. (Author's interviews in Beijing and Shanghai. 2016–2017)

with the strong possibility of a two-front war. Interestingly, China's role in the 1971 war between India and Pakistan was not as critical. While China rhetorically supported Pakistan, it did not come to its ally's aid in any meaningful way. Part of this may be because China was still in the throes of the Cultural Revolution as well as the fact that China was aware that in all likelihood Pakistan would be divided and China wanted to be able to have diplomatic relations with the newly formed state of Bangladesh (Garver 2001). Perhaps the two best explanations for Chinese inaction during the dismemberment of Pakistan are found in the fact that the war took place in December and the logistical challenges of moving troops and military supplies over the Himalayas would have been extremely difficult, if not impossible to accomplish. In addition, and of greater importance, India had signed a treaty with the USSR in August of 1971, which included security guarantees.[5]

Nuclear weapons have also played a significant role in the Sino/Indian and Indian/Pakistani rivalries. India's 1974 'peaceful nuclear test' sent a warning to both Islamabad and Beijing. Beijing countered by becoming a critical source of arms to Pakistan. During the 1970s, China spent approximately 450 million U.S. dollars on loans and grants to its 'all weather ally' (Stockholm multiple years). In what is understood as a tit-for-tat move to counter India's support for Tibetan exiles, Beijing armed and trained insurgents in India's northeast. In particular, Naga insurgents were armed in Yunnan and sent back into India where they did considerable damage to Indian security forces battling the insurgency (Garver 2001). The 1970s also saw the rivalry spread to smaller regional states on both China's and India's periphery. Beijing actively courted Nepalese, Sri Lankan, and Burmese leaders. Deng Xiaoping even visited Nepal in 1978 and Bangladeshi leader Zia Rahman visited China in 1977. India made a point of siding with the Cambodian rebel leader Heng Samrin, who fought against the Chinese backed Khmer Rouge. India also set up an informal alliance with China's enemy Vietnam (Holslag 2010).

Perhaps the greatest point of escalation in the Sino/Indian rivalry in the decades following the 1962 war came in the form of Chinese technical assistance to Pakistan's nuclear weapons programme. The Chinese government has never acknowledged this assistance, but according

---

[5] The author would like to thank Sumit Ganguly for pointing this out to him.

to John Garver, in the early 1980s, China was instrumental in helping Pakistan develop a nuclear bomb. Blueprints for the actual device as well as supplies of uranium hexafluoride were provided to Pakistani technicians. The apparent rationale for this move was to guarantee the survival of Pakistan in the event of another war with India, thus ensuring that China's rival, India, would not be able to completely dominate South Asia (Garver 2001).

As the 1980s unfolded, the rivalry between China and India experienced escalation and de-escalation. The 1986 announcement of the creation of the Indian state of Arunachal Pradesh, (what Beijing considers 'South Tibet') represented a serious heightening of tensions for China. As a result, troops were mobilized by each side, and there were even reports of armed skirmishes between PLA and Indian troops. However, this escalation was eased following Rajiv Gandhi's visit to China in 1988 (Pardesi 2019).

Overall, the first four decades of the Sino/Indian strategic rivalry in many ways mirrors the time frame under review in this book. The early years of the rivalry exhibited both spatial and positional attributes. A lack of trust on each side was fused with a bitter territorial dispute that gradually escalated to war in 1962. The aftermath of the war forever altered the balance between the two states and set the stage for a new form of rivalry that as the 21stcentury began would begin to take on maritime dimensions (Colley 2021A).

Part II: The Sino/Indian Rivalry in the 1990s and the Birth of a Modern Navy

In 1991, the IN was a long way from becoming a realistic force able to project power to any distant shore. One of the best empirical examples of the limitations of the IN during this period can be found in New Delhi's inability to protect Indian flagged oil tankers during the 1980s Iran/Iraq war. During the Tanker War of the late 1980s, when the Iranian military targeted oil tankers leaving Iraqi and Kuwaiti ports with anti-ship missiles, Indian flagged ships were the largest number attacked yet the IN was unable to project any power to the region (Menon 2012). Instead this task was left to the U.S., which in many instances reflagged various ships with American flags. In addition, the IN had failed to evacuate overseas Indians in the Persian Gulf during the 1991 Iraq War.[6] The 1991 Gulf War was a critical juncture for New Delhi in many ways as the crises resulting from Iraq invading Kuwait and the subsequent American led war to force Saddam Hussein's army out of Kuwait had a major impact on India's economy. India was heavily dependent on the Gulf region, both as a source of remittances from members of the Indian diaspora and as a source of energy. The war in the Gulf caused a near economic collapse in the Indian economy, thus acting as a catalyst for significant economic reforms in India (Haokip 2011; Mukherji 2016). Superficially, it appeared that India did have a navy that possessed substantial combatants. As can be seen in Table 3.1, in 1991 the IN had 56 major warships and submarines, however many of these platforms were obsolete and lacked significant firepower in the form of missiles. Even though the IN had two aircraft carriers at this time, the Vikrant was less than 20,000 tons and was retired in 1996. (In contrast, an American Nimitz class carrier is over 100,000 tons and the Chinese carrier Liaoning is roughly 65,000 tons.) (Joe 2021A)

The Maintenance and Escalation of the Sino/ Indian Strategic Rivalry

The events in Beijing on the night of 3 June 1989 forever altered China's foreign relations. The international press had come to Beijing in May to report on Soviet Primer Gorbachev's rapprochement with China. The real story was not the hand shaking between Soviet and Chinese leaders, but the massive demonstrations taking place just outside the Great Hall of the People in Tiananmen Square. The decision to use lethal force and the live broadcasting of the Tiananmen Massacre horrified the international community.[7] (As will be discussed in the next chapter, this also marks the re-emergence of the Sino/U.S. strategic rivalry.) In the aftermath of

---

[6] Author's interviews with scholars and experts in New Delhi in June 2016.
[7] The vast majority, if not all, of the killings actually took place outside of Tiananmen Square. (Author's discussions with individuals who were present in the square on the night of 3 June 1989. Beijing 2006–2012)

the massacre, Beijing found itself internationally isolated. It was in this context that Chinese leaders sought to improve their relations with New Delhi. Beijing saw an opportunity to forge a world not dominated by the West and thought China and India should work together to achieve this (Garver 2016).

Unfortunately, for China's weakened leaders, the era of third world solidarity was over. Upon assuming office in 1991, Indian Prime Minister P.V. Narasimha Rao viewed China as a long-term threat. With India losing its Soviet backer, the Sino/Indian rivalry continued to develop in the early 1990s. A major reason for this was Beijing's continued close relations with Islamabad, to which it continued to sell arms, including missiles that directly threatened India.[8] From 1993 to 1997, China supplied 51 per cent of all of Pakistan's arms imports. These included fast attack boats armed with anti-ship missiles (Garver 2016). In addition, Beijing insisted that security ties with Islamabad were not linked to India. As can be seen in Graph 3.1, China was a major source of Pakistani arms imports from 1991 to 2018. These arms transfers, which range from fighter-bombers, to missiles, to submarines and frigates are a major source of rivalry maintenance and escalation between India and China.

When the U.S. demanded that China break ties with Iran, primarily over its nuclear programme, Beijing did not sever ties with Pakistan (Garver 2016). While China's close ties with Pakistan were a serious concern to India, the new leadership in India was much more realistic about the dangers the modern world posed. Many of India's decision-makers believed that the 'Wooly-headed Third Worldism' had disguised China's strategic moves in the region that greatly diminished India's security. This new realist approach towards India's foreign relations rejected China's appeals to join up with India to oppose Western hegemony (Garver 2016. P 736). While Pakistan still constituted a significant threat to India, as the Indian security policy developed in the 1990s, the focus was increasingly on China.[9]

Prior to the 1990s, the Indian navy was unquestionably neglected. The so-called Cinderella service had a very small piece of the overall

[8] Author's interview with a security specialist in a New Delhi think-tank. New Delhi June 2016.
[9] Author's interview with a security specialist in a New Delhi think-tank. New Delhi June 2016.

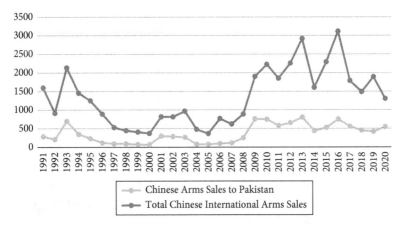

Graph 3.1 Chinese Arms Sales to Pakistan 1991–2020 (Stockholm. Multiple years in Trend Indicator Values)[a]

[a]SIPRI calculates these values in the 'Trend Indicator Value'. According to SIPRI, 'The TIV is based on the known unit production costs of a core set of weapons and is intended to represent the transfer of military resources rather than the financial value of the transfer. Weapons for which a production cost is not known are compared with core weapons based on: size and performance characteristics (weight, speed, range and payload); type of electronics, loading or unloading arrangements, engine, tracks or wheels, armament and materials; and the year in which the weapon was produced. A weapon that has been in service in another armed force is given a value 40 per cent of that of a new weapon. A used weapon that has been significantly refurbished or modified by the supplier before delivery is given a value of 66 per cent of that of a new weapon.' Stockholm International Peace Research Institute. Website. https://www.sipri.org/databases/armstransfers/background

military budget. In the first decades after independence, the naval budget varied from 5–10 per cent of the military budget. It was not until the late 1980s under Rajiv Gandhi, that the naval budget saw a real increase. In fact, in 1990, an ambitious 25-year naval modernization programme was announced, but this quickly faltered with the collapse of the USSR, and more fundamentally the financial crisis of 1991 (Mohan 2012). While India was slowly recovering from the crisis, the rivalry with China continued to be maintained. By the early 1990s, Indian naval advocates started to fear the possibility of the Chinese taking advantage of India in the maritime domain (Scott 2006). The first major PLAN forays into the IOR took place in 1993, when Chinese warships visited Bangladesh, India, and Pakistan (Koh 2016). This was in addition to consistent reports that the Chinese were setting up an intelligence gathering base and stockpiling arms in the Coco Islands in Myanmar, which are north of the Andaman and Nicobar Islands.

It needs to be noted that these reports were not based on reliable evidence, but as the strategic rivalry literature makes clear, perceptions, and worst-case scenario thinking matter (Mohan 2012). As the rivalry data set in Table 3.1 demonstrates, the early 1990s did witness maintenance and some escalation in the rivalry, but the frequency and severity of the rivalry were not as intense as it was from the late 1990s and afterwards. While we do find upgrades to naval platforms in the first five years of the period under review, given the very limited defence budget of this period Indian naval development was not as impressive as in later years. (In U.S. dollars, the entire Indian military budget did not exceed 10 billion dollars until the late 1990s.) (The Military Balance- IISS data)[10]

Even though the IN did not enjoy a large budget in the early 1990s, it did receive increases in the percentage of the defence budget.[11] Between 1990 and 1996, the IN's budget rose to approximately 13 per cent, and in the decade from 1996 until 2006, it enjoyed 15 per cent of the budget (Sawhney 2014). The 1994 decision to open negotiations with Russia on the acquisition of the aircraft carrier Admiral Gorshkov is interesting in that this was one of the few orders the Indian government placed for major new warships in the early 1990s (Cohen and Dasgupta 2010). This was at a time when the IN already had two carriers in its fleet. The most likely explanation for the plan to acquire the Gorshkov has less to do with rivalry and more to do with ship replenishment, as the Vikrant was nearing retirement. Overall, even though the rivalry with China was present in the early 1990s, the Indian government did not have the financial capability to heavily invest in new naval platforms. Of greater importance, is the fact that China's own military modernization was just getting started. The threat perceptions and instances of rivalry escalation that would characterize the 21st-century had yet to come to fruition. Interestingly, the IN did start to modernize its platforms in the late 1990s, just as the rivalry with China began to increase, and at the same time that China started to make significant investments in naval hardware as a response to the American navy.

---

[10] Although it did not exceed 10 billion dollars, it did rise significantly in Indian Rupees. In 1991, the entire defence budget was 157 billion rupees, by 1997 this had more than doubled to 356 billion rupees (The Military Balance various years).

[11] Please see Graphs 3.2 and 3.3.

Table 3.1 Maintenance and Escalation in the Sino/Indian strategic Rivalry: 1991–2020. (Points of escalation considered critical junctures are in bold)

(Author's database relying on multiple sources)

Number	Year	Description of Dispute
1	1991 to Present	Continuation of border infractions. Regular violations of sovereignty.
2	Early 1990s to 2005	Regular reports that China was setting up an intelligence base in and positioning arms on Coco Island in Burma.
3	1993, March	**Chinese warships make a port call in Pakistan.**
4	Mid-1990s	China renovates its 14 airfields in Tibet with new communication and command equipment. Also deploys SU-27 there. Increases pressure on India's northern border.
5	1996	China and U.S. work on the Nuclear Comprehensive Test Ban Treaty. Threatens India's nuclear deterrent.
6	1997–present	**Visits by PLAN warship visits to IOR states become a regular occurrence.**
7	1998, April	China allegedly assists Pakistan with the firing of an intermediate-range ballistic missile.
8	1998, May	Indian nuclear tests. China cited as the reason.
9	1998, May	**Indian Defense Minister calls China the 'potential number one threat'.**
10	1998, May	**Indian Prime Minister says India must prove its strength against China**
11	1998	**China hints that it might take a pro-Pakistan stance on Kashmir**
12	1998	**China starts to cooperate more with Pakistan. Supplies guidance systems, motors, and steel for Pakistani missiles.**
13	1998, July	**American President Clinton visits Beijing and speaks of an internationalization of the Kashmir issue with China. New Delhi views this Chinese interference in India's internal affairs.**
14	1998-1999	China lobbies the U.S., France, and Russia to only sanction Indian and not Pakistan for nuclear tests.
15	2000	**PLAN port calls to IOR states increase in frequency.**
16	2000–2010	Every month the Indo-Tibetan police report around a dozen unannounced Chinese military patrols in the disputed border areas
17	2001, May	**PLAN warships make a port call in Pakistan.**

Continued

Table 3.1 *Continued*

Number	Year	Description of Dispute
18	2001	Announcement by Chinese Premier Zhu Rongji that China pledges money to build a port in Gwadar Pakistan.
19	2001	China's Prime Minister visits Male. Raises Indian concerns about Chinese activities and influence in India's backyard.
20	2002	U.S. Chairman of the Joint Chiefs of Staff visits India to expand military relations. Perceived as a way to hedge against China.
21	2003– present	**PLA joint military exercises with IOR states become a regular occurrence.**
22	2002–2007	Sri Lanka receives at least 140 million dollars worth of military equipment from China. Increases Indian concerns of Chinese encirclement and adds credence to the idea of 'The String of Pearls'.
23	2004, July	Chinese patrol temporarily arrests an Indian intelligence team ten kilometres inside the Line of Actual Control (LAC) in Arunachal Pradesh's Subansiri district.
24	2005	Chinese psychological warfare against India starts. Articles in official Chinese newspapers start to discuss the possibility of a new war with India.
25	2005	India and the U.S. sign a New Framework for Defense Relations, laying out a ten-year program. This is a direct hedge against China and its activities in the IOR.
26	2005	India gives the Seychelles the INS Tarmugli (fast attack craft) to counter Chinese influence there.
27	2005, November	PLAN warships make a port call in Pakistan.
28	2000s	**India sees China as blocking a permanent seat on the UN Security Council for India**
29	2006	**China completes the railway line to Lhasa. Significantly enhances the PLA's ability to mobilize for war with India.**
30	2006	**Reports that China might build a naval base in the Maldives**
31	2006	**Chinese policy hardens towards India, China withdraws Article 7, that states that China might be prepared to give up its claim to all of Arunachal Pradesh**
32	2006	**Chinese ambassador to India claims all of Arunachal Pradesh**
33	2006	Chinese border incursions in Ladakh and Tawang

Table 3.1 *Continued*

Number	Year	Description of Dispute
34	2007	Chinese President Hu Jintao visits the Seychelles. Perceived by New Delhi as increasing Chinese influence in the IOR.
35	2007	Chinese helicopter flies over the western sector of the LAC
36	2007, November	Chinese demolition of unmanned Indian forward posts in the Dollam Valley—causes public outrage
37	2007	China signs an agreement with Sri Lanka to develop a port at Hambantota in Sri Lanka
38	2007	Chinese Foreign Minister Yang Jiechi meets Indian Foreign Minister Pranab Mukerjee in Germany and tells him that the mere presence of a population in disputed territories does not affect Chinese claims
39	2008	PLAN takes a major step in increasing its presence in the IOR by joining anti-piracy patrols in the Gulf of Aden. Significantly increases Indian concerns of Chinese (PLAN) encirclement in the IOR.
40	2008	Indian Foreign Minister Mukherjee visits Beijing and is stunned to see Chinese claims to various territories claimed by India.
41	2008	**Chinese attempt to undermine approval of the Indo-U.S. civilian nuclear initiative at the Nuclear Suppliers Group in the fall of 2008**
42	2008–onward	India starts to counter Chinese airfields in Tibet with SU-30MKI jets in the eastern sector
43	2009, January	Chinese warships force an Indian SSK to surface after an intense standoff near the Bab-el-Mandeb Strait in the Gulf of Aden
44	2009, February	Chinese President Hu Jintao visits Mauritius to speed up the development of a Chinese Special Economic Zone. Further reinforces Indian concerns of 'The String of Pearls'.
45	2009, March	Beijing demands that the Asian Development Bank delete a reference to Arunachal Pradesh from a 2.9 billion dollar proposal for a four year Country Partnership Proposal—or scuttle the deal
46	2009, August	3 PLAN warships make a port call in Pakistan.
47	2009	**PLAN port calls to the IOR region skyrocket.**
48	2009–2010	The PLA uses a helicopter to patrol the border with India, increases tension and adds to concerns of Chinese containment.

Continued

Table 3.1 *Continued*

Number	Year	Description of Dispute
49	2010, March	3 PLAN warships make a port call in Pakistan.
50	2010–present	PLA joint military exercises with IOR states increase.
51	2010	A posting on the Renmin Ribao's 'Great Power Forum' calls for a showdown with India to solve the territorial dispute once and for all. Renmin Ribao is the People's Daily newspaper. The official newspaper of the CCP.
52	2010, September	A 450 million dollar deal is finalized by the Chinese to modernize Colombo's port by China Merchant Holdings—through a joint venture
53	2011, March	Three Chinese warships make a port visit to Pakistan.
54	2011, July	**Chinese warships challenge the INS Airvant while it is visiting Vietnam**
55	2011, December	**Chinese Defense Minister Liang Guanglie visits the Seychelles. Sparks rumours that the Seychelles will offer China a base, this is denied by China, but China does confirm that it is considering the Seychelles as a relief and supply station for the PLAN**
56	2012, September	3 PLAN warships make a port call in Pakistan.
57	2013, July	PLAN warships make a port call in Pakistan.
58	2013	**Border standoff during Chinese Prime Minister Li Keqiang's visit to India**
59	2013	**Announcement of the Chinese Belt and Road Initiative.**
60	2014	**PLA joint military exercises with IOR states skyrocket.**
61	2014	**Border standoff during Chinese President Xi Jinping's visit to India lasts for 20 days**
62	2014	For the first time three PLAN warships transit the Straits of Lombok and Sunda.
63	2014	PLAN deploys eight warships in search of MH 370. Asks India to allow four PLAN warships to search the Andaman Sea, India says no.
64	2014, September	3 PLAN warships make a port call in Pakistan.
65	2015	Chinese White Paper on Defense calls for far greater power projection
66	2015	**Announcement of a PLAN base in Djibouti. Increases concerns in New Delhi that the 'String of Pearls' is turning into a reality.**
67	2016, January	3 PLAN warships make a port call in Pakistan. (Would have been scheduled in 2015.)

Table 3.1 *Continued*

Number	Year	Description of Dispute
68	2016, September	Xi Jinping visits Bangladesh and offers Dhaka 24 billion dollars in infrastructure investment
69	2017, Summer	**Border standoff between Chinese and Indian forces at Doklam**
70	2017 Summer	14 PLAN warships transit the Indian Ocean at the same time. Conduct live fire exercises. At same time as Doklam standoff.
71	2017, August	Three PLAN warships dock in the Maldives
72	2017, December	Maldives rushed through the Maldives-China Free trade Agreement- reward for China's support- reverses the 'India-first policy'
73	2017, December	China signs 99 year lease with Sri Lanka for the port of Hambantota.
74	2018 February	**China tells India to stay out of the Maldives Crisis**
75	2018, February	**11 PLAN warships patrol near the Maldives. Perceived in New Delhi as a deterrent to stay out of political crisis in the Maldives.**
76	2018, March	President Abdulla Yameen of the Maldives demands India take back 2 helicopters for search and rescue— India suspects he was acting at China's request.
77	2019, June	China continues to deny India entry to the Nuclear Suppliers Group.
78	2019	China's ambassador to Pakistan says China will stand by Pakistan on the issue of Kashmir.
79	2019	Indian military exercises in Arunachal Pradesh
80	2019, September	Scuffle breaks out between Indian and Chinese soldiers in Ladakh.
81	2019, November	Indian Navy ejects Chinese research ships from India's exclusive economic zone near the Andaman and Nicobar Islands.
82	2020, January	China and Pakistan conduct joint Naval Exercise 'Sea Guardians-2020', in the northern Arabian Sea. Their sixth joint exercise.
83	2020, May	Tensions along the disputed border
84	2020, June	**Deadly encounter along disputed border in Aksai Chin. At least 20 Indian soldiers and an undisclosed number of Chinese troops killed.**
85	2020, September	**For the first time in decades shots fired along disputed border.**
86	2020, Fall	Chinese build military installations near Doklam.

The Late 1990s: A Period of Rivalry Escalation and the Rise of the BJP

By the mid-1990s, Indian analysts began to speak of what they perceived as 'creeping encirclement' and containment by the Chinese. In the middle of 1996, Beijing moved with Washington to prevent the spread of nuclear weapons, India saw this as an attempt to deny it the ability to defend itself from its nuclear-armed neighbour (Garver 2016). David Scott argues that it was also in 1996 that many in New Delhi started to fear a rising Chinese maritime threat in the IOR (Scott 2006). In addition, by the mid-to-late 1990s the Gujral Doctrine, which was named after Indian Prime Minister Inder Kumar Gujral, made its appearance. This doctrine made a stronger Indian presence in India's periphery a top priority and was seen as a way to respond to the increasing Chinese presence in the area (Holslag 2010). It was also in the late 1990s that the IN started to increase its modernization efforts. From 1995 until 2000, the number of missile cells in the IN navy increased from 126 to 185. Perhaps of greater significance is the fact that many new technologically sophisticated platforms started to enter the IN. The first of the Delhi class destroyers, which was equipped with 18 missiles, entered in 1997. Importantly, orders for new warships also began in the late 1990s. New kilo-class submarines and frigates were ordered during this period (Cohen and Dasgupta 2010). As previously mentioned, the IN also started to receive a greater proportion of the defence budget in the late 1990s.[12] One note-worthy example of the increasing importance of the navy is found in the Standing Committee on Defense, which in 1998 recommended the IN get 30 per cent of the military budget (This was not fulfilled, but the recommendation is important.) (Ladwig 2012).

The year 1998 was a critical year in India's relations with China. The electoral victory of the Bharatiya Janata Party (BJP) brought to power a much more realist orientated government that viewed China as a threat. Under the leadership of Atal Bihari Vajpayee India published the 'Strategic Defense Review—The Maritime Dimension—A Naval Vision' in May. This document was an in-house study that argued the IN must be powerful enough to defend India's maritime interests. It also called

---

[12] Please see Graph 3.3.

for the need to deter a naval challenge in the Indian Ocean Region. The document was specifically aimed at China when it spoke of coercion or intervention by outside powers (Scott 2006). The 1998 document also coincides with what was starting to emerge as a general pattern of PLAN port calls and incursions into the Indian Ocean. These voyages were of significant concern to security officials in New Delhi who believed that India must respond with its own form of naval modernization. First and foremost, the document is strong evidence that the top levels of the Indian government were actively working to counter the PLAN in the IOR with a stronger Indian navy. Many of the warships and submarines that took to the seas in the decade after 1998 would have been ordered in the late 1990s. Any doubts about the new leadership's perceptions of China were settled when India tested five nuclear devices in mid-May of 1998, and stated that the tests were designed to send a signal to China. Prime Minister Vajpayee's letter to American President Clinton is concrete evidence of Indian fears of China. In the letter Vajpayee stated:

I have been deeply concerned at the deteriorating security environment, specially the nuclear environment, faced by India for some years past. We have an overt nuclear weapon state on our borders, a state which committed armed aggression against India in 1962. Although our relations with that country have improved in the last decade or so, an atmosphere of distrust persists mainly due to the unresolved border problem. To add to the distrust that country has materially helped another neighbor of ours to become a covert nuclear weapons state. At the hands of this bitter neighbor, we have suffered three aggressions in the last 50 years. And for the last ten years we have been the victim of unremitting terrorism and militancy sponsored by it in several parts of our country, specially Punjab and Jammu & Kashmir. (Vajpayee 1998)

Even after the Clinton administration leaked the above letter to the *New York Times*, Vajpayee did not back down in his assertion that China was a grave threat to India. In a speech in the Lok Sabha on 29 May 1998, he stated 'there is a threat, a primary security challenge from China ... We are for a better relationship with China even today. But at the same time, you should not forget that *unless we prove our might,*

unless we prove our strength, (my emphasis) peace is not possible'
(Vajpayee in the Lok Sabha; cited in Holslag 2010. P 51). A week and
a half before this statement, George Fernandes, the Indian Minister
of Defense, stated that China was the 'potential threat number one'
(Holslag 2010. P 51). It is also important to note that Fernandes was a
strong supporter of naval modernization. The IN received a 14 per cent
increase in its budget from 1999 to 2000 (Mohan 2012). It was with the
BJP, which held power from 1998 to 2004, that the IN really started
to experience significant modernization, although modernization
was also continued by the Manmohan Singh government after 2004
(Scott 2007–2008). The IN of the 1990s and early 2000s was primarily a
Corbettian force designed to protect India's territorial waters from hostile threats. In 1998, the IN still had 19 attack submarines and was gradually upgrading its surface combatants in the form of new destroyers,
frigates, and corvettes (The Military Balance 1998). Considering New
Delhi's clear designation of China as a threat and the increases in the
naval budget, as well as the ordering of new warships and submarines,
the link between the PLAN and Indian naval modernization becomes
clearer. It was also in the late 1990s that the PLAN started to make consistent port calls in the IOR, by the early 2000s, these would become
a regular occurrence (Janardhan and Colley 2020). These port visits
greatly increased Indian concerns about Chinese long-term ambitions
in the IOR and Indian defence planners sought to counter the PLAN in
the maritime domain.

India's nuclear tests in May of 1998 did come with certain consequences. New Delhi's concerns of Chinese containment were exacerbated
by the reaction of the international community, and in particular, China's
to the nuclear tests. From 1998 to 1999, Beijing lobbied France, Russia,
and the U.S. to sanction only India and not Pakistan. In fact, during this
time China started to cooperate even more with Pakistan. Islamabad was
supplied with guidance systems, specialty steel and motors for missiles
(Garver 2016).

The 1999 Kargil War between India and Pakistan demonstrated the
critical role a more modern navy could play for New Delhi in its rivalries with its neighbours. While the kinetic fighting was reserved for the
high Himalayas, the IN played an important role by dispatching a large
task force of submarines and warships 13 miles off the coast of Karachi.

This effectively blockaded Pakistan and has been referred to as a 'silent victory' for the IN (Rehman 2012. P 63). With the conventional threat from Pakistan receding at the beginning of 2000, the Indian Ministry of Defense started to shift its maritime presence from the Arabian Sea to the Bay of Bengal. The goal was to have the Eastern Command berth two carriers and to take possession of the new diesel electric submarines that were coming into service (SSKs). Admiral Raman Suthan, who was the commander of the Eastern Fleet, was quite blunt in the reason for the emerging shift, he stated, 'we keep hearing about China's interest in Coco Island and we are wary of its growing interest in the region and we are keeping a close watch' (Reuters 2007). The Ministry of Defense also acknowledged that the Far Eastern Command needed to increase its capabilities beyond policing and argued that the IN should 'maintain control over the Andaman Sea as China's principal maritime gateway' (India's Upping 2007). With Pakistan no longer the critical threat it had been for much of India's history, and with China starting to increase its influence in the IOR and taking steps perceived to be aimed at containing India, it is no surprise that India shifted its strategic naval posture. It is important to note that by 2000, the PLAN was well into a modernization programme that was aimed at countering the American navy. Many of these new warships started to make voyages into the IOR, thus dramatically increasing Indian threat perceptions about Chinese containment. India's shift away from the Arabian Sea and towards China's entry point, the Andaman Sea, is best illustrated in the establishment in 2001 of India's first joint command, the Andaman and Nicobar Command (Mukherjee 2015). According to Raja Mohan, the main objective of this command was to counter the emerging PLAN activity in the IOR (Mohan 2012). As will be elaborated on in a later section of this chapter, this command was plagued with bureaucratic rivalries and was for a time considered a failure, but it is important from a perspective of how Chinese activities and increasing forays into the IOR were a driving force behind changes in Indian maritime strategy.

China's Failed Attempts to Alleviate
the Rivalry: 2001–2004

In the post-1989 world, one of Beijing's greatest concerns was to find its neighbours balancing against it with the U.S.[13] This scenario started to play out in the early 2000s, with increasing ties between Washington and New Delhi, as well as India's deepening ties with Japan and the gradual evolution of India's 'Look East Policy', to the 'Act East Policy', which sought a greater security role for India in East and South East Asia.[14] One issue of significant concern to New Delhi was the continuing Chinese development of Tibet. New Delhi believed the railway that was being constructed in the early 2000s that linked Lhasa with Qinghai province would allow the PLA to mobilize 10–12 divisions in a month (Joshi and Mukherjee 2018). China tried to reduce tensions with India by putting the border issue in the background and sending high-level officials to India. For example, Chinese National People's Congress head Li Peng visited India in 2001, while Chinese Premier Zhu Rongji visited in 2002 and Defense Minister Cao Gangchuan in 2004.[15] These were followed by Prime Minister Wen Jiabao in 2005, and President Hu Jintao in 2006 (Garver and Wang 2010).

Even though Beijing was attempting to restart relations with New Delhi, Indian concerns with China were too great to overcome. American President Clinton's 2000 visit to India was a major step in reconciliation between the U.S. and India since the 1998 nuclear tests. By 2002, American arms sales to India had begun and under the George W. Bush administration, Washington retreated from UN Security Council Resolution 1172 that called for India to abandon nuclear weapons. One challenge for Beijing was that Sino/Indian talks were considered all talk and little action. While there were discussions on the territorial dispute, Beijing failed to make genuine movement on this issue, which New Delhi wanted to solve. While Chinese leaders visited India in succession, the Americans

---

[13] Author's interviews with Chinese security experts in Beijing. Beijing. Fall 2016 and spring 2017.

[14] Author's interviews with Indian Security scholars in New Delhi. New Delhi. May and June 2016.

[15] It should be noted that although Cao Ganchuan was the Minister of Defense, the most powerful military leader in China is the Head of the Central Military Commission.

and the Indians were preparing the groundwork for the New Framework for the Defense Relationship, which laid out a 10-year detailed programme for defence cooperation (Garver and Wang 2010). Beijing was oblivious to the fact that its increasingly muscular navy was causing New Delhi's threat perceptions to rise.[16] In addition to increasing port visits, the Chinese military also started to carry out regular joint military exercises, many of them in the maritime domain, with IOR states (Allen et al. 2017). This further increased New Delhi's concerns of Chinese containment.

While these events were unfolding in the early 2000s, the dynamics of the strategic rivalry were at work. As will be elaborated in much greater detail in the next section, various aspects of the rivalry were at play and there were calls for more modern and technologically sophisticated naval hardware. As previously stated, when one considers that it can take 5–10 years for a naval platform to take to the sea from the time it was ordered, most of the platforms that joined the IN in the 2010s were ordered in the early 2000s. Nonetheless, many of them were 3–5 years behind schedule because of inefficiencies and bureaucratic red-tape (Menon 2012). With this being the case, as Table 3.2 shows, many of the major platforms and submarines were ordered in the early 2000s.

Overall, the period from 1991 to 2004 is consistent with the punctuated equilibrium model of rivalry escalation and maintenance. The fact that the IN did not make major gains in its fleet is best explained by a lack of available funds.[17] Once the Indian government had the ability to finance a modern navy and threat perceptions increased significantly with constant Chinese adventures into the IOR, we find a commensurate level of naval modernization. It is this phenomenon that the second half of this chapter directly addresses.

---

[16] Author's interviews with Indian security experts. New Delhi. Summer 2016.
[17] Author's interviews in New Delhi. Summer 2016.

Table 3.2 Indian Naval Hardware from 1991–2030. (The Military Balance—IISS) Annual Reports 1991–2020; Authors interviews.)

Year	CVG	DDG	Frigates	Corvettes	Subs	Nuclear Subs	Missile Cells	Total major combatants[a]	Seaman
1991	2	5	20	10	18	0	92	56	52,000
1992	2	5	21	13	17	0	106	58	55,000
1993	2	5	17	15	15	0	110	54	55,000
1994	2	5	18	15	15	0	118	55	55,000
1995	2	5	18	17	15	0	126	57	55,000
1996	2	5	19	18	19	0	130	63	55,000
1997	1	6	18	19	17	0	150	61	55,000
1998	1	6	18	19	19	0	152	64	55,000
1999	1	7	13	24	16	0	184	61	53,000
2000	1	8	12	19	16	0	185	56	53,000
2001	1	8	11	24	16	0	298	60	53,000
2002	1	8	11	24	16	0	298	60	53,000
2003	1	8	16	23	19	0	342	67	55,000
2004	1	8	16	26	16	0	394	67	55,000
2005	1	8	17	28	19	0	682	73	55,000
2006	1	8	17	28	19	0	682	73	67,700
2007	1	8	24	25	16	0	604	74	55,000
2008	1	8	15	24	16	0	616	64	55,000

2009	1	8	14	24	16	0	593	63	55,000
2010	1	8	12	24	16	1	595	61	58,350
2011	1	10	12	24	15	1	664	63	58,350
2012	1	10	10	26	15	1	530	63	58,350
2013	1	11	12	24	15	1	708	63	58,350
2014	1	11	13	24	14	1	839	63	58,350
2015	2	12	13	24	13	1	901	65	58,350
2016	1	13	13	24	14	1	962	66	58,350
2017	1	14	13	22	14	1	965	64	58,350
2018	1	14	13	21	14	1	1017	63	58,350
2019	1	14	13	19	14	2	1001	63	67,700[b]
2020	1	13	13	23	15	2	947	67	66,100
2025[c]	2–3	17	20	28	20–25	4–6	1,500	90	N/A
2030[d]	2–3	20	20	30	25	10–14	1,800	100[e]	N/A

[a]This figure includes carriers, destroyers, frigates, corvettes, and submarines.

[b]This number includes 7,000 naval aviation personnel and 1,200 marines.

[c]Estimated. Based on Author's interviews in New Delhi and various academic and policy publications.

[d]Ibid.

[e]Some sources state that New Delhi would like to have a 200 ship navy by 2030. The number of major combatants is not specified. Please see Kliman et al. 2019.

Part III: The Push for a Blue Water Navy.
2005–2020

*Whatever power controls the Indian Ocean has, in the first instance,
India's sea-borne trade at her mercy, and in the second, India's very
independence itself.* Jawaharlal Nehru (Chellany 2015)

During the 1990s the IN made limited progress in its modernization, this
was primarily the result of two factors. First, the Indian defence budget
was relatively small in the 1990s, thus hampering the IN's ability to purchase large numbers of new platforms. This is shown in Graphs 3.2 and
3.3, which demonstrate Indian naval spending, and the percentage of
the overall military budget the IN was allocated during the period under
review.

However, it needs to be noted that the IN was able to modernize in
different ways by increasing the lethality of existing platforms. The
second main reason for the slow pace of modernization relates to the
relatively limited threat perceptions emanating from the sea. The

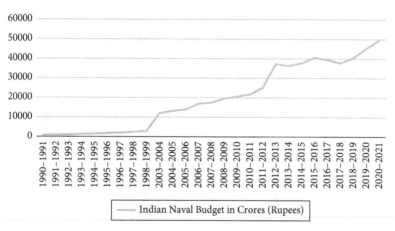

Indian Naval Budget in Crores (Rupees)

Graph 3.2 Indian Naval Budget in Crores (Rupees) 1990–2021 (Institute for
Defense Studies and Analysis Multiple Years)[a]

[a]One crore is equal to 10 million rupees. Please see the yearly papers on Indian defense
spending published by the Institute for Defense Studies and Analyses in New Delhi. http://
www.idsa.in/.

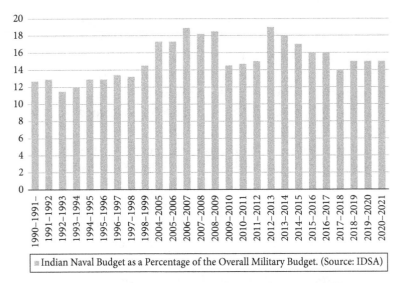

Indian Naval Budget as a Percentage of the Overall Military Budget. (Source: IDSA)

Graph 3.3   Indian Naval Budget as a Percentage of the Overall Military Budget. 1990–2021 (Institute for Defense Analysis. Multiple Years)

Indian military was primarily preparing for land warfare with either or both of its strategic rivals, China and Pakistan. This 'sea blindness' gradually began to change towards the mid-to-late 1990s as the rivalry started to become increasingly positional with escalation taking place in the maritime domain, and more recently it frequently involves other IOR states (Xavier 2020; Hall 2019). By the time the BJP came to power in 1998, a consensus emerged that the threat posed by China was no longer just confined to the Himalayan borders. As Beijing made increasing forays into the IOR, military planners, and in particular, the BJP, started to emphasize the increasing threat the PLAN posed for India's national security (Scott 2006). By the late 2000s, Indian strategic planners were acutely aware of the challenge/threat China posed to India's interests not just in the IOR, but also to overall Indian national security. This continuing strategic rivalry is the primary driver of India's naval modernization and while this is the main reason, as this section will make clear, it is not the only one. Closely related, and firmly embedded in the two cases examined, is the influence of bureaucratic politics. As will be demonstrated, the

IN has played a role in promoting the 'China threat' and the need to defend one's maritime interests including protecting India's SLOCs, although this is closely connected with the dynamics of strategic rivalry. Finally, the role of nationalism is a lesser driver. All of these factors contribute to the process; however, I will argue that strategic rivalry is the best explanation and the top reason cited by most experts in this field.[18]

Starting in 2005, and continuing to the present day, the IN started to make major progress in its modernization efforts. From 2004 to 2015, the number of missile cells increased from 394 to 901, and every surface warship, except one, was equipped with multiple advanced weapons systems and radars (The Military Balance 2004 and 2015). In addition, by 2015, Indian (and some foreign) ship yards were busy constructing dozens of high tech surface combatants, ranging from at least two aircraft carriers, multiple destroyers, corvettes and frigates, to advanced submarines including SSKs, SSNs, and SSBNs (Ensuring Secure Seas 2015; Various interviews). In late 2019 reports emerged that the IN wanted to have a 200 vessel navy by 2030. This ambitious target would establish the IN as a formidable blue water navy (Kliman et al. 2019). However, Sunil Lanba, the former Chief of Naval Staff, admitted that this time frame may not be very attainable and stated that 2050 was a more realistic goal for a 200 warship navy. Of note, Lanba did mention that as of December 2018, New Delhi was constructing 32 warships and submarines. In addition, another 56 warships and 6 submarines had been approved (Woody 2018). In the words of a foreign naval attaché in New Delhi with deep knowledge of the Indian navy, India was trying to do a 'great leap forward', going from a Corbettian, low tech navy with limited power projection capabilities, to a Mahanian navy with big platforms that have the ability to project power throughout the IOR and beyond.[19] When tracing the process of this evolution in the modernization of the IN, it is helpful to begin at the point where New Delhi firmly rejected Beijing's attempts to reduce the rivalry, the mid-2000s.

---

[18] During the fieldwork stage of this book, nearly every expert interviewed agreed that the perceived threat posed by China was either the chief driver or directly related to the chief driver of India's naval modernization. Author's interviews. New Delhi May and June 2016.

[19] Author's interview with foreign military Attaché. New Delhi, summer 2016.

As the previous section made clear, China's efforts to court India away from the embrace of the Americans were not successful. By the early to mid-2000s, there was a general consensus that the IN needed to start to counter China in the IOR. As can be seen in Graph 3.3, starting in the late 1990s, China started to carry out and then increase its 'Confidence and Security Building Measures' (CSBM) with states in the IOR. From Beijing's perspective, these measures were perfectly innocuous and are what sovereign states engage in when they have increasing interests in a particular region. However, from India's point of view, at best they were seen as meddling in India's backyard, and at worst, a deliberate effort to contain India.[20] In attempts to counter China's increasing influence in the IOR, India also started to conduct its own CSBMs with regional states. As Graph 3.3 also demonstrates, Indian CSBMs also expanded rapidly in the 21st century.

Empirical examples of India's attempts to counter Chinese influence can be seen in both the Seychelles and the Maldives. As Chinese power expanded in the Seychelles in the early 2000s, New Delhi provided that country with the INS Tarmugli, a fast attack vessel in 2005. As reports began to circulate that the PLAN might be setting up a naval base in the Maldives, India's Defense Minister visited the capital, Male, and provided the government with the 260-ton fast attack craft. Defense Minister A.K Antony visited the Maldives and reported that India would base two helicopters there and would set up radar systems in 26 atolls, which would be integrated with India's own coastal radars. According to Raja Mohan, these actions were specifically aimed at China (Mohan 2012). As will be elaborated on below, these Chinese actions would come to be part of what would be termed 'The String of Pearls' (Pehrson 2006).

By 2006, Beijing's policy towards New Delhi started to harden. Although China recognized Sikkim as a part of India in 2005, in 2006 discussions on solving the border disputes came to a sudden end. China withdrew its suggestion that it might be willing to give up all of Arunachal Pradesh, and Chinese border incursions increased in both Arunachal Pradesh and Ladakh. Interestingly from a rivalry perspective, Beijing informed New Delhi that it had been working on a border

---

[20] Author's interviews with Indian experts in New Delhi. June 2016.

agreement until the Indians started to turn towards Washington (Garver 2016). It may well be that Beijing was serious about a border swap (India keeps Arunachal Pradesh and China keeps Aksai Chin) as it (Beijing) does have a commendable record on compromise in territorial disputes (Fravel 2008). However, even though China was pushing its short-lived charm offensive, it was not reducing the escalation of the rivalry in the disputed territories. Even as Chinese leaders were visiting New Delhi with the goal of halting the budding strategic relationship between the U.S. and India, Chinese military patrols actually increased. The Indo-Tibetan Police reported that from 2000 to 2007 the number of annual violations increased from 90 to 140 (Holslag 2010). This seemingly contradictory policy of engagement and low-level escalation may not have been a calculated strategy from Beijing. Scholars and experts in both Beijing and New Delhi have speculated that the noticeable increase in border violations by the PLA may have been driven by local level commanders who either did not know of the larger political game being played out, or may not have cared.[21] As will be seen in a later section, this game was repeated with deeper consequences in 2014 during President Xi Jinping's state visit to New Delhi.

Perhaps of greater importance to the rivalry explanation was the gradual increase of PLAN activities in the IOR starting in 2000. As Graph 3.4 demonstrates, the PLAN started to make regular port calls in the IOR starting in the late 1990s. These became common by the end of the first decade of the new century and skyrocketed after 2008. In fact, in January 2015, Senior Colonel Yang Yujin, who is the spokesperson for the PLA, said that tours of PLAN subs and warships in the IOR will become normal and their frequency will increase in the future (You 2016). While the Indian government usually does not directly call out who it considers to be a threat in its region, various government documents offer important insights into which states are considered threats. Of theoretical significance, these increasing PLAN forays into the IOR are direct evidence of the rivalry linkage

---

[21] Author's interviews with scholars and experts in New Delhi in June 2016, and Beijing spring 2017.

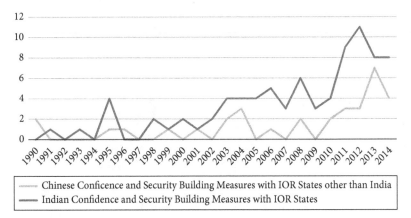

Graph 3.4 Number of Indian and Chinese Confidence and Security Building Measures in IOR States (Koh 2016)

playing out as New Delhi has made it clear that it perceives China as a threat. In addition to the increasing PLAN forays into the IOR, Beijing also raised significant concerns in New Delhi with its expanding use of joint military exercise with IOR states. As depicted in Graph 3.5, from 2003 until 2017, the PLA carried out 96 military exercises with IOR states, of which 17 were with India's arch-rival Pakistan (Allen et al. 2017).

Official Indian Navy Documents.

The various Maritime Doctrine documents published by the Indian navy are helpful in understanding the goals of the IN. The 2004 Indian Maritime Doctrine called for it to be more competitive in the IOR and recommended a maritime destiny for the IN. It was also clear about what it perceived to be China's 'attempts to strategically en-circle India' and about 'China's exertions that tend to spill over into our maritime zone in the Indian Ocean' (Indian Maritime Doctrine 2004. P 54, 71—Cited in Scott 2013. P 488). The 2004 version also stressed the importance to control choke points in the IOR, as well as critical islands and trade routes (Scott 2007–2008). The following

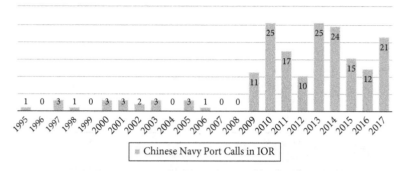

Graph 3.5 Number of Port Calls by the Chinese Navy in the IOR: 1995–2017 (Allen et al. 2017; 2017 data derived by author)

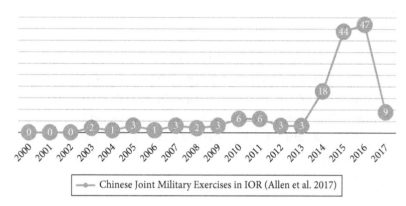

Graph 3.6 Number of Chinese Joint Military Exercises in IOR (Allen et al. 2017; 2017 data compiled by author from multiple Chinese sources.)[a]
[a]Ibid.

year the 'Maritime Capability Perspective Plan' called for a 160 ship navy equipped with 90 front line large platforms, which included destroyers, frigates, and carriers (Scott 2013). The calling out of Chinese forays that 'spill over' into India's maritime zones is strong evidence that a rivalry linkage is at play. Chinese leaders' concern over the 'Malacca Dilemma', where American warships could sever Chinese SLOCs and block critical choke points, has led the PLAN to reinforce its ability to protect such vital geographic points and sea-lanes from the Americans.[22] In carrying out patrols to safeguard its SLOCs, the PLAN is encroaching into India's sphere of influence, thus alarming New Delhi. By highlighting Chinese attempts to 'encircle India' and pointing to the vulnerability of various choke points, the Indian government is clarifying the linkage between Chinese naval modernization and Indian naval modernization.[23]

It is important to note that Chinese maritime experts are also increasingly aware of the Indian navy's ability to disrupt Chinese SLOCs. According to the well-respected professor of Chinese maritime security, You Ji, Beijing has devised two war plans for India in the event of a spillover from the Sino/U.S. rivalry. The PLA's two '1.5 war doctrines' specifically deal with India. In the first scenario, if the Chinese military is drawn into a war in the East or South China Seas with the U.S., China must be ready to fight India in the Himalayas. In the second '1.5 war doctrine' if a maritime war breaks out in East Asia, the IN may block China's SLOCs in the IOR, thus causing the PLAN to engage the IN in the Indian Ocean. These plans demonstrate considerable concern that the IN would capitalize on China's vulnerability and seek to disrupt China's SLOCs in order to help the U.S. and to strengthen India's position vis-à-vis China (You 2016).

The 2007 Indian Maritime Strategy was in line with calls for far greater power projection. The document, which analysed the coming 15 years, saw a stronger navy as a main feature of Indian diplomacy and it mentioned Mahan and his influence (Scott 2013). The strategy also noted the importance of controlling choke points 'as a bargaining chip in the international power game, where the currency of military power remains a stark reality. Importantly, the document mentions China and how it is working to establish a presence in the IOR (Holmes and Yoshihara 2009). Pant and Joshi have argued that the 2007 document was 'China focused' and that the 2007 MALABAR naval exercises with the United

---

[22] Author's interviews with Chinese security experts were in wide agreement that a core driver of PLAN modernization is the ability to protect Chinese SLOCs and maritime choke points from the American navy. Beijing 2016–2017.

[23] The ability to disrupt Chinese SLOCs and to block choke points that are vital to China is a primary goal for the modernization of the IN. Author's interviews with Indian defence experts. New Delhi Summer 2016.

States Navy (USN) were designed to signal to China the evolving shift in the balance of power in the Indo-Pacific (Pant and Joshi 2015).

The 2009 document argues that the IN is centred around sea control and that carriers are the most substantial contributors to this strategy. It also states that submarines are an essential component of a sea denial strategy. Notably, the document specifically points out that the primary objective of the IN is to deter military adventurism (Indian Maritime Doctrine 2009). This last part is crucial for multiple reasons. The 2009 document does not mention China by name, but it is widely understood in New Delhi that 'military adventurism' is a reference to Chinese activities in the IOR. India security experts, both in government think tanks and in academia, argue that New Delhi does not have any issue with the USN in the IOR. In fact, when pressed about the use of Diego Garcia, they universally stated that this is not a threat to India. Even the 1971 Enterprise incident, (where the Nixon Administration sent the aircraft carrier Enterprise into the Bay of Bengal in a show of gunboat diplomacy in support for Islamabad as India was splitting Pakistan in half) while still remembered, has been forgiven.[24] What most troubles Indian security planners is the increasing Chinese presence in the IOR.

The most recent document from the IN 'Ensuring Secure Seas: Indian Maritime Security Strategy', was published in 2015. It has a strong focus on securing Indian SLOCs in the IOR and speaks of a desire for sea control and states that the IN is being deployed around this concept. The ability to exercise sea denial with submarines as an offensive measure, in order to reduce the enemies' freedom of action is also cited as a major strategy. While not directly calling China out as an enemy, the document makes clear that there has been 'no reduction in the potential threat from traditional sources' (Ensuring Secure Seas 2015. P 6). A further signal that China is a significant driver comes from the statement that likely sources of conflict would be from states that have a history of aggression against India, and those with continuing disputes or maintaining hostile postures to India's national interests. Although the document notes other drivers include the ability to sustain economic growth, the protection of SLOCs, ensuring the safety of the diaspora community and Indian overseas investments, according to people who took part in preparing the report,

---

[24] Author's interviews with multiple Indian security experts. New Delhi May and June 2016.

China is a major factor. One of these people asserted that India wants external powers out of the IOR, but that India 'does not have a problem with the USA'. When asked why India is building up its forces, this person stated, 'the answer is clear—China'. Specifically, the individual mentioned that in the absence of China, there would be no need for some of the large platforms taking to the sea.[25] As will be elaborated below, the 2015 document argues that in terms of procurement, the IN has gone from a 'buyer's navy' to a 'builder's navy', and recently a 'designer's navy' (Ensuring Secure Seas 2015. P 130). This last point is very important to the sustainability of the IN. If India has the ability to conduct serial production of platforms, this demonstrates a level of standardization and technological maturity. However, there are some doubts about the efficiency of India's ability to produce platforms and submarines in a consistent and timely manner with delays of three to five years not uncommon (Menon 2012).

The String of Pearls and Increasing PLAN Incursions into the IOR

A major source of concern in security circles in New Delhi is the concept of the 'String of Pearls'. This argument, originally put forth in the mid-2000s, argued that China was surrounding India with the building of various port facilities in the IOR in states that neighbour India (Pehrson 2006). Security planners in India contend that these port facilities have the ability to harbour PLAN warships and submarines and would be of critical strategic value to China in the event of hostilities with India. The idea that these ports, which now run from Djibouti in the Horn of Africa, to Malacca in the Strait of Malacca, would pose a critical risk to India is a topic of considerable debate in New Delhi.

Active duty members of the Indian military who are based in various think tanks view the 'String of Pearls' as a long-term threat to India. Other members stated that these were not bases in the traditional sense, but China wants these for short of war scenarios. In peacetime, they can be used for a number of activities, such as surveillance and mapping

---

[25] Author's interview with individual who took part in the preparation of 'Ensuring Secure Seas'. New Delhi. May/June 2016.

out details of the ocean floor. Notably from their perspective, the String of Pearls gives China the ability to do many things and can be used for both coercion and dual use capability.[26] A former IN officer believes the 'String of Pearls' to be very real and argued that India has started its own 'counter encirclement strategy' by sending warships into East Asian waters.[27] Another former IN officer, who now works in a New Delhi think tank, argued that there will 'soon be a low-level Chinese naval base in Pakistan or Sri Lanka', and that China 'wants a naval foothold in the IOR'. Interestingly, this expert stated that Pakistan wants a PLAN base in the Chinese constructed port in Gwadar Pakistan, but so far Beijing has refused to agree to this request. This individual also argues that China's new 'One Belt, One Road Initiative' was the 'String of Pearls version 2.0'.[28]

Indian fears of Chinese encirclement in the Indian Ocean have been exacerbated by various Chinese publications. Several researchers from the PLAN naval research institute have called for China to build military bases around the Indian Ocean ranging from Sittwe in Myanmar, to Hambantota in Sri Lanka, to Gwadar in Pakistan, to the Seychelles and as far west as Dar-es-Salam in Tanzania (Li et al. 2014). One Chinese analyst even called for bases to be used as interlocking footprints that can support each other (Lim 2020). Zhang Jie, a researcher from the Chinese Academy of Social Science (CASS), has argued that Gwadar should provide supplies to Chinese fleet, which will strengthen the capacity of PLAN operations in the IOR. Zhang also points out that Gwadar alone cannot fulfil China strategic goals in the region and that Beijing needs to construct several 'strategic fulcrums' that can support each other (Zhang 2015). It is worth noting that many of the ports being constructed in the IOR do have the ability to accommodate major Chinese warships. Chart 3.1 depicts the depths of seven ports in the IOR that are frequented by PLAN warships. All can take in the PLANs Type-071 Yuzhao-class amphibious warfare vessel, which has a draft of roughly 7 meters (Erickson and Collins 2015). Closely related to the 'String of Pearls' is the 'Pearl Chain', while details of this are discussed in the China chapter, this spinoff

---

[26] Author's interviews with members of the Indian military. New Delhi May/June 2016.
[27] Author's interview with a retired member of the Indian navy. New Delhi. May 2016.
[28] Author's interview with a retired member of the Indian navy in a New Delhi think tank. New Delhi June 2016.

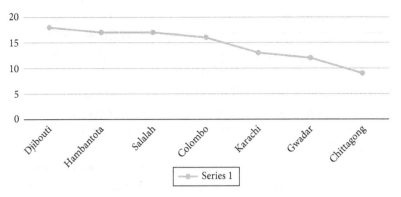

Chart 3.1 Selected IOR Ports with Depths in Meters (Erickson and Collins 2015)

is designed to militarize the ports/bases and make them combat ready to defend Chinese interests in the IOR (You 2016).

Finally, one of the biggest sources of the perceived threat from China emanates from increasing frequency of Chinese naval forays into the IOR. Many of these PLAN vessels make calls in ports considered to be in the 'String of Pearls'. As can be seen in Graph 3.4, which illustrates PLAN IOR port visits, PLAN excursions into the IOR have increased dramatically from the mid-2000s. While these visits are in no way unlawful, they significantly contribute to rivalry escalation and reinforce negative perceptions of Chinese activities in what India considers its backyard.

While New Delhi's perceptions of the 'String of Pearls' are congruent with the psychological dynamics of strategic rivalry, many scholars and economists hold different perspectives on the issue. One very well-respected scholar of international security based at a top New Delhi university argued that concerns over the 'String of Pearls' were not real. This scholar pointed out that in the event of hostilities between India and China, China would be at an enormous disadvantage due to the great distance PLAN warship would have to travel to reach the ports. Apart from this, many of the ports are within the range of Indian bombers that have the ability to quickly cripple them. In the case of the facilities at Gwadar in Pakistan, the port is at the end of a very narrow peninsula and could easily be taken out of service with precision-guided munitions. This scholar believed that the IN tries to play up the importance of the 'String' because it can be a useful tool in the bureaucratic struggle for funding. Calling China out as a dire threat and using the 'String of Pearls' as concrete proof of this is a more convincing way to justify a larger naval budget.[29] Other scholars and analysts agreed with this assessment. Many pointed out the geographic and logistical challenges China confronts in its forays into the IOR. With its new submarines now starting to come into service, just a few of these positioned at strategic choke points could pose enormous problems for PLAN platforms entering the IOR. Several noted that while the academic and think tank communities cast enormous doubt on the utility of the ports, the policy and government circles are much more ardent and believe in the potential threats posed by them.[30] Oddly enough, while the rivalry between the two states continues to experience periods of significant escalation, China has become India's number one trade partner. As seen in Graph 3.7, bilateral trade has increased enormously since the beginning of the 21st century.

Gulf of Aden Anti-Piracy Patrols

The anti-piracy patrols conducted by the PLAN off the coast of Somalia and in the Gulf of Aden are also a cause of concern for the Indians. While some interpret these manoeuvres as a positive example of China contributing to the security of the global commons and demonstrating that China's rise is peaceful, many in the security establishment in New Delhi see these as opportunities to increase China's presence in the IOR. China's first anti-piracy deployment took place in 2008 and since that year, the PLAN has carried out at least three different deployments a year with at least three warships sent out at a time (Koh 2016). By the beginning of 2019, the PLAN had escorted over 6,600 vessels, of which 3,400, or 51.5 per cent were foreign flagged. In addition, the Chinese navy had rescued over 70 ships that were in danger (Chinese Naval 2019). These patrols have created a permanent PLAN presence in the IOR, and the PLAN has made use

---

[29] Author's interview with Indian security scholar at a New Delhi university. June 2016.
[30] Author's interviews with think-tank scholars and analysts in New Delhi. June 2016.

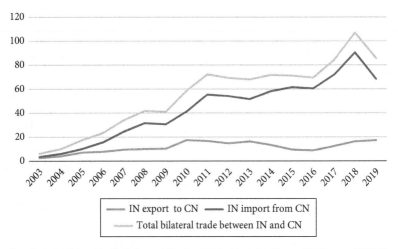

Graph 3.7 China-India Bilateral Trade: 2003–2019 (In Tens of Billions of USD)
Source: World Bank.

of berthing rights in Oman, Djibouti, and Yemen (Mohan 2012). This increasing activity has not gone without incidents between the IN and the PLAN. On 15 January 2009, there were reports that PLAN surface combatants in the Gulf of Aden and an Indian Kilo-class submarine were locked in an intense standoff near the Bab-el-Mandeb strait. The report stated that a Chinese ship forced the Indian submarine to surface after the Chinese ships sent an anti-submarine helicopter to help track the submarine. Raja Mohan writes that the submarine had been trailing the Chinese warships since they entered the IOR on their way to the Somali coast. This report was denied by New Delhi (Mohan 2012).

The Gulf of Aden patrols have been an enormous learning experience for the PLAN. According to an American naval officer who dealt directly with the PLAN during these patrols from 2008 to 2014, the PLAN at first did not want to work with the other states on the patrols. He stated that the PLAN pressured the Central Military Commission to allow them to become actively involved in the patrols. From 2009 to 2010, the PLAN just sent ships and did not communicate with other countries warships, the officer said that 'nobody knew what they were doing'. By 2012, the PLAN had gone through a learning process and even wanted to chair some of the 'Shared Awareness and Deconfliction' (SHADE) meetings that were held on the patrols in Bahrain.[31]

India was more concerned about what the PLAN might discover about operating in the IOR than anything else. PLAN commanders could learn about different currents in the ocean, as well as how to deal with logistical challenges. Important from a strategic perspective, the PLAN could conduct research on water temperatures, salinity gradients, the terrain of the sea floor, and other essential issues relevant for submarine warfare.[32] In fact, China has already conducted extensive research on weather patterns and the geology of the sea floor in the vicinity of Sri Lanka and other parts of the IOR. Maritime strategists in China are rapidly trying to overcome their lack of knowledge of the underwater terrain in waters both close to China and in the IOR. According to a report by the U.S. Naval War College, on a daily basis 5–10 Chinese 'scientific research vessels' can be found in the Indo-Pacific and this fleet has expanded rapidly. When it was set up in 2012 the research fleet had 19 ships, but by the end of 2017 it had 50 vessels with 10 other oceanographic research vessels being built. The Qingdao National Lab is working on a massive project that seeks to construct an integrated network of both fixed and mobile sensors that will be able to monitor the underwater contours of the Indo-Pacific. The lab has also worked with the Maldives on the physical oceanography of the sea in waters close to the island nation. While a large part of the data gathered is for commercial use, it also has military applications (Martinson and Dutton 2018). The authors of the report point out the potential applications of such research:

Temperature is a key factor affecting underwater sound propagation. The ability to know and predict the location of currents, eddies, and other oceanic phenomena confers an advantage to submarine commanders seeking to elude detection. To maximize the performance of sonar and other systems used to detect foreign submarines, navies must develop accurate oceanographic models for all of the ocean areas where they intend to operate (Martinson and Dutton 2018. P 12).

Just as Beijing is strongly opposed to American research vessels in waters close to China, India is equally concerned with similar Chinese

---

[31] Author's phone interview with retired American naval Officer . January 2017.
[32] Author's interview with Indian maritime security expert. New Delhi. Summer 2016.

vessels in its backyard. In fact, in the fall of 2019 Chinese survey ships were spotted in the Bay of Bengal close to the Andaman and Nicobar Islands. While these ships were asked to leave by the IN, there is speculation in the Indian media that they were attempting to locate American 'fish hook sensors' that are designed to track Chinese submarines entering the Indian Ocean. In fact, in December 2019 the Chinese ship Xiang Yang Hong 06 is reported to have deployed at least 12 underwater gliders in the Bay, which can travel up to 12,000 kilometres and drop to depths of 6.5 kilometres (Kannan 2021). Four Chinese scientists from the South China Sea Institute of Oceanology in Guangzhou who were working on mapping the sea floor around Sri Lanka under a BRI project were killed in the 2019 Easter bombings in Sri Lanka (Zastrow 2019). The PLAN's increasing familiarity with the northern Indian Ocean is now widespread in its officer corps. According to a China security specialist in Washington D.C., every PLAN surface commander has now done a Gulf of Aden patrol.[33]

The 2017 PLAN foray into the IOR and the 2018 Standoff over the Maldives

During the summer of 2017 a major point of Sino/Indian rivalry escalation took place in the Indian Ocean. From June to August of that year four separate PLAN flotillas entered the Indian Ocean. Most of the vessels were armed with missiles and included a sophisticated Yuan-class SSK and its support ship which also visited Karachi (Koh 2018). In a significant display of rivalry escalation, the PLAN flotilla conducted live-fire exercises on the high seas (You 2018; Colley 2021A). Crucially, these warships (which totalled 14 in August (Gurang 2018)) conducted their exercises while a major 72 day border standoff was taking place between Chinese and Indian troops along the disputed territory in Doklam (Singh 2019). The signal Beijing sent to New Delhi was that the PLA had the political cover to carry out simultaneous escalation on land and at sea. As will be detailed below, this event caused New Delhi to respond with a new naval strategy designed to track Chinese warships.

[33] Author's interview with scholar of Chinese security. January 2017.

The standoff at Doklam and the significant PLAN operations in the Indian Ocean in the summer of 2017 caused great concern in New Delhi. Within six months, another major point of escalation took place in the Maldives, which is emerging as a critical point of contention between New Delhi and Beijing. In the run up to a political crisis in February 2018, the former president of the Maldives, Abdulla Yameen, moved to end military cooperation with India and openly embraced the Chinese, thus increasing concerns in India that Male was drifting into China's sphere of influence. The crisis was between Yameen and the political opposition, which looked to India for support. India, which has long had considerable political influence in the Maldives, was warned by China to not intervene in the crisis (Pattanaik 2019). A critical action by Beijing was the movement of a PLAN flotilla consisting of 11 warships, including several destroyers, a frigate, and three supply ships towards the Maldives in February 2018 (Tham et al. 2018). According to Abhijit Singh this coincided 'just as India moved aircraft and ships southwards and debated the merits of intervening in the archipelago' (Singh 2019. P. 203). The Indian media took note of the PLAN flotilla and wondered on how it was that the PLAN had the ability to challenge the IN so close to India's shores (Dutta 2018). A well informed Indian expert on maritime security believes that this was a strong signal from Beijing to New Delhi to not intervene in the Maldives. This individual thinks that China was prepared to restore peace in the Maldives if it had been deemed necessary. At the same time there was a belief that an Indian intervention would have produced consequences for India from China.[34]

Nevertheless it is very unlikely that Beijing would have risked a military confrontation with India in India's backyard. The timing of the flotilla also adds scepticism to the idea that Beijing was deliberately carrying out an act of military coercion against India. The flotilla of 11 warships would have needed to have been dispatched weeks in advance. While China may have predicted the political crisis, it is highly unlikely they were planning to engage in a shootout with India. Regardless of Beijing's rationale, this event demonstrates why rivalry matters. The very fact that Beijing warned New Delhi not to intervene in the crisis, and happened to have well-armed warships in the vicinity of the Maldives, gave Beijing the

---

[34] Author's interview with Indian naval expert. New Delhi. 2018..

opportunity to escalate the rivalry on the high seas. The ability to carry out some form of strategic leverage or military coercion over India is what matters most. This military presence is not a one-off event. According to the Chief of Staff of the Indian Navy, China maintains a constant force of between 6–8 warships in the northern Indian Ocean (Admiral Sunil Lanba 2019). This force pales in comparison to the PLAN's actual blue water capacity. The PLAN is estimated to have over 100 warships that are capable of carrying out operations in the Indian Ocean. Given these assets, the PLAN is believed to be able to field a constant force of 18 warships in the Indian Ocean (Becker 2020). This situation in itself is a cause of great alarm to Indian decision-makers. When coupled with a perceived attempt to intimidate India through gunboat diplomacy, it constitutes a major point of rivalry escalation.

Overall, Chinese activities in the IOR contribute enormously to escalation in the Sino/Indian rivalry. The PLAN has even deployed nuclear-powered submarines into the IOR, a move that New Delhi has considered a 'red line' not to be crossed (Singh 2015; Holmes and Yoshihara 2013).

Box 3.1 Major Points of Rivalry Maintenance and Escalation in the Sino/Indian Rivalry[a]

- Increasing PLAN presence in IOR
- Perceptions of Chinese containment of India in India's strategic community
- Saliency of the 'String of Pearls' in India
- Continued Chinese arms sales to Pakistan
- Regular PLAN port visits to Pakistan
- Increasing Chinese leaders visits and agreements with IOR states
- Continued border infractions in the disputed territory
- 2017 PLAN foray into the IOR with 14 warships conducting live-fire exercise
- 2017 Doklam crises
- 2018 Maldives political crisis

[a]*These* are from 1991–2015, and are primarily from an Indian perspective.

These PLAN forays into India's backyard have led some to call for an 'Indian Monroe Doctrine', which would keep outside powers (except the USN) out of the IOR (Holmes and Yoshihara 2009). As will be demonstrated in the next section, the dynamics of strategic rivalry and accompanying escalation, while not the sole driver of the IN's modernization, are the best explanations of this phenomenon. India's navy would likely modernize in one way or another in the absence of the strategic rivalry with China, but it would not be calling for such powerful platforms and nuclear-powered submarines.[35]

The Role of China as a Driver in Indian Naval Modernization: 2005–2020

When comparing the Indian Navy's weapons acquisitions over the period under review, one finds significant variation in the choice of warships. The inability to fund significant systems in the 1990s is part of this reason, but this is only a partial explanation. Weapons systems and significant upgrades to existing platforms were ordered in the 1990s, and especially in the late 1990s as the BJP took power. The story from 2005 until 2020 is helpful in that it allows one to empirically measure the firepower of both new platforms, and to examine what surface combatants and submarines the government has ordered for the future. Significant variation is present in both of these. This variation is consistent with a navy that is transitioning from a Corbettian navy to one that aspires to project power in a more Mahanian force structure. In the late 1990s and the early 2000s, PLAN forays into the IOR were a cause of significant concern to New Delhi, even though these voyages may have been about securing Chinese interests from the U.S. navy.[36] By 2010, these incursions became a common occurrence and increased in the number of warships and accompanying firepower, thus leading to calls for India to build a more powerful navy. Kondapalli argues that originally PLAN

---

[35] The majority of experts interview for this book argued that the rivalry with China has caused significant variation in the acquisition of weapons platforms. Author's interviews with Indian experts. New Delhi, May and June 2016.

[36] Please see the China chapter for an analysis on Chinese SLOCs and the role the U.S. plays in threat perceptions.

forays into the IOR were a case of the 'flag following trade', however in recent years the PLAN is attempting to influence the structure of maritime power in the IOR (Kondapalli 2018). For Indian leaders this is a significant and rapidly increasing threat that must be countered with a much more powerful IN.[37] Concerns about China were so great that in 2011 a high-level task force called the Naresh Chandra Committee was set up to look into challenges posed by China. The participants viewed China as trying to contain India in Tibet and in the Indian Ocean. Crucially the committee recommended that India needed to prepare the military for the China challenge, while also continuing to build bridges with Beijing (Joshi and Mukherjee 2018).

As New Delhi modernized its navy there were more calls for the acquisition of modern aircraft carriers and nuclear-powered submarines, both SSNs and SSBNs. As Ganguly and Thompson point out these are the two hallmark icons of blue water navies and power projection in the post-1945 era (Ganguly and Thompson 2017). India's undersea warfare programme has gone from a navy reliant on older SSKs, to one that is now acquiring advanced SSKs with the capability to harness AIP,[38] and more fundamentally, is building and ordering a robust fleet of nuclear-powered submarines that are China specific.[39]

Evidence that the increasing Chinese presence in the IOR was a major driver of IN modernization can be seen in statements from top-ranking Indian defence officials (Colley 2021A). Speaking in 2009, Admiral Sureesh Mehta, the Chairman of the Chiefs of Staff Committee and the Naval Chief of Staff, stated that, 'on the military front, our strategy to deal with China must include reducing the gap and countering the growing Chinese footprint in the Indian Ocean Region' (Special Correspondent 2009). His successor as Naval Chief of Staff, Nirmal Verma also argued:

China is establishing footholds all over the IOR ... this is not something we can stop but our strategy certainly needs to factor in these developments. India's strategy to minimize and control the Chinese influence in the Indian Ocean region is to reduce the military gap through

---

[37] Author's interviews with Indian security specialists. New Delhi. Summer 2016.
[38] AIP allows a diesel electric submarine to stay submerged for significantly longer periods of time without have to surface. This allows the SSK to be much more difficult to detect and destroy.
[39] Author's interviews with Indian naval expert. New Delhi, June 2016.

'internal balancing' (Naval buildup) and countering the Chinese presence through 'external balancing with the US. (Scott 2013. P 505)

It is difficult to dismiss the above quotations from the heads of the Indian navy as simply bureaucratic politics and attempts to exploit the China threat for increased naval funding. These leaders do have an interest in perpetuating fear of Chinese containment, but as will be discussed next, arguments based solely on bureaucratic politics are not well supported in the Indian case. As previously argued, bureaucratic factors are embedded in strategic rivalries. The budget of the IN from 2005–2007 was 17.3 per cent of the defence budget, while the budget for 2007–2008 was 18.26 per cent. This needs to be compared with the budget from 1992–1993 which was 11.2 per cent and from 1998–1999 which was 14.5 per cent (Institute for Defense multiple years). From 2005–2008 the government of India pursued a major naval modernization drive. By March of 2006, the IN had on order 27 new ships and had plans for at least a three-carrier navy. Project 71 called for a new generation of indigenous aircraft carriers and the keel of one of these was laid at Cochin shipyard in 2005. A second carrier was to be commenced in Cochin in 2010. Regarding submarines, the second half of the 2000s saw the government move to procure much more modern and lethal SSKs and nuclear-powered boats. Although in 2004, India's Kilo-class boats were upgraded with Klub-S cruise missiles, in 2006 the government finally cleared a 30-year submarine construction building programme. This initiative involved an agreement with France to build six states of the art Scorpene class SSKs equipped with AIP. In addition, the government launched the 'Request for Proposals (RFP) in 2007 to build six additional SSKs. There were also calls to build 24 more modern blue water frigates and destroyers (Scott 2007–2008). As can be seen in Table 3.1, many of these warships started to take to the seas after 2010 (The Military Balance—IISS data).

The transition from a Corbettian navy to a more Mahanian force is best seen in the increasing size and types of platforms that the IN started to acquire in the late 2000s. By 2010, Raja Menon argued that the 'short-legged ships' had been decommissioned. These ships were being replaced with modern platforms designed to travel far greater distances and project Indian naval power. By 2010, the average tonnage of ships had doubled from 2,000 to 4,000 tons. From 2002 until 2009, many SSKs were fitted with advanced missiles and the surface combatants had significant technological upgrades that allowed them to stay interconnected through data-link. Also in 2010, the government issued an order for the next generation of submarines under the program 75-I, which was rumoured to be worth over 10 billion U.S. dollars. Each SSK would be about 2,500 tons and were be equipped with state of the art missiles (Menon 2012). The Delhi-class of destroyers are nearly 25 per cent larger than the previous Rajput-class destroyers and the new frigates that started to enter service in the 2000s were also much larger, the Shivalik was nearly the size of the Delhi-class DDG (Holslag 2010). According to the Indian Navy, in the process of modernization, the traditional dividing lines between DDGs and Frigates has been blurred, Traditionally the distinction was made by size, but new classes of DDGs are between 6,000 and 10,000 tons, while frigates are between 3,000 and 6,000 tons (Indian Maritime Doctrine 2009). While the most modern Kolkata-class DDG is the only Indian destroyer to be equipped with a phased array radar (PAR) system and a vertical launching system (VLS) that can fire surface-to-air missiles, four improved Visakhapatnam-class destroyers are scheduled to be commissioned by 2025. These vessels will also be equipped with PAR and VLS (Joe 2021B). Furthermore, corvettes are frequently between 500 and 3,500 tons (Indian Maritime Doctrine 2009). Walter Ladwig has measured the overall tonnage of the IN in 1991 and 2011. He found that the aggregate displacement of ships was 30 per cent greater in 2011 (217,426 tons versus 167,657 tons). This increase of 30 per cent is yet one more measure of the more muscular blue water trajectory of the IN (Ladwig 2012). These new platforms that were being constructed in various docks were far superior to anything the Pakistanis could field in a naval engagement.

Not surprisingly while New Delhi was busy building a navy capable of projecting power, the Sino/Indian rivalry continued to have periods of escalation. As demonstrated above, there were plenty of episodes of rivalry maintenance and escalation. Several of these episodes are noteworthy. In 2007, the Chinese Foreign Minister met his Indian counterpart in Hamburg and told him that the 'mere presence' of population in Arunachal Pradesh did not affect Chinese territorial claims. Then in 2008, at a Nuclear Suppliers meeting China's attempt to undermine approval of the Indo-U.S. civilian nuclear initiative by blocking approval of an exemption from some NSG rules. The group needed a consensus and failed to achieve one. The subject of Arunachal Pradesh came up again in 2009, when Beijing demanded that the Asian Development Bank delete a reference to the state from a 2.9 billion dollar plan for a four-year Country Partnership Proposal, or they threatened to scuttle the deal (Garver and Wang 2010). From a strictly security standpoint, in 2010 a posting on the Renmin Ribao's (*People's Daily*: the official newspaper of the Communist Party) 'Great Power Forum', spoke of a 'showdown with India that would solve the territorial dispute once and for all.' The fact that this was published in the government's official news portal sent a clear message to India. It should also be noted that this was part of an increase in what Garver and Wang call a 'psychological warfare' campaign aimed at India starting in 2005 (Garver and Wang 2010). In 2011, escalation also took place on the high seas. On 22 July, the PLAN challenged the INS ship Airvant while it was visiting Vietnam. Indian naval visits to ASEAN states increased dramatically from an average of just over one-and-a-half per year in the 1990s to four-and-a-half per year during the 2000s (Colley and Ganguly 2019). Multiple scholars and experts pointed out that these exercises are both a part of India's 'Look/Act East Policy', but from a strategic perspective that are a direct 'tit-for-tat' response to PLAN activities in the IOR. New Delhi is carrying out exercises in the South China Sea, which it knows will irritate Beijing.[40]

Further evidence that India was actively countering China's increasing assertiveness and voyages can be found in Defense Minister A.K. Antony's statement, 'we cannot lose sight of the fact that China has been improving its military and physical infrastructure. In fact, there has been an increasing assertiveness on the part of China. We are taking all necessary steps to upgrade our capabilities' (Wojczewski 2016. P 37). Naval Chief Sureesh Mehta directly called for India to counter China by stating 'Our strategy to deal with China must include reducing the military gap and countering the growing Chinese footprint in the Indian Ocean Region ... along with a reliable stand-off deterrent' (Joshi 2009). When analysing these statements in light of the modernization of the IN, a close causal connection becomes apparent. According to Holmes and

[40] Author's interviews with Indian security experts. New Delhi. May and June 2016.

Yoshihara of the U.S. Naval War College, China has violated the three 'red lines' that would cause India to accelerate naval build-ups. These red lines are the forward deployment of PLAN nuclear submarines in the IOR, a militarized String of Pearls,[41] and efforts to shut India out of the South China Sea[42] (Holmes and Yoshihara 2013). Former Naval Chief Admiral Arun Prakash has implored the government to acknowledge the threat the PLAN poses and to take it seriously. He has stated 'It is time for India to shed her blinkers ... and prepare to counter the PLA Navy's impending power-play in the Indian Ocean' (Mathew 2009).

Considering that China has violated what India has sketched as red lines, India has responded with naval acquisitions and future orders. While it is difficult to directly link specific warships and other equipment to a particular issue, there are some platforms and systems that are China specific and that have been ordered because of the strategic rivalry with Beijing. According to an extremely well-informed individual in New Delhi, India's nuclear submarine programme is China specific in that it has been manufactured to 'take the war to China in the event of hostilities'. This statement was backed up by six other experts who specialize in Indian security.[43] A former Indian navy officer argued that the platforms are for both China and other contingencies. He stated that the real problem in the IOR is the PLAN and that New Delhi is looking for warships to counter this threat. He mentioned that in the past 20 years the rivalry has moved from Pakistan to China, and that Pakistani equipment is not considered a problem. He did point out that platforms can have multiple roles and can be used in crises and other conflicts. However, he agreed that the strategic weapons are for a China contingency.[44] Other platforms are also designed to counter the PLAN. An analyst at a security-orientated think tank in New Delhi argued that since 2005, China has been driving specific platforms. He cited platforms equipped with anti-submarine warfare technology, such as corvettes and frigates. The P8 anti-submarine planes purchased from the U.S. were another response that is China specific. He stated that in the absence of the PLAN

---

[41] I count the Chinese naval base in Djibouti as breaking this threshold.
[42] The 2011 incident previously mentioned breaks this threshold.
[43] Author's interviews with Indian security experts. New Delhi. May/June 2016.
[44] Author's interview with retired Indian Navy officer. New Delhi. June 2016.

in the IOR there would be no need for anti-submarine platforms and technology.[45]

A prominent security scholar at a top New Delhi university argued that China was a foil for naval modernization in that it is used to justify the navy. However, he was also very clear that China is a major driver of India's power projection efforts and Mahanian inclination. In line with the psychological dynamics of strategic rivalries, he said that New Delhi must assume the worst-case scenario when it comes to the PLAN's presence in the IOR.[46] Views that China is a major factor were shared by a former Indian Ambassador to East Asia, while also pointing out that naval modernization has economic and a security provider components.[47] A well-respected security scholar at a prominent New Delhi think tank stated that there are several drivers of Indian naval modernization. She argued that the ability to keep extra-regional powers out (except for the U.S.) was a major concern for New Delhi and the increasing PLAN presence in the IOR are the two key drivers. However, she did believe that China is the 'key driver'.[48]

Analysts in government-run think tanks also point to China as a major if not the major driver of naval modernization. One stated that in the early 1990s the process of modernization had stalled, but was accelerated by the development of the PLAN in the 1990s and then later by PLAN forays into the IOR. He also said that we have not yet seen the real Indian response to Chinese submarines in the IOR as this will take time. He argued that this was what the Indian and American navies relations are about and that there is a great deal of information sharing between the two navies on key choke points in the IOR. When directly asked why India is building up its naval forces, he stated that the 'answer is clear—China. No China equals no need for platforms'. Importantly he stated that the government has plans to develop five SSBNs and six SSNs.[49] Other scholars at government-run think tanks agreed that China was a main driver of naval modernization. In a joint interview, two of them pointed

[45] Author's interview with security analyst in New Delhi think tank. New Delhi. June 2016.
[46] Author's interview with university professor in New Delhi. New Delhi. June 2016.
[47] Author's interview with retired Indian Ambassador to East Asia. New Delhi. June 2016.
[48] Author's interview with security scholar in New Delhi think tank. New Delhi. June 2016.
[49] Author's interview with naval scholar at a government run think tank in New Delhi. June 2016.

out that what China does today in the IOR will increase in the future and that China's intentions in the region are not benign. They firmly believed that the port in Gwadar is a naval base and has the infrastructure for submarines and other PLAN warships.[50] They stated that the best way for India to counter the PLAN is for the IN to build up its own capabilities to deal with the PLAN. They acknowledged that China is one of the drivers, and that the IN should not be overly China centric, but that China is a very important factor. They also agreed with other experts that Pakistan was not a problem, but when combined with the Chinese navy, it is a real problem.[51] A naval attaché from a Western country that has deep ties with India and has extensive knowledge of the IN, argued that China is not the only driver, but is very important and that the big platforms are being built with China in mind. The officer also mentioned the role of humanitarian operations and how they can also be used as a justification for some of the modernization. This individual said that the South China Sea incursions by India and the MALABAR exercises, as well as the training of Vietnamese submarine crews, are designed to irritate China. Interestingly this person said that the IN has neglected the role of submarines and that the surface warfare is 'in vogue' in the IN. On the strategic side of naval modernization this individual thought that the 'risk fleet' approach to naval modernization was accurate in that India is trying to build up a large enough navy to dissuade China from engaging the IN in the IOR. They did feel that India's current push towards a Mahanian navy with nuclear submarines and carriers was not correct and that India needs a more Corbettian approach.[52] In terms of the interconnected nature of the Sino/U.S. and Sino/Indian maritime rivalries, Box 3.2 supports rivalry linkage in that it summarizes some key points of evidence demonstrating that Indian naval modernization is linked to Chinese attempts to counter the American navy.

A significant point of escalation that is particularly provocative to New Delhi was the border incursions in September 2014, which lasted

---

[50] The belief that Pakistan will host a future Chinese naval base is also supported in the 2017 American Department of Defense's Annual Report to Congress on the PLA (Annual Report to Congress 2017. P 4).

[51] Author's interview with naval scholars at a government run think tank in New Delhi. New Delhi. June 2016.

[52] Author's interview with western government official in New Delhi. New Delhi. June 2016.

Box 3.2 Evidence that Indian Naval Modernization Is Linked to Chinese Naval Modernization

- 1998: Internal Indian Document '*The Strategic Defense Review: The Maritime Dimension—A Naval Vision*' called for the Indian Navy to be able to deter a military challenge from China.
- From the late 1990s on, a consensus emerges in New Delhi that PLAN modernization constituted a threat to India that needed to be countered by the Indian navy.
- As the PLAN develops the ability to protect Chinese SLOCS from the U.S. in the IOR, New Delhi has responded with its own form of naval modernization.
- 2001 Andaman and Nicobar Command set up in response to Chinese activities in the IOR.
- PLAN warships increasingly challenging Indian naval vessels in the IOR.
- Chinese attempts to protect critical choke points from the U.S. have caused India to also develop naval capabilities designed to counter the PLAN in these regions. (Examples: Purchase of SSKs, development of SSNs and advanced anti-submarine technology)
- Over the past decade, the PLAN has crossed multiple Indian 'red lines' in the IOR, thus causing the IN to respond. A direct cause of this is the SSN program, which has the ability to 'take the war to China.'[a]
- Widespread agreement in India that large platforms such as new DDGs, frigates, and corvettes are heavily centred on maintaining the PLANs vulnerability in the IOR.
- Anti-submarine warfare program is 'China specific'.
- High levels of agreement in the academic, policy, and government/military communities in New Delhi that PLAN modernization is causing Indian naval modernization.
- Statements from top leaders that India must build up a powerful navy to counter the PLAN. Ex: Indian Naval Chief Sureesh Mehta 'Our strategy to deal with China must include reducing the military gap and countering the growing Chinese footprint in the Indian Ocean Region.'

- 2017 IN initiates 'Mission Based Deployments' (MBD). In direct response to PLAN incursion in the IOR. These consist of 24/7 naval patrols in the Indian Ocean.

aAuthor's interview with Indian Defense official. New Delhi. June 2016.

for 20 days (Koh 2016). These violations occurred as Chinese President Xi was in New Delhi visiting Indian Prime Minister Modi. According to several scholars in New Delhi, these incursions left a very negative impression on Modi. The question of whether President Xi was aware of this was asked, and many in the New Delhi policy community believe that Xi authorized these incursions. Prime Minister Modi even raised this issue in the official press conference with Xi (which is unusual), instead of behind closed doors.[53] The effects of this escalation are difficult to pinpoint, but it certainly added ammunition to the anti-China faction in India.

The most recent critical juncture in New Delhi's naval response to the PLAN is the previously mentioned August 2017 PLAN foray where 14 Chinese warships conducted live-fire exercises in the Indian Ocean. This event set off alarm bells in New Delhi and led to the initiation in October 2017 of the 'Mission Based Deployment plan' (MBD) (Colley 2021A). The objective of this is to provide 24/7 surveillance of the PLAN in the Indian Ocean. The IN deploys up to 15 warships at a time while conducting this mission in different parts of the Indian Ocean (Koh 2018). While the IN had been monitoring PLAN warships for years, frequently with the assistance of the American navy, this represents a clear strategy for responding to the Chinese in the region. It also requires the IN to make use of its new and modern warships. During one monitoring mission the IN tracked five PLAN warships that were sent to the vicinity of The Maldives in a patrol that New Delhi believes was designed to coerce India into not intervening in the February 2018 political crisis in that country (Koh 2018). Gurpreet Khurana, an officer in the IN, has also written that the MBDs are a response to China's Belt and Road Initiative (Khurana 2019). One of India's top analysts on maritime security argued that the MBDs were the product of a cumulative process of increasing PLAN operations

[53] Author's interviews with scholars and analysts in New Delhi. New Delhi. May and June 2016.

in the IOR, but that the events of the summer of 2017 were the decisive factor. He mentioned that Indian naval vessels are now found throughout the IOR from the Strait of Malacca, to the Strait of Hormuz, where they monitor the PLAN. According to this analyst, one of the biggest concerns in the IN is the excessive wear and tear on the warships as they are now required to conduct regular operations far from home ports.[54]

If the IN is to maintain constant surveillance of Chinese warships in the IOR, it will need to sustain its naval modernization. In 2018 the IN was composed of 137 warships including 15 submarines. According to Admiral P. Murugesan, the Vice Chief of the Indian Navy, India plans to have a 200 vessel navy by 2027. Interestingly, he revealed that for every two to three warships that enter service, one is retired. In addition, he mentioned that the IN will continue to make foreign acquisitions and plans to purchase three Grigorivich-class frigates from Russia (Indian Navy 2018). The purchases from Russia are helpful, but from a long-term perspective, the fact that 30 warships were being constructed in December of 2018 demonstrates that New Delhi is serious about sustaining a long-term naval modernization process. Indian Naval Chief Sunil Lanba commented that in the Indian Ocean the IN had the advantage of 'balance of power' over the PLAN, but China holds the advantage in the South China Sea (Shim 2018). While the IN may not be able to confront the PLAN head-on in the South China Sea, from a tactical perspective it does not need to. With geography on its side, all the IN needs to do is develop a 'risk feet' that has the ability to inflict unacceptable damage on any PLAN flotilla that would enter the IOR with the goal of engaging the IN.

Such geographical advantages are not to be underestimated. Any Chinese flotilla in the Indian Ocean would be forced to operate thousands of kilometres from home ports and would have to face a small, but well trained Indian SSK force upon entry into the Indian Ocean at very narrow choke points. This 'asymmetrical' relationship where India actually enjoys a substantial strategic and tactical advantage over China is frequently downplayed. Cooperation between Washington and New Delhi in anti-submarine warfare and upgrades such as the positioning of Jaguar fighter bombers equipped with anti-ship missiles in the Andaman and Nicobar command, would present a formidable barrier to PLAN access to

---

[54] Author's interview with Indian maritime security analyst. New Delhi. 2018..

the northern Indian Ocean (Colley and Hosur Suhas 2021). Interestingly, just before his retirement in 2009, former Navy chief Admiral Sureesh Mehta stated that the Indian military is no match for China and that if war broke out between India and China that India was 'doomed'. The admiral further stated that there was no way India could bridge the expanding gap between the two militaries (Singh 2009). This analysis may hold true in a conventional war between China and India where India is forced to fight on China's terms, but this will likely never happen as any kinetic fighting would take place along India's borders with China, or in the Indian Ocean, thus providing New Delhi with a Strategic advantage (Colley and Hosur Suhas 2021; O'Donnell and Bollfrass 2020). Chinese security analysts are also very aware of the geographical advantages India enjoys over China in the Indian Ocean. Shi Hongyan views India's Andaman-Nicobar command as an 'iron curtain' that can form a blockade against China's entry into the Indian Ocean (Shi 2012).

A point of friction between India and China that has not received close attention is the Chinese decision to sell Bangladesh two Ming-class submarines. While these SSKs were designed in the 1970s, the PLAN used them as training submarines in the 1990s. Apparently Bangladesh could not afford the more advanced Kilo or Yuan class SSKs, so Beijing sold them the Ming's at a discount. The sale of two obsolete SSKs to Dhaka may not appear to be a significant point of rivalry escalation for New Delhi, however, the fact that Chinese crews will be training the Bangladeshi submarine crews is of significant concern to India. The vessels will be constructed at Bangladesh's Kutubdia naval base, which is close to India's future SSBN base at INS Varsha. The Chinese crews will have to map out the contours of the floor of the Bay of Bengal, thus acquiring vital strategic information on the potential places where future Indian SSBNs may be concealed or carry out deterrence operations. Conscience of this issue, India reached out to Dhaka and offered to train the crews at India's submarine academy at Visakhapatnam, however, Indian submariners are not familiar with the Ming-class SSK and thus could not effectively assist Bangladesh (Why China's Submarine 2017). A retired Indian naval officer argued that China was pursuing an 'organic approach' to Bangladesh in that their goal is to make Dhaka dependent on Beijing for technology, training, and future repairs. He mentioned that India could have trained the Bangladesh submarine crews had they purchased Kilos. However by purchasing Ming-class submarines, this ensures that only China can assist Dhaka, thus ensuring a constant Chinese naval presence in Bangladesh.[55]

Is China Pushing India and America Closer Together?

The increasingly warm ties between New Delhi and Washington are a major manifestation of the linkages between the two rivalries under review in this book. While the next chapter provides an analysis of Chinese perspectives of this evolving relationship, a brief note is in order on the significance of this development. Since the beginning of the century, Washington and New Delhi have established a solid working relationship between their militaries. Important foundational agreements have been signed such as the 2005 'New Framework for Defense Relations', and the signing of three key agreements, the 2016 U.S.-India Logistics Exchange Memoranda of Agreement (LEMOA), which covers logistical issues such as supplying naval vessels. The 2018 'Communications Compatibility and Security Agreement' (COMCASA), which increases interoperability between the militaries, and the 2020 signing of the Basic Exchange and Cooperation Agreement for Geospatial Intelligence (BECA), helps with issues such as targeting and navigation information from American systems (Colley 2021A; Joshi 2020). These agreements are controversial in India as they are seen by the political left as eroding Indian autonomy and independence in strategic affairs. This powerful desire to be able to pursue an independent course of action in international affairs and not play a junior partner to the Americans is a structural force in Indian politics. However, with perceptions of increasing Chinese assertiveness in India's backyard and the coming to power of Prime Minister Modi, India is rapidly shedding its apprehensions over actively working with the Americans (Bajpal 2017). The core driver of the warming of ties between India and the U.S. is China.

While military-to-military ties are expanding, including tri-service exercises between the American and Indian navies, air forces, and armies in the 2019 'Tiger Triumph', India has not, and will not for the foreseeable

[55] Author's interview with retired Indian naval officer. New Delhi, 2018. .

future, join America in any arrangement that even hints of an alliance (Parpiani and Singh 2020). A publication from the U.S. Army War College notes that the U.S. seeks to deepen interoperability and cooperation between the two militaries. The two authors of the report also note that the U.S. hopes that India will be able to counterbalance rising Chinese power and influence in Asia. Crucially, the authors argue that this is a 'misplaced hope' as India does not see itself as fulfilling such a role (Ganguly and Mason 2019. P 24). The same report argues that navy to navy exercises, while commonplace, is more about public relations, than about strategic interoperability. Due to New Delhi's unwillingness in bilateral and multilateral training exercises to link India warships with electronic combat systems with American and other countries, real interoperability between India and its partners is not possible. Because of the lack of technological integration, the Malabar exercises have been categorized as having the same level of sophistication as the battle of Trafalgar. A similar comparison has been made with joint exercises between the American and Indian Air Forces where the Indian Russian Mig and American fighters do not even turn on their electronic warfare equipment, thus leading one expert to call this a 'photo opportunity' (Mason 2021. P 26).

It needs to be noted that even though American desires for increases in interoperability are proceeding at a very slow pace, compared to two decades ago, the U.S. and India have made enormous progress in this field. Washington may be too accustomed to dealing with its formal allies where meaningful integration between militaries is a common occurrence and appears to have unrealistic expectations of what is politically possible in India on this front. With this said, the dynamics of the Sino/India rivalry will likely continue to push New Delhi into Washington's embrace.

Why Strategic Rivalry Is the Best Explanation

This book does not attempt to argue for a single cause to naval modernization. A phenomenon as vast as this is frequently the product of multiple factors. Instead, I argue that strategic rivalry is the most compelling explanation. A crucial component of the growth of the IN is the links between the Sino/U.S. strategic rivalry with the Sino/Indian strategic rivalry. Box 3.3 provides various points of evidence that leaders in New Delhi have selected China as their primary rival. From scholarly works, to policy papers, to official government statements, and to in-depth interviews, the perceived and real threat emanating from China is the largest, but not the only driver of India's naval modernization. Strategic rivalry influences the way that events are understood. Preconceived ideas and

---

Box 3.3 Evidence that Indian Leaders Have Selected China as Their Primary Rival.

- 1990s: Indian Government Defense Scholars: Development of PLAN in the 1990s pushes Indian navy to modernize.
- 1998: China called out as primary rival by Indian Prime Minister Vajpayee.
- 2004: Indian Maritime Doctrine: Argues that PLAN excursions are spilling over into India's maritime domain, thus constituting a threat.
- 2007: Indian Maritime Strategy: Document is China focused and states that the PLAN is working to establish a presence in the IOR.
- 2009: Indian Naval Chief of Staff Admiral Sureesh Mehta: 'India must counter the PLAN footprint in the IOR.'
- 2009: Indian Maritime Doctrine: Primary goal of the Indian Navy is to deter foreign military adventurism (Chinese) against India.
- 2015: Indian Maritime Security Strategy: 'No Reduction in the potential threat from traditional sources' China.'
- 2016: Planner of many of India's official documents on drivers of Indian naval modernization: 'The answer is clear—China.'
- Statements by Indian officials such as Indian Naval Chief of Staff, Nirmal Verma 'India must carry out internal balancing (Naval buildup) to counter China'.
- The October 2017 decision to initiate the 'Mission Based Deployment plan' to counter the PLAN in the IOR.
- A clear majority of India's strategic leadership (54 per cent) see China's assertiveness as India's 'biggest external challenge'.

perceptions are both reinforced and justified through the process of rivalry escalation and maintenance. Empirical evidence of this is found in a recent Brookings India survey of India's strategic community where a clear majority of the leadership (54 per cent) view China's assertiveness as India's 'biggest external challenge' (Jaishankar 2019). Furthermore, the punctuated equilibrium model of rivalry maintenance and escalation provides a solid framework for analysing the rivalry. As the model predicts, Sino/Indian relations have experienced significant periods of escalation over the period under review. Regular PLAN ports calls in the IOR, and especially with Pakistan, serve as significant points of escalation for Indian decision makers. This when coupled with a steady expansion of PLAN missions in the IOR and ports calls by Chinese submarines, some of them nuclear powered, have raised threat perceptions. In addition, the carrying out of live fire exercises in the Indian Ocean by the PLAN in 2017, which led to the initiation of India's MBD, provides concrete support to the explanatory power of the model. As predicted, rivalries experience periods of lower-level maintenance, interspersed with periods of intense escalation. These episodes of significant tension have directly led to calls in New Delhi to conduct a significant form of naval modernization. This section examines competing explanations of Indian naval modernization and finds that while these are plausible, they either fall short, or are embedded in the strategic rivalry model.

Challenges to Bureaucratic Politics Explanations

The focus on how various bureaucratic entities and actors influence politics is a valuable approach to understanding political behaviour. However, when seeking to understand the process of naval modernization in India, this model falls short of adequately explaining this phenomenon. Another barrier to using bureaucratic politics as an explanation is that it is nearly impossible to disentangle it from strategic rivalry. Bureaucracies are frequently drivers in their own right in maintaining and escalating rivalries. Entities ranging from Foreign Ministries, to Ministries of Defense, often have vested interests in perpetuating a rivalry to the point where it can become a self-fulfilling prophecy.

The nexus between bureaucratic politics and strategic rivalry can be seen in the fact that the policy establishment believes that it must account for a worst-case scenario when it comes to how to deal with the Chinese (Singh 2015). The navy has also challenged the traditional land bias of the Indian military. As China increased its military capabilities on the Tibetan plateau, the IN argued that it needed the ability to interdict Chinese SLOCs in the Indian Ocean (Mukherjee 2015).

There are also structural challenges in the IN that prevent it from exercising significant influence. The IN wants platforms, but its power is held by the executive branch, and only officers from this branch can exercise command of warships, aircraft, or submarines. These individuals are the only ones who can have any chance of climbing to the highest ranks in the IN. Also in the IN, individual identities of officers do not have the same parochial feelings as their counterparts may have in other navies. In addition, leadership in the navy at the highest level is chosen on the basis of seniority, and it would be a real challenge for a particular community to establish a long-term dominance over the IN as a whole. From 1991 to 2011, the IN was led by aviators, submariners, and others. It would be very difficult for a particular group to advocate a specific trajectory for a prolonged period (Ladwig 2012). It is equally important to note that the Indian armed forces were never encouraged to take part in decision making at the level of national security, and especially of that relating to foreign policies at the political-military level (Bhaskar 2012).

The creation of the position of Chief of Defence Staff (CDS) on 1 January 2020 is a significant development in the military bureaucracy. While it is too early to analyse the power of this new position, the appointment of Bipin Rawat, the Army Chief, may not bode well for the Indian Navy. While General Rawat will not exercise an actual command, he will chair a committee of the three service chiefs. This will theoretically enhance the Indian military's ability to perform joint operations between the services. The CDS will still be under the Defense Minister, but it will be able to exercise influence through a well-staffed office of over 60 people who will be able to advocate various policies (India's Armed Forces 2020). How the CDS influences (or fails to influence) the modernization of the IN has yet to be seen. However, with China's increasing activities in the IOR, the potential for it to take the side of the navy is a strong possibility. The bloody border clashes with China in the summer of 2020 have added a sense of urgency to reforms in the Indian military. As Mukherjee points out, this may result in the military having greater influence in defence policy, but this is resulting in a rebalancing strategy that favours the ground forces and focuses more on the immediate threats on the northern borders (Mukherjee 2021).

Multiple interviewees also agreed that on its own, bureaucratic politics does not offer a convincing explanation. One scholar argued that the 'String of Pearls' is not real, but the navy needs to promote this and continues to advocate this belief. He stated that 'China is an excuse/threat that enables the government to justify the navy—without a China threat, it would be very hard to justify the blue water navy.' Another scholar pointed out that the rivalry has taken on a life of its own and is used to justify the navy.[56] One interviewee from a top New Delhi think tank, pointed out that the new commanders in the navy are not submarine people, and these people have a bias towards power projection.[57] Perhaps the greatest liability of the bureaucratic argument is the fact that there is an increasing Chinese naval presence/threat in the IOR. If we found no Chinese threat and increasing naval budgets, the bureaucratic model would likely have much greater explanatory power. The PLAN in the IOR is an empirical reality that is a primary cause of the continuing Sino/Indian rivalry.

Overall, the bureaucratic model on its own fails to offer a convincing explanation for India's naval modernization. However, when coupled and embedded in the strategic rivalry approach, it does have utility.

Arguments Based on Nationalism

Nationalism and great power status are not very helpful for explaining Indian naval modernization. Nationalism may be a powerful unifying force, but no scholarly work cited it as a primary driver, nor did experts interviewed for this book. Nationalism is best understood as playing a secondary role as a driver of Indian naval modernization. This is also the case for China, as cited next, where nationalism does influence although

---

[56] Author's interviews with a security scholars at a top New Delhi university. New Delhi. June 2016.
[57] Author's interview with security scholar at top New Delhi think tank. New Delhi. June 2016.

to a lesser degree. With the exception of India's aircraft carrier building programme, nationalism is not helpful. This argument was reinforced in multiple interviews, in particular, by a scholar who is also on active duty in the IN who spoke of carriers for their symbolic value, but who did not believe that this was a main cause of naval modernization.[58] Ladwig has also stated that nationalism/great power status is present in India, but he does not agree that this is a main driver of the IN (Ladwig 2012). In the absence of convincing evidence that nationalism or great power status are the main drivers, they should be viewed as secondary explanations.

The role of humanitarian missions as a driver of IN modernization is also best viewed as a secondary explanation. While India does have humanitarian considerations in the use of the IN, this role does not call for ballistic missile submarines, or multiple aircraft carrier battle groups complete with state-of-the-art guided-missile destroyers. The ability to come to the aid of victims of natural disasters can be carried out by an aircraft carrier, but aircraft carriers are extremely expensive and the funds for such programmes would be much better spent on different ships, such as hospital ships and vessels that have the ability to launch amphibious operations. Those who cite humanitarian reasons in interviews as a reason for naval modernization, specifically mentioned that this was a peripheral issue. On force replenishment, not a single expert interviewed cited this as the primary driver. Of key importance, force replacement would simply keep the IN as primarily a green water fleet with a few token vessels that can project power beyond India's exclusive economic zone of 200 miles and empirically this is not what we are witnessing.[59]

A final note is in order on the protection of SLOCs. This was cited by many individuals during both interviews and in written academic work. However, the protection of SLOCs argument is very closely tied to keeping outside powers (China) out of the IOR. As has been cited multiple times above, New Delhi does not have a problem with American naval power in the IOR. The only viable strategic and long-term threat to India's SLOCs would come from a rival power. This rival power (China) is embedded in the strategic rivalry explanation. While Pakistan and Somali pirates may be a nuisance, they are not threats that are severe enough to justify the

---

[58] Author's interviews with Indian naval experts in New Delhi. New Delhi. May and June 2016.
[59] Ibid.

acquisition of the naval hardware the IN has acquired. Pirates on rubber speed boats armed with AK-47s and RPG-7s may drive up insurance premiums for the world's shipping companies, but they do not demand carrier battle groups and sea launched ballistic missiles to counter them.

Conclusion

Over the period examined in this book, the IN has evolved from a relatively unsophisticated green water fleet, into a fleet that could defend India's periphery, and a force that now has the ability to project power to nearly every corner of the IOR and increasingly to destinations farther afield. The Mahanian impulses of the IN are unmistakable. As one foreign naval attaché with extensive knowledge of the IN stated they are 'leapfrogging' from a Corbettian to a Mahanian force. Perhaps of greater importance, this individual stated, that the platforms now in service are fully operational.[60] How quickly the IN is able to put to sea the warships and submarines that it has on order is yet to be seen. If the past is any guide, these platforms currently on order will experience significant delays of many years. The recent stagnation of the defence budget is a cause of concern and likely a source of delay for platforms. The 2020–2021 defence budget barely keeps up with inflation and New Delhi spends more on pensions for retired military personnel, than on active duty personnel (Panda 2020). Although it needs to be noted that the IN saw a 44 percent increase in its capital allocation for 2022–2023 compared to 2021–2022. While this is very helpful for the modernization of the IN, it is unknown if this will continue in the future (Peri 2022). An author of multiple editions of the IN's doctrine reports stated that the IN has plans for five SSBNs and six SSNs.[61] There are also reports that the IN has plans for two additional indigenous carriers, one of these will be 65,000 tons and may be nuclear (Rajagopalan 2016). The variation from a Corbettian force to a force that has many hallmarks of Mahanian power projection is remarkable.

---

[60] Author's interview with foreign military attaché in New Delhi. New Delhi. June 2016.
[61] Author's interview with naval scholar in government think tank in New Delhi. New Delhi. June 2016.

There is no comprehensive approach that completely explains Indian naval modernization. As argued above, explanations based on nationalism and desire for great power status may be helpful for one or two platforms (primarily carriers) but beyond this, they are insufficient. Both protection of SLOCs and bureaucratic models do have merit, but when they are fused with the strategic rivalry approach, they have the most utility. In the absence of a Chinese maritime threat, we would still see some form of Indian naval modernization, but it would likely be very different. Many of the platforms that are in existence or on order would have a very difficult time being justified in the absence of a maritime threat emanating from China. The China threat lobby does play a bureaucratic role, but this role is only possible with a strategic rival to justify such exorbitant costs. As can be seen in Table 3.1, I have also provided projections of platforms that are on order. These future platforms are included in this chart, because they were in the works during the period under examination.[62]

The India case does not have the equivalent of a Taiwan crisis or a Belgrade Embassy bombing, which provided a catalyst for a Chinese blue water navy. The continued maintenance and escalation of the Sino/Indian strategic rivalry is the most comprehensive explanation of the drivers of Indian naval modernization. While not directly related to the maritime domain, the violence that erupted along the disputed border in June 2020 was a major point of rivalry escalation. At least 20 Indian soldiers were killed as well as an undisclosed number of Chinese troops. This was the first deadly encounter between Chinese and Indian forces in 45 years (India and China 2020). Such lethal confrontations demonstrate the challenges of trying to terminate, or at least reduce tension in a strategic rivalry. While China and India have taken part in various confidence building measures over the years, these are clearly unable to eliminate the underlying structural aspects of the rivalry. For example, since 1981 discussions on resolving the dispute have been held every single year, but have produced no major breakthroughs. These include eight rounds of vice-ministerial meetings in the 1980s, fifteen meetings of joint

---

[62] These platforms and submarines were specifically mentioned to the author people either directly involved in the procurement process, or by Indian experts in naval security. I have also included data on future platforms listed in scholarly articles. Author's interviews with experts in New Delhi. New Delhi. May and June 2016.

working group from 1989–2005, as well as twenty-one meetings of special representatives at level of national security advisor since 2003 (Fravel 2020). In addition, the informal meetings between Prime Minister Modi and President Xi in 2018 and 2019 have also failed to resolve the border issue. The re-inclusion of Australia into the Australia-India-Japan-U.S. Quadrilateral Security Forum (QUAD) in the fall of 2020 is further evidence that recent perceptions of aggressive Chinese behaviour in South Asia are fuelling a maritime response to Beijing buy not just India but by the other QUAD members (Rawat 2020).

Of vital importance to the Sino/Indian rivalry, the Sino/U.S. rivalry shows no signs of losing momentum and may be headed for further escalation in the near future. This will reinforce calls in Beijing to construct a more robust navy that is capable of deterring the American navy from a kinetic attack. While this may increase Chinese security, it will only erode Indian security and will lead to continued PLAN incursions and rivalry escalation with India in the IOR, thus continuing to drive and justify IN modernization.

4

The Renewal of the Sino/American Strategic Rivalry and the Evolution of the Chinese Navy

In July 2017, two Chinese warships set sail from Zhanjiang in China's southern province of Guangdong with an undisclosed number of crew. Their destination was the country of Djibouti, next to the horn of Africa, where they were set to open China's first foreign military base. The establishment of this military instillation represents a milestone in the evolution of the Chinese navy and Chinese maritime strategy. While some Chinese commentators downplayed the significance of the base and even refused to call it a base (they used the term 'supply station') *The Global Times*, owned by the *People's Daily*, did not mince words.[1] The paper was unambiguous in stating that 'this is the PLA's first overseas base and it is not a commercial supply station' (Djibouti Base 2017). The empirical reality of the Djibouti base is one measure of how much the PLAN has developed since the end of the Cold War.

China, like India, has, for the past several hundred years, been a continental power with little need for a powerful navy. For much of the PRC's modern history land warfare and perceived threats emanating from China's borders represented the greatest strategic threats to Beijing. Just after the dawn of 'New China' in 1949, Mao launched the PLA into a bitter land war on the Korean Peninsula, where they battled a technologically superior American led force to a stalemate. Less than a decade later, China found itself in a short, but bloody war,

---

[1] The Chinese government has been very hesitant to publically call the base a 'base'. There has long been an ideological aversion to China having overseas military bases. These have historically been vilified as products of hegemonic powers.

The Nexus of Naval Modernization in India and China. Christopher K. Colley, Oxford University Press. © Oxford University Press 2022. DOI: 10.1093/oso/9780192865595.003.0005

with India fought along their frozen Himalayan border. While the perceived threat from India was present after 1962, the real continental threat to China came from the north from the USSR. Mao was so concerned about a Soviet invasion that he ordered China's defence industries to relocate into China's vast interior, where he believed they would be safer from a Soviet attack. In the early 1970s, Mao and President Richard Nixon were able to overcome the first Sino/U.S. rivalry and worked together to counter Moscow. As the Cold War began to thaw, and China's relations with the USSR improved with a visit to Beijing from Soviet Premier Gorbachev, the Chinese military fell into a state of neglect. By reaching out to Washington, Mao, and later Deng Xiaoping, found a way to alleviate pressure from the Soviet Union. Notably for this study, this also called for an emphasis away from defence spending, and more resources geared towards economic development. For much of the 1980s, the PLA had to fend for itself and in an era of budget cuts, it had to generate its own sources of income. In fact, in order to fund itself and cover costs the PLA took part in business opportunities and commercial deals (Bickford 1994). By the time the PLA marched into Beijing on 4 June 1989 and massacred thousands of unarmed Chinese civilians, the Chinese military was an obsolete force that would struggle to defend against any technologically sophisticated foreign rival (Tiananmen Square Protest 2017).

The events of June 1989 also resurrected the dormant Sino/American strategic rivalry.[2] In the aftermath of Tiananmen, international sanctions were immediately placed on Beijing. Even the George H.W. Bush administration was forced to enact harsh sanctions after a horrified American public demanded action after watching live coverage of PLA soldiers' machine-gunning unarmed protestors in the streets of western Beijing.[3] The sanctions ended the close cooperation Chinese and American security officials had enjoyed since the early 1970s. The CCP firmly believed that it had done what was necessary to preserve order in China and blamed hostile foreign forces, specifically

---

[2] The original rivalry began shortly after the CCP came to power in 1949 and lasted until the early 1970s, when Mao and Nixon reestablished ties.

[3] The Bush Administration was originally reluctant to punish China too harshly, as they wanted to preserve a united front against the Soviet Union (Mann 1999).

singling out the U.S. for trying to weaken and split China (Mann 1999). Importantly, the PLA, which throughout the 1980s had enjoyed access to American military technology, was banned from purchasing or obtaining American equipment. It was against this backdrop that the 1991 Gulf War took place.

The 1991 Gulf War was a critical juncture for the modernization of the PLA. Chinese defence officials believed that the American led war would become bogged down in heavy fighting with battle-hardened Iraqi divisions, who were fresh off the battlefield from their eight-year war with Iran. Chinese confidence in Iraqi military hardware (much of the Iraqi heavy armour and field guns were of Chinese origin) and Saddam Hussein's 'million man army' evaporated. Within a couple of weeks, a punishing, technologically sophisticated American air war first blinded the Iraqi military and then destroyed it from afar. The lesson for China was clear: large army's with low levels of technology were a thing of the past. The 'revolution in military affairs' had arrived (Shambaugh 2002).

From the time the Gulf War ended in early 1991, until the end of the decade, the PLAN would go from a dilapidated and neglected force that was historically ignored by leaders who heavily favoured the army, to a force that was beginning to take on a major role in Chinese strategic thinking. This period would witness the Sino/U.S. rivalry come very close to armed conflict on several occasions and would see the accidental destruction of a Chinese Embassy by American bombs.[4] The 1990s also saw the rivalry started to evolve from a spatial one that narrowly focused on disputed territory, to a more positional rivalry that extended beyond Taiwan. By the dawn of the 21st century, the PLAN began to take on a much greater role and started to develop a more Mahanian oriented force structure that would produce nuclear-powered submarines, advanced destroyers, and aircraft carriers. The year 2015 was important for the PLAN. In May, the Ministry of Defense issued a new White Paper

---

[4] Many Chinese experts involved in Sino/U.S. relations believe this bombing to have been intentional. When pressed as to what the Americans would gain from destroying the Chinese Embassy, none could offer a convincing answer beyond American containment. Some also believed that the Embassy was bombed to destroy pieces of an American F-117 stealth fighter that had been shot down by Serb anti-aircraft artillery and pieces were being stored in the Embassy. No concrete evidence has ever emerged to prove this theory.

that openly called for 'open seas protection' (China's Military Strategy 2015). In December, the Chinese government announced that it would open a naval base in Djibouti, thus fulfilling a key component of a blue water navy.

This chapter will argue that China's strategic rivalry with the U.S. is the primary driving force behind the PLAN's modernization. Like the previous Indian chapter, this argument is not monocausal. Other arguments such as nationalism, the security dilemma, and bureaucratic politics models do offer some utility, but on their own, they are insufficient to cause sustained naval modernization. This chapter provides a granular analysis of the period from 1991 to 2020 and demonstrates why China's rivalry with America caused Beijing to modernize its navy.

What Should We Be Looking For?

The primary goal of this chapter is to connect critical junctures/major points of rivalry escalation to decisions regarding the purchase or construction of naval hardware. This is not an easy task, but it is essential to the argument that strategic rivalry is the main driver. This chapter casts a spotlight on these junctures and then analyses the open-source material as well as making use of in-depth interviews with experts to establish a link between cause and effect. Different periods of the rivalry produced different responses from leaders in both China and the U.S. I will demonstrate that by the end of the first decade of the 2000s, the rivalry had solidified to such an extent that both Washington and Beijing realized the rivalry would be long-lasting and each started to make long-term strategic plans that accounted for both the rivalry and naval platforms. We should also be cognizant of the changing nature of the PLAN over the period under review. The PLAN transformed from a navy centred on access denial in the 1990s, to a force seeking to project into the open seas in the late 2000s. In addition, I examine instances where the Sino/U.S. rivalry spilt into the Sino/Indian rivalry, thus contributing to Indian naval modernization. Overall, readers should be looking for concrete evidence that strategic rivalry is the main driver, while also closely examining other competing explanations.

Organization of Chapter

This chapter is divided into three main sections. The first part examines the state of the PLAN at the dawn of the rivalry and traces the evolution of its modernization until 2004, when it was primarily a force centred on Corbettian strategies of naval warfare. This section exposes the most important critical junctures in the rivalry that took place during this period. The second part will examine the PLAN's push towards a more Mahanian/blue water centred navy from 2004 until 2020. This period witnessed the PLAN evolve from a force centred on access denial, to one with increasingly sophisticated platforms and submarines designed to protect Chinese interests in the open oceans. The final section of the chapter focuses on the main explanation—rivalry—as well as the competing arguments. It demonstrates that arguments centred on nationalism, with the exception of the aircraft carrier programme, are not well supported, while the security dilemma and bureaucratic politics models, struggle to offer convincing explanations.

Section I: The Resurrection of the Sino/ U.S. Strategic Rivalry and the Birth of the Modern PLAN

The events of 4 June 1989 shaped the political culture and foreign relations of China in a profound way. In the immediate aftermath of the massacre, both the Chinese and American intelligence agencies attempted to insulate the carefully crafted nearly two-decades long strategic partnership between Beijing and Washington.[5] George H.W. Bush even secretly sent his National Security Director, Brent Scowcroft, to Beijing at the end of June to try to stop the careening relationship from completely falling apart. Scowcroft's mission was to maintain communication between the White House and Deng Xiaoping and to let him know that Bush was being forced to adopt sanctions against China. Deng told Scowcroft that the U.S. was to blame for the Tiananmen incident as they had a history of interfering in China's internal affairs. In addition, Deng

---

[5] Author's discussion with former American Embassy official in Beijing. Beijing. 2016.

ignored the political reality in Washington and told the National Security Advisor that it was up to the U.S. to find a way out of the mess and that China had no intention of repenting (Cohen 2010). Although Deng had to take a hard stand against the U.S., many of the lower-level officials in the Chinese government who managed the day-to-day security relationship with Washington were fully aware of the political consequences of Tiananmen. They went to their American counterparts and told them that they knew sanctions were coming and there would be a heavy political price to pay for the massacre, but they pleaded with the Americans to 'keep the lines of communication open between Chinese and American intelligence agencies'.[6]

Even though Bush tried to preserve the ties between Beijing and Washington, the political damage of 4 June could not be overcome in the U.S. Bush was frequently attacked during his 1992 failed re-election bid as Bill Clinton and Al Gore accused his administration of 'coddling dictators' in Beijing (Mann 1999). Bush was also ignoring public opinion by trying to maintain a working relationship with China. In February 1989, a public opinion poll found that 72 per cent of Americans had a 'favourable' perception of China, but only 31 per cent had a 'favourable' opinion of China in the first poll taken after the massacre (Cohen 2010). In fact, research by Page and Xie demonstrates that even after two decades this favourability rating has never fully recovered from the pre-June 1989 mark (Page and Xie 2010). In regards to rivalry initiation, I argue that the second Sino/U.S. strategic rivalry traces its origins to June 1989, and has been maintained ever since.

The Gulf War

Saddam Hussein's August 1990 invasion is an unlikely place to locate a major critical juncture in the current Sino/U.S rivalry, but this event culminated in the dramatic defeat of his 'million-man army' in only a couple of weeks at the hands of a technologically superior American led military force. Chinese security analysts were confident that as the American military faced off against the battle tested Iraqis, they would

---

[6] Author's discussion with a former American intelligence official. 2016–2017 academic year.

become bogged down in a protracted ground war that would result in thousands of American casualties and eventual American withdrawal. Instead, the swift American victory shocked the PLA and more importantly, demonstrated to them that a new era of warfare had arrived. It is important to note that while this was not a direct point of rivalry escalation between China and the U.S., it is still a critical juncture between the two and it played an enormous role in the strategic thinking of the Chinese leadership and the PLA. The Chinese believed that their concept of a 'people's war', which relied on China's massive population and seemingly unlimited manpower to fight foreign powers in wars of attrition, (as they did during the Korean War) could defeat any foreign power foolish enough to challenge China. In addition, much of the Iraqi Army's hardware was purchased from China. Over a two-month period in early 1991, China's military strategy was undermined in what is referred to as 'The Revolution in Military Affairs' (RMA) (Shambaugh 2002; Fravel 2019).

In the immediate aftermath of the war, the Chinese leadership ordered a massive review of Chinese military tactics and strategy. Rivalry escalation in the form of American arms sales to Taiwan, especially the 1992 decision by the Bush administration to sell Taipei 150 F-16s, added to the urgency. While this sale was a significant point of escalation in the early 1990s, it was largely for domestic American political calculations.[7] Concrete evidence that the Gulf War and perceptions of American interference in Chinese affairs drove Beijing to reform the PLA are found in the meetings held by Admiral Liu Huaqing and his colleagues on the Central Military Commission (CMC). These meetings produced policy recommendations designed to speed up weapons development and culminated in the 'Military Strategic Guidelines for a New Era' (MSG: *Junshi Zhanlue Fangzhen*) (Cheung 2015). The MSG were crafted by the Chinese leadership and were designed to guide the development, planning, and utilization of the armed forces. The revisions were carried out between 1991 and 1992, and were unveiled in January of 1993 when Chinese leader Jiang Zemin gave a speech that argued that major shifts in the domestic, regional, and international environments were necessary to change the

---

[7] During the summer of 1992, Bush found himself trailing Bill Clinton in the polls. In an effort to try and win over Texas, he approved the sale of the F-16s in an attempt to create jobs at General Dynamic's struggling factory in Texas (Mann 1999).

previous MSG. According to Liu Huaqing's memoirs, a meeting was then set up in June 1993 that called for a better strategic direction and the development of long-term force modernization and better military combat capabilities (cited in Cheung 2015).

The participation of Liu Huaqing in constructing strategy and a major overhaul of the PLA is essential. From 1992 to 1997 Liu was one of seven members of the Politburo Standing Committee (PBSC) and this gave him enormous influence in the formal levers of power in China. More importantly, paramount leader Deng Xiaoping was sidelined after 1994 due to health problems. (Deng was not on the PBSC.) Crucially, Jiang Zemin had yet to achieve greater power as he was still vying for control with rivals and trying to placate the PLA (Shirk 2007; Garver 2016). This meant that Liu would likely have been able to influence policy even more as the PBSC was without a dominant figure or rival military commander. As will be demonstrated in the third section of this chapter that focuses on competing arguments for PLAN modernization, Liu's time on the PBSC is the last time a member of the Chinese military has had such a formal position of power. His failure to secure a green light for China's aircraft carrier programme casts serious doubt on the PLA and PLAN's ability to operate as effective organizations in a bureaucratic politics model.

The Yinhe Incident

In the summer of 1993, the Chinese merchant ship *Yinhe* (Milky Way) left port in northeast China for a long voyage to Iran. Upon leaving its initial port, the CIA informed the White House that the ship was transporting chemical agents that were essential for the production of chemical weapons. The American Embassy in China informed the Chinese authorities about the supposed cargo, and Jiang Zemin gave his personal assurance to American Ambassador Stapleton Roy that the ship did not contain chemical agents. Ambassador Roy then told Bill Clinton that he believed Jiang and that he did not think the Chinese leader would lie about this. Clinton did not accept Jiang's guarantee and American warships closely followed the *Yinhe* and stopped it on the high seas as it neared Iran. The Americans then insisted that the ship be searched for contraband and after a team from Saudi Arabia carried out an inspection, no chemical agents were found.[8] The Chinese Government was outraged over what they perceived to be a blatant violation of Chinese sovereignty on the high seas. More importantly, the PLAN was helpless to assist the Chinese vessel. With no viable long-range warship to escort the *Yinhe*, let alone stand up to the American Navy, the Chinese were defenceless in what they perceived to be American hegemony and bullying of China (Medeiros 2009).[9]

The *Yinhe* incident is frequently ignored by scholars and analysts of Chinese security, but it had a profound impact on Chinese leaders. Chinese scholars and government think-tank experts argue that it was an early critical juncture in the push for modernizing the PLAN. It is described as 'a great humiliation' and the government vowed to 'never let it happen again'. A prominent expert on Chinese security at a top government think tank argued that the *Yinhe* incident was even a greater catalyst for the modernization of the PLAN than the Gulf War. He stated 'the *Yinhe* incident was very important, it made China feel it should have the ability to defend China's national face, to not be humiliated ... This incident showed China that the USA has a double standard on freedom of navigation. China then knew it needed to develop naval power.'[10] One of the few Western references to the *Yinhe* does point out that it was a critical juncture. Erickson and Goldstein of the U.S. Naval War College have argued that the incident was a major event that drove the acquisition of new nuclear-powered submarines. They state that the 'PRC high command was "extremely furious" but had no recourse—at this moment the leadership 'redoubled its efforts to build a capable and superior SSN that could protect China's shipping in distant seas.' This argument is also supported by Liu Huaqing in his official memoir (Erickson and Goldstein 2007. P 185). How an SSN would help in the event of an interdiction on the high seas is not clear, but the incident's influence on the push for naval modernization is widely recognized. In a possible tit-for-tat response to America's naval presence in China's periphery, in October 1994, a Chinese nuclear-powered Han-class SSN stalked the American aircraft

---

[8] During the course of field work a source told the author that chemical agents were originally on board the ship, but these were removed during the stop in Shanghai. Author's discussion with Chinese expert. Beijing 2016.

[9] Author's personal interviews. Beijing 2016–2017 academic year.

[10] Author's personal interview. Beijing 2016.

carrier Kitty Hawk and was then engaged by American aircraft (Bussert and Elleman 2011).

The events of the early 1990s played a significant role in setting the stage in the Sino/U.S. rivalry. The massacre in June 1989, coupled with the American sanctions and arms sales to Taiwan, led leaders in Beijing to view Washington as a threat that was trying to undermine national stability and bring about the demise and eventual collapse of the CCP. Concrete evidence that the Tiananmen massacre and subsequent events caused the rivalry to resurface is found in The Tiananmen Papers.[11] Chinese Premier Li Peng ordered the Ministry of State Security (MSS) to prepare a report for all Politburo members that blasted the U.S. for seeking to overthrow the Chinese government. Chinese leaders also accused the U.S. of trying to organize democratic forces in socialist countries in attempts to topple communist regimes. In addition, the MSS accused the American State Department of attempting to arm China's floating population (mostly migrant workers) and turn it into an anti-government-armed force. Other Chinese leaders including Li Xiannian, who was President of China from 1983 to 1988, and was Chairman of the Chinese People's Political Consultative Conference in 1989, argued that the U.S. aimed to create chaos in China and remove the CCP. Deng Xiaoping also condemned the U.S. for allegedly trying to overthrow the CCP (The Tiananmen Papers).[12] American attempts to punish China over Tiananmen also included forcing the World Bank and the Asian Development Bank to withhold loans to China, and negotiations on China joining the World Trade Organization were suspended for three years (Nathan and Scobell 2012).

Concerns were undoubtedly increased with perceptions of American bullying that accompanied the Yinhe incident along with the shock of the American victory in Iraq, led Beijing to overhaul its military strategy and tactics. The drive for greater firepower would intensify enormously

[11] The Tiananmen Papers are top-secret documents smuggled out of Beijing by a Chinese government employee. These documents detail the Chinese leadership's decision to use lethal force against their own people during the upheaval in the spring of 1989.

[12] It is important to note that the perception that the U.S. was behind the Tiananmen protests is still held today by many members of Chinese academia. When this author mentioned this to members of America's intelligence community, they laughed and stated, 'if only we were that good'. Author's discussion with members of American intelligence community. U.S. 2007.

in 1995 and 1996 as Beijing was confronted with perhaps the most important critical juncture in the history of the current rivalry.

The 1995/1996 Taiwan Crisis

During the early 1990s, the process of democratization started to gain traction in Taiwan and by 1994, Taiwan was quickly moving towards a democratic transition. Adding to Beijing's fears were various actions carried out by lawmakers in Washington. In April 1994, a bill passed in Congress with a provision that directed the State Department to improve ties with Taipei. The Taiwan Policy Review, as the act was known, was signed by President Clinton and upgraded ties between Taiwan and the U.S. in several small ways. For example, American officials could now meet with Taiwanese officials in their respective offices, instead of in an 'unofficial venue'. While these small incremental changes annoyed Beijing, they were minuscule when compared to what followed (Garver 2016).

In early 1995, Taiwanese leader Lee Teng-hui requested a visa to make a visit to Cornell University, where he had graduated from in 1968 with a PhD in agricultural economics. Fearing the issuance of a visa would lead to further rivalry escalation, the State Department informed Beijing that the visa would not be issued (Fravel 2008). It is important to note that in April of 1995, Lee stated that China and Taiwan were 'two political entities', this was perceived in both Beijing and Washington as a break with the goal of a peaceful cross-Strait unification. Beijing also viewed this statement as a path towards formal Taiwanese independence and thus the breakup of 'China' (Garver 2016). The State Department made it very clear to China that Lee would not be issued a visa and Secretary of State Warren Christopher told Chinese Foreign Minister that the Clinton Administration was opposed to issuing one (Shirk 2007). However, both the Chinese and the White House ignored the role Congress plays in Taiwan policy. Increasing congressional pressure forced Clinton to change positions after the Senate voted 97 to 1 and the House voted 396 to 0 in support of issuing Lee a visa (Cohen 2010).

Lee used the 1995 visit to Cornell as his kickoff for the 1996 Taiwanese presidential election. John Garver argues that the PLA had little understanding of the workings of domestic American politics, and many in Beijing saw this move as concrete evidence of American attempts to weaken and split China. The rising political storm put Chinese leader Jiang Zemin in a very awkward position. While Jiang was the Party Secretary, he did not have the authority over the military that previous Chinese leaders held. In particular, when Deng Xiaoping selected Jiang as the future paramount leader, he lobbied the PLA leadership to give Jiang their full support. In this context, Jiang had to pay attention to pressure from the PLA and come up with a strong military response to what was perceived to be American and Taiwanese 'separatists' attempts to divide China (Garver 2016).

The PLA started to carry out military manoeuvres in the form of missile tests aimed at Taiwan in early July 1995. These original tests lasted two months and were an attempt by Beijing to demonstrate its resolve and willingness to use force to prevent a formal Taiwanese declaration of independence (Fravel 2008). By late 1995, Beijing's coercive diplomacy had succeeded in reducing Taiwanese support for Lee (Garver 2016). Crucially, there had not been an American military response. This changed in December, when American officials believed the PLA exercises had become large enough to require an American show of force. The American carrier USS Nimitz was on its way from Japan to the Persian Gulf and was ordered to transit the Taiwan Strait, the first American carrier to do so since Sino/U.S. relations were restored in 1979. The carrier's transit was kept a secret for six weeks until the end of January when it was explained as the result of bad weather (Garver 2016). The American demonstration of gunboat diplomacy did not resolve the rising tensions, and instead locked China and America into a cycle of rivalry escalation.

On 4 February 1996, Beijing further escalated the rivalry by conducting more military drills and missile firings in the vicinity of Taiwan. Codenamed 'Express 60', this was a test to deploy large PLA forces opposite Taiwan within 60 hours. These exercises continued into March with various firings of ballistic missiles around key Taiwanese ports. The result of the military tests and drills was public panic in Taiwan as people rushed to stores to buy essentials such as oil, rice, and toilet paper. So many people were exchanging Taiwanese dollars for U.S. dollars that extra planeloads of USD were flown in and banks started to limit the amount of money people could use in a transaction. The Taiwanese stock market also took a major hit (Garver 2016; Cohen 2010).

On 8 March, the PLA started to fire missiles in brackets off the coast of Kaosheng and Keelung. The Clinton Administration decided this act had to be challenged and announced the deployment of the USS Independence aircraft carrier battle group to the vicinity of Taiwan. Three days later the Americans announced the additional deployment of the USS Nimitz aircraft carrier battle group. The deployment of two aircraft carrier battle groups is enormously important to rivalry escalation and represented the most powerful display of American against China since 1971 (Shambaugh 2002; Garver 2016). Had Washington decided to send just one carrier and its accompanying ships, the signal to Beijing would have been less severe. One battle group is a symbolic gesture of support. A single battle group would also not be ready to engage in any meaningful combat activities. Two battle groups are a major escalation, arguably just short of war. Given the state of the Chinese military in 1996, two battle groups would have been able to do significant damage to the PLA/PLAN had they engaged in any kinetic action. As can be seen in Table 4.1, the PLAN did not have a single 'modern' submarine, and only three of the PLAN's surface combatants were considered 'modern'. Each American battle group has at least six other warships in addition to the super-carrier. The Americans would have had up to 15 state-of-the-art warships and submarines, complete with air cover, up against a technologically inferior, and never tested in combat PLA and PLAN.[13]

Even though it was faced with a formidable naval challenge, Beijing did not back down. Neither side wanted a full-scale war, but they also had to demonstrate their resolve. Beijing actually continued to escalate the conflict as it ordered more exercises to last from 18–25 March. Once the Taiwanese election was over on 23 March (with Lee as the victor) Washington and Beijing took steps to return to normalcy (Fravel 2008; Garver 2016). By this time, the damage was complete and this critical juncture would prove to be arguably the biggest turning point in the

---

[13] The size of carrier battle groups, or carrier strike groups, can vary in size. According to the American Navy, a battle group is composed of at least six warships. Each battle group has 1 aircraft carrier with an air-wing of 65–70 aircraft, 1 guided missile cruiser, 2–3 guided missile destroyers, 1–2 nuclear powered attack submarines, and one oilier/supply ship. In addition, the group has at least 7,500 personnel (The Carrier Strike Group).

Table 4.1 Chinese Naval Hardware from 1991 to 2030.[a]

Year	CVG	DDG	Frigates	Corvettes	SSK	Nuclear Subs[b]	Total Major Vessels[c]	Sailors
1991	0	18	37	N/A	88	5 [1]	148	260,000
1992	0	19	37	N/A	88	5 [1]	149	260,000
1993	0	18	38	N/A	40	6 [1]	102	260,000
1994	0	18	37	N/A	43	6 [1]	104	260,000
1995	0	18 <5%>	37 <8%>	0	43 <0%>	6 [1] <0%>	104	260,000
1996	0	18	36	0	56	6 [1]	116	265,000
1997	0	18	36	0	54	6 [1]	114	280,000
1998	0	18	35	0	57	6 [1]	116	260,000
1999	0	18	35	0	64	6 [1]	123	230,000
2000	0	20 <20%>	40 <25%>	0	60 <7%>	6 [1] <0%>	126	220,000
2001	0	21	41	0	62	6 [1]	130	250,000
2002	0	21	42	0	62	6 [1]	131	250,000
2003	0	21	42	0	62	6 [1]	131	250,000
2004	0	21	42	0	62	6 [1]	131	255,000
2005	0	21 <40%>	43 <35%>	N/A	51 <40%>	8 <25%>	123	255,000
2006	0	25	45	N/A	50	5	125	255,000
2007	0	25	47	N/A	53	5	125	255,000
2008	0	29	45	N/A	54	9 [3]	128	255,000
2009	0	27–28	48–50	N/A	54–55	9 [3]	133	255,000
2010	0	25 <50%>	49 <45%>	0	54 <50%>	9 <22%>	137	255,000
2011	0	26	53	N/A	49	9 [3]	137	255,000
2012	1	13–26	53–65	N/A	48–53	8 [3]	132	255,000
2013	1	14–23	52–62	N/A	49–55	8–9 [4]	132	255,000
2014	1	13–24	49-54	8	51	8–9 [4]	140	235,000
2015	1	21 <81%)	52 <67%>	15	53 <59%>	9 <100%>	151	235,000
2016	1	23	52	23	51	9 [4]	159	235,000
2017	1	21	57	27	47	9 [4]	162	235,000
2018	1	21	59	37	48	13 [4]	169	240,000
2019	1	27	59	41	48	13 [4]	179	250,000

Continued

Table 4.1 *Continued*

Year	CVG	DDG	Frigates	Corvettes	SSK	Nuclear Subs[b]	Total Major Vessels[c]	Sailors
2020[d]	1–2	32 <85%>	56 <85%>	(24–30)	62 <75%>	13 <100%>	191	N/A
2021	2	31	46	55	46	12 [6]	161[e]	260,000
2030[f]	4–6	34	68	26	75	24	232	N/A

[a]Data is derived from the International Institute for Strategic Studies annual data sheets found in 'The Military Balance', as well as data compiled by the Andrew Erickson of the China Maritime Studies Institute at the U.S. Naval War College and from Rick Joe (Erickson 2017B; Joe 2021B). Percentage of warships designated as 'modern' comes from Andrew Erickson who utilizes data from the American Office of Naval Intelligence (ONI). (Erickson 2017B) <%> indicates 'approximate percentage modern' by ONI, or the editors from the China Maritime Studies Institute. This means a platform of submarine has the ability to launch ICBMs or ASCMs. Modern ships are also able to carry out multiple missions, or they have been significantly upgraded since 1992. (Erickson 2017B) For multiple years the percentage of modern ships is not listed in either data set and therefore this information is not available.

[b][] represents the number of SSBNs

[c]For the years after 2008, the total number is not clear. Rough estimates are provided instead.

[d]Estimates by Erickson 2017B, as well as Author's interviews with Scholars of Chinese security. China and the USA. 2007–2012, and 2016–2017 Academic Year.

[e]This number includes six Principal Amphibious Ships (The Military Balance 2021) and three 055 cruisers not listed in the The Military Balance—IISS 2021 data. (Joe 2021B)

[f]Ibid.

strategic rivalry. Both sides had tested each other and had learned just how far their rival was prepared to go over the issue of Taiwan. For the Chinese leadership the most important takeaway was learning that the Americans were willing to protect Taiwan, even if that risked a military confrontation with China. Beijing also realized very quickly that they were not at all prepared to deal with an American military intervention in the Taiwan theatre. For the Americans, the key takeaway was that Beijing was willing to go to war over Taiwan, even if this meant a potentially catastrophic confrontation with the American navy. American scholar Susan Shirk has referred to the Taiwan issue as 'a matter of regime survival', in that the CCP cannot afford to allow Taiwan to become a de-facto independent state without going to war to prevent this. While Shirk's argument hinges on the unproven forces of Chinese nationalism, she is correct in her analysis of the societal pressures the CCP would face if Taiwan declared independence (Shirk 2007).

The 1995/96 Taiwan Crisis as a Driver
of PLAN Modernization

There is nearly universal agreement that the 1995–1996 Taiwan crisis was a significant critical juncture in the Sino/U.S. strategic rivalry. The key question is how much of a shock, and how much influence did it have on actual naval modernization and the procurement of naval hardware?

In terms of the punctuated equilibrium model of rivalry maintenance and escalation, the events of 1995/96 were profound. Prior to this juncture, the leadership in Beijing did not realize the extent to which Washington would go to protect Taiwan from Chinese coercion. For the first time since the Vietnam War, the Chinese and American military were on the brink of a kinetic confrontation. The Chinese leadership viewed the demonstration of American military power as a clear violation of Chinese sovereignty and direct interference in what Beijing perceived to be an internal Chinese matter. Dramatically increasing Beijing's threat perceptions was the fact that the Chinese military not only lacked the ability to detect the approaching American carrier battle groups but once the carriers arrived, the PLA and PLAN were helpless in forcing the Americans out of the theatre (Cole 2016). A professor of international security at one of Beijing's best universities described the crisis as a 'total state of helplessness for China'.[14] Many of the decision makers in China vowed to never again let such a situation happen (Holmes 2012). Scholars based in Chinese government think tanks as well as a scholar of Chinese security working at the American Indo-Pacific Command, view the crisis as 'China's Cuba crisis'. They argued that just as the Cuban missile crisis had a major impact on Soviet naval modernization, the Taiwan crisis played a similar role in China.[15]

It is clear that the crisis had a major effect on Chinese leaders, but how can we tell if it led to naval modernization? While building up one's navy can take decades, there is solid evidence that the crisis caused Beijing to increase its naval capacity and procurement. It is important to note that the Chinese government had limited financial resources in the 1990s, and

---

[14] Author's personal interview with Chinese academic. Beijing. Spring 2017.
[15] Author's personal interviews with Chinese and American scholars. Shanghai and Beijing. 2016/2017 academic year.

as a result the leadership set out to build a naval force that was able to keep outside powers (the U.S. Navy) at a safe distance.

Concrete evidence that the crisis drove naval modernization is found in multiple sources. A well-respected Chinese academic who is based at an elite Beijing university and has given lectures to the top levels of the Chinese government stated that the Taiwan incident directly caused the Chinese leadership to modernize the PLAN. Specifically, this scholar said the purchase of Russian Sovermenny DDGs and Kilo class SSKs were the result of the crisis. He also said that most of China's current fleet of warships and submarines were custom designed to counter the American navy, although he did mention that the aircraft carrier programme is not America specific.[16] This argument is also supported by Western scholars. Carlson and Bainchi state that after the Taiwan crisis, Chinese leaders reacted quickly bought Russian Project 956E Sovremenny-class guided-missile destroyers. Each DDG was armed with Shtil SAMs (Surface to Air Missiles). Prior to this episode, the Chinese military had not considered the use of long-range SAMs. In addition to the SAMs, the Russians also provided the Chinese with various anti-ship cruise missiles (ASCMs) such as the SS-N-22 Sunburn, and area defence SAMs such as the SA-N-7A Gadfly. Apart from the Russian acquisitions, overall there was a dramatic increase in the purchase and development of naval systems designed to deter the Americans from getting involved in any sort of Taiwan scenario (Carlson and Bainchi 2017).

The argument that the Chinese were developing their own version of a 'risk fleet' was supported by numerous Beijing based experts who believed the PLAN was following a Corbettian approach to modernization from the early 1990s until roughly 2005. The 'strategic suspicion' between China and Washington was also frequently cited as a driver. Another influential security scholar at a top Beijing university argued that 'without the American threat/rivalry/provocation, there would be no reason to build the navy'.[17] A retired U.S. navy officer, who was in the office of the Military Attaché in the American Embassy, noted that during his frequent meetings with the Chinese military, he would often hear about the 1995/96 Taiwan Crisis, and how important it was to the PLAN.[18]

---

[16] Author's interview with Chinese scholar. Beijing. 2016/2017 academic year.
[17] Author's interviews with Chinese scholars. Beijing 2016/2017 academic year.
[18] Author's phone interview with retired naval Captain. 2017.

Chinese language sources also demonstrate the role that the crisis played as a driver of modernization. Major General Luo Yuan spoke of the need to modernize the military and to accelerate the development of new weapons which are driven by America's behaviour vis-à-vis Taiwan (Lin 2010). Wang Fifeng and Ye Jing speak of an American plan to join with Japan in a military alliance directed at China, with the goal of building an 'anti-submarine chain' against China (Wang and Ye 2005). In a different article Ye Jing states that China's second generation nuclear powered SSN will make it very difficult for the U.S. to carry out direct intervention if there is a military conflict in the Taiwan Strait (Ye 2005).

Bernard Cole, widely recognized as one of the world's foremost authorities of the PLAN, points out that submarines also significantly benefitted from the crisis as the navy began to acquire Russian Kilos and started to develop and test their own versions of SSKs. Cole sums up his view of the role the crisis played in the quote:

It is unlikely that the modernization of China's submarine force began by coincidence with the PLA's realization of its shortcomings following U.S. naval intervention in the Taiwan imbroglio in 1996. The events of the mid-1990s no doubt spurned PLAN modernization of its surface combat fleet, as well. In particular, the PLAN realized its weaknesses in specific naval warfare areas, and more generally in lack of standardization, interoperability, and joint operations (Cole 2016. P 82).

Prior to the mid-1990s, the PLAN submarine force was large, with 93 vessels in 1990, of which 88 were SSKs, 1 was an SSBN, and there were 4 SSNs. Vitally, not a single vessel was considered 'modern' by the American Office of Naval Intelligence. They were unable to fire any missiles.[19] It is important to note that eight submarines did take part in the crisis, but all were obsolete (Bussert and Elleman 2011). In fact, many of the SSKs in the PLAN in the 1990s were Romeo and Ming-class boats that dated to the 1950s (Glosny 2004).

While Beijing was fully aware that it needed to modernize its fleet, the Chinese military, and the PLAN, in particular, had to deal with relatively limited financial resources. As demonstrated in Chart 4.1, China's military budget was relatively small and many of the available resources went towards salaries and various costs associated

[19] Please see data Table 4.1.

with providing for several million service members. As will be elaborated next, the official budget of the PLAN remains a state secret in China. However, various scholars and analysts have provided educated guesses of the amount money the PLAN might receive each year. One estimate was that the PLAN was able to spend 3.1 billion dollars a year on procurement in 1997, a year after the crisis (Raska and Bitzinger 2014). Whatever the real amount, it was clear to both the Chinese leadership and the PLAN that China did not have the economic resources to compete on the high seas with the USN. Faced with this situation, Chinese decision makers actively pursued a navy that would have the ability to protect China's coastline, while also posing a significant risk to the USN if it chose to intervene in any future Taiwan scenario.

The decision to pursue an access denial naval strategy in the 1990s and early 2000s reflects a rational strategic decision by Beijing. Yoshihara and Holmes of the U.S. Naval War College argue that the PLAN's strategy of keeping rivals out of designated waters, or deterring them from entering in the first place, is a practical approach to naval power (Yoshira and Holmes 2010). This strategy was heavily reliant on building up a credible deterrent, which was centred on SSKs. The concept of the 'risk fleet' was alive and well in the minds of Chinese security strategists. As the data on Chinese naval hardware in Table 4.1 demonstrates, in 1990, the PLAN was considered obsolete. However, by 2010, the PLAN had 54 SSKs with 50 per cent classified as 'modern' boats. In addition, they also had six SSNs, of which three were 'modern'. The PLAN commissioned 31 submarines from 1995–2005, and from 2002–2004 alone it launched 13 new submarines (Erickson et al. 2007). Major General Huang Bin explained the strategic logic behind China's asymmetric strategy by stating that the destruction of an American aircraft carrier is:

> The focal point of doctrinal development ... We have the ability to deal with an aircraft carrier that dares to get in our range of fire ... The U.S. likes vain glory; if one of its aircraft carriers could be attacked and destroyed, people in the U.S. would begin to complain and quarrel loudly, and the U.S. President would find the going harder and harder. (Cited in Goldstein and Murry 2004. P 191)

Chinese planner's fixation with destroying, or at least disabling an American carrier mirror earlier Russian war planes, which believed certain gaps in carrier defences could be exploited. With tactics designed around multi-wave and multi-sector cruise missile attacks, strategists thought they could accomplish their goal. Leaders in the PLAN believed it would require 8–10 direct hits by ASCMs to disable a carrier. This would require a coordinated simultaneous attack that unleashed a wave of 70–100 missiles (Goldstein and Murry 2004). A 2002 study by the Dalian Naval Academy calculated that 20 anti-ship missiles would be necessary to disable an American Arleigh Burke-class destroyer (Yan et al. 2002). The PLAN was also fully aware of the advantages submarines would have in a Taiwan scenario. The shallow water of the Taiwan Strait is ideal for the PLANs diesel electric submarines. Chinese SSKs can conceal themselves between the different layers of underwater thermals and the rocks and shoals where the acoustics are very poor. This would significantly reduce the enormous technological advantage American warships and submarines hold over the PLAN (Goldstein and Murry 2004).

Glaser sheds light on how the procurement process in the mid to late-1990s was influenced by the American involvement in the Taiwan issue. Importantly, she demonstrates that procurement issues are discussed in the CMC and starting in the late 1990s, procurement strategy and Taiwan strategy started to converge. The role of the USN was crucial to this fusion as procurement decisions were heavily influenced by the priority to deter the USN from coming to the aid of Taiwan in the event of a Chinese attack on the island. In firm agreement with both a Corbettian model of naval development and the influence of a strategic rivalry, decisions were made to develop near-term capabilities, while postponing larger long-range platforms that were not as relevant to the Taiwan scenario.

The role of the bureaucracy in the PLA must not be completely dismissed. The literature views various bureaucracies as embedded in the rivalry process and the perceived American 'interference' in the Taiwan issue provided the PLA with a frame that vilified the Americans and justified greater resources to be directed to the military. General Chen Bingde, the Director-General of the General Armaments Department, called American involvement in Taiwan and the Taiwan Relations Act as examples of American hegemony and interference in China's internal affairs (Glaser 2015).

The Chinese response also gave the PLAN the opportunity to build a force that was capable of denying the Americans access within the 'first island chain'. This 'chain', which is depicted on Map 4.1, extends from Japan to Taiwan and then follows the 'Nine Dash Line' in the South China Sea, which is firmly in line with Corbett's theory of naval modernization for states with low levels of resources. In fact, the Taiwan crisis may have set back the Chinese aircraft carrier programme by up to a decade as Beijing saw the urgency of developing more practical, and in the context of a war with American, more lethal hardware.

Not fully recognized are the structural changes the crisis likely initiated. Prior to the mid-1990s, the PLAN was a second-class citizen in the Chinese military. This is not surprising considering that the senior officials in the PLA and the Chinese government came of age in an era when the threat of a Soviet land invasion was not only real, but also at certain times it was expected. In the absence of a realistic threat from the sea, the PLAN did not require a significant budget or endless resources. The PLAN was also the victim of inter-service rivalry within the military. Generals in the Chinese Army would frequently treat the PLAN as mostly an appendage to the Army, and senior officers resisted moves towards joint operations (McVadon 2007). In fact, as late as the mid-1990s, the PLAN was commanded by Generals, and not Admirals (Erickson et al. 2012). From an organizational perspective, the crisis exposed just how

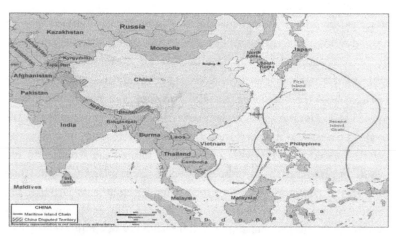

Map 4.1 East Asian Island Chains (Annual Report to Congress 2008)

helpless and vulnerable the PLAN was to defend what is considered to be a 'core interest'. While the major reforms and evolution or strategy would take years, if not decades to implement, the crisis captured the attention of China's leaders and demonstrated to them the necessity of having a capable and potent navy that was able to defend China's interests.

Thus, an access-denial strategy was adopted and Chinese leaders realized such a navy would not have to be able to engage the Americans on the high seas, but could either deny the USN access into the Taiwan theatre, or at least have the ability to cause Washington to reconsider such a move. The purchase of Russian warships and submarines, as well as Russian ASCMs is evidence of this. Over the next decade, the PLAN would develop a robust area denial capability able to inflict significant damage on any American surface warships that ventured within the first island chain. While the 1995/96 Taiwan Crisis was a huge event, another major critical juncture would take place just three years later with the destruction of the Chinese embassy in Belgrade.

China's Anti-Access and Area Denial Strategy from 1996 to 2004

The period from 1991 to 1996 demonstrated to the Chinese leadership the serious inadequacies of the PLAN if it were to engage in modern warfare. The years from 1996 to 2004, following the Taiwan Crisis, are best explained as China's attempt to build a navy that had the ability to deter the USN from encroaching into China's sphere of influence. The PLAN during this period, however, was relatively short on funds and as a result had to purchase or construct a naval force that could pose a significant 'risk' to any American naval foray sent to assist Taiwan. As will be demonstrated in the second half of this chapter, this period differs enormously in terms of the force structure the PLAN was acquiring. As previously stated, the post-2004 PLAN sought a more blue water trajectory, while the pre-2004 PLAN was much more geared towards a navy centred around Julian Corbett's theory of naval power.

Because the Chinese leadership could not compete on the high seas with the USN, the PLAN started to develop more lethal SSKs and began a significant push to build stealthy and capable nuclear-powered submarines. Empirical evidence of these efforts to modernize the SSK fleet is seen both in the purchase of Russian Kilo-class SSKs and in the percentage of SSKs that were considered 'modern'. For example, as Table 4.1 demonstrates, in 1995, the PLAN did not have a single 'modern' SSK in its entire fleet, however, by 2005, nearly 40 per cent of the PLAN's SSK fleet was considered 'modern'. The data for PLAN DDGs and Frigates is nearly identical over the same period. As mentioned above, from 2002 to 2004, it launched 13 new submarines. These early 2000s launches would have been ordered in the late 1990s as part of the PLAN's 'assassin's mace' programme aimed at access denial. Retired American Admiral Michael McDevitt argues that the PLAN's strategy during this time is a variant of the Soviet strategy of sea denial in the 1980s. He states, 'by electing to mimic the Soviet approach, Beijing has opted for a maritime strategy that is at once affordable, militarily practical, and comprehensive' (McDevitt 2007. P 370). The late 1990s was not without its own share of technological challenges for the PLAN. In 1998, and again in 2000, several Kilo-class SSKs were sent back to Russia because of technical problems (Glosny 2004). The late 1990s also saw the beginning of the anti-ship ballistic missile (ASBM) programme, apparently initiated by Jiang Zemin in the immediate aftermath of the 1995/96 Taiwan Crisis. The primary goal of the ASBM programme was the ability to target American aircraft carriers that were far out to sea, but were coming to the aid of Taiwan.[20] In 1997, Jiang Zemin even urged the PLAN to 'build the nation's maritime Great Wall' (Bussert and Elleman 2011).

The PLA and PLAN Budget

An important component of Chinese naval modernization is the PLAN's annual budget. Unfortunately, this information is considered a state secret in China, thus we are only able to come up with rough estimates of the actual amount.[21] Most experts interviewed believed the 2015–2019 budget to be approximately 25–30 per cent of the overall PLA budget.[22]

[20] Author's interview with Chinese academics. Beijing 2016–2017 academic year.
[21] Please see Liff and Erickson 2013 for an excellent analysis of China's defence spending.
[22] Author's interviews with multiple experts in China and the U.S. 2016–2017 academic year.

(Please see Chart 4.1 for the official overall PLA budget for the period under review.) A political military advisor for the American Navy estimated the PLAN received roughly 20 per cent of the overall budget 15 years ago, and now is allocated 30 per cent.[23] There are a number of methodological problems associated with comparing the perceived PLAN budget to other militaries. Apart from the challenges laid out by Modelski and Thompson above, Liff and Erickson are sceptical of figures approaching 30 per cent of the budget. They argue that rampant inflation has likely mitigated the actual impact of the increases in the Chinese military budget (Liff and Erickson 2013). In addition, the PLA budget (and PLAN) does not include the acquisition of foreign weapons (Bussert and Elleman 2011). Comparisons with the American budget are also not very helpful. For example, every soldier in the American military is paid on average 18,000 USD, while only 2,000 USD is paid to his or her Chinese counterpart (Cole 2016). A large share of the increases in the Chinese defence budget goes to improving the living standards of Chinese personnel, and not to building military hardware. In fact, the PLA in general struggles to recruit well-educated people and has recently invested in improving living standards for its personnel.[24] Overall, a rough figure of 25 per cent of the military budget is a good estimate of the PLAN budget as a percentage of the overall PLA budget. This figure would be more appropriate for the years 2010–2020. For the years prior, we do not have reliable estimates.

The Sino/U.S. rivalry between the 1995/1996 Taiwan Crisis and the Belgrade Embassy bombing three years later stabilized and was relatively calm, but it still experienced maintenance. Under the Nye Initiative, which attempted to redefine the security alliance between Tokyo and Washington in post-Cold War terms, from 1997 to 1998, the U.S. and Japan agreed to jointly work together to develop theatre missile defence systems (Silver 2000).[25] From 1996 to 1997, the U.S. also moved to reassert its security relationship with Australia in ways that were of concern to the Chinese government. In addition, the Americans sought to upgrade their bi-lateral military relationships in South East Asia following

---

[23] Author's interview with Political Military Advisor to the U.S. Navy. 2017.

[24] Author's interviews with Chinese security scholars. 2016–2017 academic year.

[25] The Nye Initiative was named after Joseph Nye who at the time was the American Assistant Secretary of Defense for International Security Affairs.

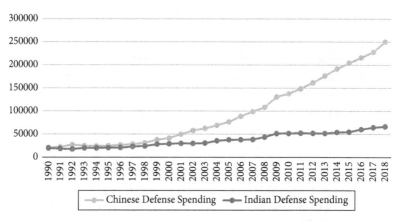

Chart 4.1 1990–2018 Annual Defense Spending in China and India (Constant 2017 Prices in USD Millions) (Stockholm-SIPRI)

the loss of Subic Bay in the Philippines in the early 1990s. Chinese commentators viewed these developments as concrete evidence of American attempts to 'contain China' and as American 'regional hegemony'. Christensen has even argued that the development of the Shanghai Cooperation Organization (SCO) in 1996 was a Chinese response to perceived American 'Cold War Thinking' and 'Power Politics'.[26] Yan Xuetong argues that by the late-1990s, the U.S. began to treat China as its main rival, and that opinions expressed in the American Quadrennial Defense Review (QDR) viewed China as a regional or global competitor (Yan 2000 cited in Christensen 2006). Liu Jianfei supports this perspective and argued that American efforts to contain China would continue (Liu 2005). Whether the U.S. was actively trying to 'contain' China is less important than Chinese perceptions that it was being 'contained' by Washington. In a rivalry perceptions matter and decision makers base their policies on perceptions.

---

[26] The term 'Cold War thinking' is usually associated with viewing the other side as a rival and enemy. It can also mean zero-sum calculations and viewing interactions through the prism of relative and not absolute gains. It frequently has an ideological component where an opposing state's values and ideology are criticized. 'Power politics' frequently means that strong powers do as they please and is associated with hegemony (Liff 2018).

One important side note to the late 1990s regarding PLAN procurement is the purchase of three aircraft carrier shells. In 1998, the aircraft carriers Varyag and Minsk were purchased, as was the Kiev in 2000 (Scobell et al. 2015). These acquisitions do not demonstrate a drive towards the blue ocean as none of these carriers were even remotely operational, but instead may demonstrate the influence of Liu Huaqing, who was on the Politburo Standing Committee (PBSC) until 1997. As will be discussed next, these purchases show that the leadership was interested in carriers, but the decision to actively build and make the carrier operational does not come until 2004.

The Destruction of the Chinese Embassy in Belgrade

On the night of 7 May 1999, the Chinese Embassy in Belgrade was obliterated by five American satellite-guided JDAM bombs (Fravel 2019). With the destruction of the embassy, the American led war in Kosovo went from a minor point of rivalry maintenance between China and the U.S. (Beijing perceived the war as an example of American hegemony and interference in other countries internal affairs) to a major point of rivalry escalation. This incident competes with the 1995/1996 Taiwan Crisis for the most important critical juncture in the rivalry.[27] The bombing led to widespread protests across numerous Chinese cities including major anti-American demonstrations in Beijing. The Chinese leadership viewed the bombing as intentional and as an American attempt to humiliate China in the international community (Gries 2004).

While the bombing was not directly related to the maritime domain, the Chinese leadership responded with a push to further acquire access denial capabilities. According to Tai Ming Cheung, immediately after the bombing the Chinese leadership and the CMC called for intensifying efforts to build major new weapons systems designed to counter the USA. Jiang Zemin pushed very hard for assassin's mace armaments and that Jiang stated that these weapons systems were what the 'enemy' feared

---

[27] Numerous Chinese interviewees argued that this event was on a par with the Taiwan crisis three years before. Author's interviews. Beijing, 2016–2017 academic year.

most and that China must target American vulnerabilities (Cheung 2015). The Chinese government also set up a New/High Technology and Engineering Leadership Small Group in 1999, which was tasked with the management and development of high-tech weapons (Cheung 2015). Numerous experts argued that the bombing was a major blow to national pride and was an enormous point of rivalry escalation and strongly influenced an upgraded PLAN. One top-level scholar even argued that the bombing was more of a critical juncture than the Taiwan Crisis.[28]

A stated goal of Admiral Liu Huaqing was to prevent hostile (American) powers from entering within the 'first island chain' by 2000. While it is difficult to put a precise time on the achievement of this goal, Bernard Cole believes that the PLAN achieved it by 2000 and was working to realize the much more difficult task of keeping the USN out of the 'second island chain by 2020' (Cole 2016). The perceived success of the PLAN obtaining this first island chain goal by 2000 was supported by several American defence attaches.[29] At the dawn of the 21st Century the PLAN was still focused on asymmetric warfare capabilities that were fixated on an American naval contingency, but as Scobell points out a 'paradigmatic change' in naval thinking was taking place, and within five years Beijing would start to transition from near seas to far seas strategy (Scobell et al. 2015). While the PLAN was focused on keeping the Americans out of East Asian waters close to China, PLAN warships did make regular visits to distant ports. As demonstrated in the India case study, many of these visits in the late 1990s and early 2000s were to IOR states. These visits significantly increased Indian threat perceptions, which led to calls for a stronger IN that could counter the PLAN in the IOR.

The Challenge of Chen Shui-bian and the Sino/ U.S. Rivalry

As the embassy bombing was a critical juncture, the year 2000 would also witness several significant points of rivalry escalation that would further

---

[28] Author's interviews with Chinese academics. Beijing 2016–2017 Academic Year.
[29] Although several attaches believed the precise timing of this achievement varied by a few years. Author's discussions with members of the Office of the Defense Attaché in the American Embassy in Beijing. Beijing. 2010–2012.

galvanize Beijing's threat perceptions of American strategy in East Asia. The 2000 Taiwanese Presidential Election, which resulted in the election of the pro-independence candidate Chen Shui-bian, caused significant unease in China. Of additional concern was the 2000 American presidential campaign where eventual winner George W. Bush called China a 'strategic competitor'. Bush's language combined with American arms sales to Taiwan automatically increased anxiety in Beijing. The situation deteriorated further on 1 April 2001, when a Chinese fighter-bomber collided with an American EP-3 spy plane that was eavesdropping on China. The death of Chinese pilot Wang Wei, and the holding of the American aircrew on Hainan Island, further complicated ties between Washington and Beijing (Gries 2004).[30] On 25 April 2001, Bush increased pressure on Beijing by stating that the U.S. would 'do whatever it took' to defend Taiwan from China (Sanger 2001). This incident was part of a pattern of mid-level maintenance and escalation as several American warships and surveillance vessels were harassed in waters close to China. The Singaporean Government's decision to upgrade Changi Naval Base (at its own expense) to accommodate American aircraft carriers was in keeping with general rivalry maintenance (Latif 2009). In addition, in 2002, the U.S. began selling arms to India and the U.S. Chairman of the Joint Chiefs of Staff made a visit to New Delhi. These developments were perceived by Chinese as American attempts to encircle and contain China (Garver 2016).

Chinese perceptions of a U.S. fixated with containing China may not hold up well to scrutiny, but the U.S. has certainly carried out steps to hedge against the rising power of Beijing. As far back as 2001, there is evidence that the U.S. was actively taking steps to prepare for China's rise. It is important to note that the term 'hedge' differs from that of 'contain'. While containment deals with actively preventing another state's rise and attempting to shut it out of the international community, while also countering it in multiple arenas (Kennan 'X' 1947) hedging is different.

---

[30] According to some sources, the 2001 EP-3 incident was a massive loss for American intelligence. While the Pentagon initially stated that the crew of the plane had used a fire axe on the plane's computer hard drives, as well as pouring hot coffee on the computers, later it was revealed that they had not completely destroyed the hard drives. Apparently, the Chinese were able to retrieve vital information from the computers and learn detailed information about American spying activities directed at China (Hersh 2010). It should be noted that this story was denied by a Pentagon official in 2012. Author's discussion with Pentagon official. 2012.

Tunsjo argues that hedging is a set of strategies that balance cooperation and confrontation so that states can be well-positioned regardless of future events (Tunsjo 2017). In this regard, the U.S. is both working with China and helping to facilitate its rise, while at the same time taking certain precautions should a stronger China attempt to challenge the U.S. or American interests in the future. The Defense Strategy Review of 2001 viewed China as 'the key case of concern', and the goal of the Pentagon was to dissuade China from countering the American military advantage. In addition, the 2001 QDR and the 2004 Global Posture Review (GPR) both had a goal of preventing China from challenging the American military (Silove 2016).

Chinese Ministry of Defense White Papers also view the U.S. as China's most important rival/enemy (China's National Defense 2000, 2002, 2004).[31] Interestingly, while Beijing identified the USN as key concern, PLAN representation on the CMC was very low. Of the 11 members of the 2002–2007 CMC, there was only one naval representative and this was Admiral Zhang Dingfa. (The previous CMC from 1997 to 2002 did not have a single naval representative (see Chart 4.1).) Other sources in the early 2000s also call out the U.S. as a threat and call for the PLAN to be strengthened in order to counter the perceived American threat. Wang Yifeng and Ye Jing speak of America's attempts to form an alliance with Japan and Taiwan that would build an 'anti-submarine chain' against China. They also argue that as China's submarine technology improves, it is increasingly difficult for the Americans and Taiwanese to detect Chinese submarines (Wang and Ye 2005).

Many of the PLAN ships and submarines that were commissioned in the early 2000s were ordered because of the critical junctures of the 1990s. The PLAN's first real attempt at a modern nuclear attack submarine the 093 Shang class SSN was launched in 2002, with a second vessel delivered in 2003. China's latest attempt at mastering the ability to fire Sea Launched Ballistic Missiles (SLBMs) is found in the 2003 introduction of the 094 Jin-class ballistic missile submarine (SSBN) (Goldstein and Murry 2004). Both of these nuclear-powered submarines are best viewed as experimental training vessels. Production of the

---

[31] Chinese Defense White Papers frequently use the term 'hegemonism', 'Cold War mentality', or 'extra-regional countries', in reference to the U.S.

093 was halted in 2003 and did not begin again until 2012 (The PLA Navy 2015). While these submarines encountered numerous problems, such as high noise levels and technical malfunctions, they are best seen as a concerted long-term effort by the PLAN to develop both a credible undersea nuclear deterrent, and the ability to field an attack submarine that can stay submerged indefinitely.[32] In support of the Corbettian argument, from 2004 to 2006, 18 SSKs were added to the PLAN. These submarines would have been ordered 4–6 years earlier, or right at the height of rivalry escalation. The PLAN also ordered two more Russian Sovremenny guided missile destroyers in 2002, which entered service in 2005 and 2006 (O'Rourke 2016). Many of these Russian DDGs were studied by Chinese engineers in an attempt to ascertain how to make their own indigenous DDGs. For example, China only built three DDGs in the 1990s, but as it made up the learning curve, production significantly increased. From 2000 to 2004, average production of DDGs and frigates stood at 1.6 per year. However, as China started to master the ability to build better and more robust platforms, Chinese shipbuilders started to engage in serial production and started to put to sea 4.2 per year from 2010 to 2014 (Fanell and Cheney-Peters 2017).

The early 2000s also saw increasing interest in China's ability to protect its SLOCs, and an emerging interest in a navy that was based more on Mahanian principles. For example, in 2002 Major General Jiang Shilang stated in the publication 'Chinese Military Science', that the competition for absolute control of critical SLOCs is a fact of life in international relations (cited in Yoshihara 2010). The PLANs transition from access denial and asymmetric warfare to a blue water navy was a gradual evolution and by 2005, Chinese scholars, and in particular, Chinese leaders, started to speak of a navy capable of projecting power and protecting Chinese interests beyond the first island chain. While the PLAN was gradually increasing its blue water capability and sending surface warships to distant ports in the IOR, as previously mentioned, New Delhi was anxiously watching as the PLAN started to learn about some of the key geographic and oceanic features and maritime challenges in the Indian Ocean. In the event of maritime hostilities with India, such information could prove

---

[32] Author's interviews with Chinese experts. Beijing 2016–2017 academic year.

vital in a kinetic confrontation. Indian defence planners are well aware of the information China can obtain from such voyages.[33]

The period from 1991 until 2004 witnessed profound transform-ations in the Chinese navy. The PLAN went from a force that was unable to even detect American carrier battle groups in China's periphery, to a force that had the ability to inflict significant damage on any American expeditionary force that would challenge Chinese interests and the pri-mary driving force behind this naval modernization was China's strategic rivalry with the U.S.

In conclusion, we know that these spikes in rivalry escalation were instrumental in driving the modernization of the PLAN. But other drivers such as nationalism and bureaucratic politics models were also present. This will be discussed in greater detail at this chapter's conclu-sion, but on their own they do not adequately explain naval modern-ization. By the first decade of the new century, the PLAN had satisfied its goal of developing the capability to inflict significant damage on the American navy in the event of a Taiwan contingency. Beijing knew that it would not be able to outright defeat the Americans, but the es-tablishment of a 'risk fleet with Chinese characteristics' was a reality. The Corbettian approach to naval modernization had achieved sig-nificant success. By the first decade of the 2000s, strategic thinking in Beijing started to look towards the open ocean and started to prepare for a much more capable and muscular naval force. In the decade from 2005 to 2015, the PLAN would make a concerted push towards a blue water navy, and would begin to make significant changes in the types of platforms and force structure of the Chinese navy. During this en-tire time, the PLAN would set its sights on the USN and the Chinese leadership would continue to perceive the U.S. as attempting to con-tain China, this would call for a much greater naval force. This same period would also witness the PLAN increasing its port calls into the IOR, thus causing rivalry escalation with Indian, which led to calls for Indian naval modernization. It is this new era that the second part of this chapter examines.

---

[33] Author's interviews with Indian security scholars. New Delhi. Summer 2016.

Part II: The Evolution of China's Blue Water Navy

By the time Jiang Zemin handed control of the PLA over to Hu Jintao in 2004, the PLAN was already starting to look beyond a Taiwan contingency and the Corbettian stage of naval modernization. While the PLAN continued to build its anti-access and area denial capabilities, Chinese decision makers were increasingly aware of the vulnerabilities China faced on the high seas. These were compounded by the continuing maintenance and occasional escalation of the Sino/U.S. rivalry and the widespread Chinese perception that the U.S was trying to contain China's rise. The second part of this chapter examines the evolution of the PLAN from a green water force designed to keep the American navy out of China's periphery, to a gradually evolving blue water navy that is able to protect China's interests far out to sea and demonstrate to China's rivals that the PLAN is a powerful force. Key to this transformation is the continuation of Chinese threat perceptions emanating from Beijing's rivalry with Washington. Specifically we should be looking for evidence that Chinese fears of the U.S.' and, in particular, the USN, were the primary driver of PLAN modernization. Of related importance, we should look for evidence that supports the links between the two rivalries in this project. As is demonstrated in Table 4.1, the PLAN started to become a much more modern and lethal force in the decade after Jiang Zemin left office. Most importantly is the percentage of modern hardware that the PLAN acquired during the decade, and how this differs enormously from the previous period of modernization.

This section will focus on four key areas during the Hu Jintao era. First, the continuing maintenance and periodic escalation of the Sino/U.S. rivalry will be examined. Second, the increasing concern with Chinese SLOCs will be analysed and how that was related to rivalry and naval hardware. Third, I will briefly discuss the Chinese navy's anti-piracy patrols in the Gulf of Aden. (The protection of SLOCs and anti-piracy patrols will also be discussed in regards to how they linked the two rivalries under review.) Finally, the issue of procurement and why certain naval platforms and submarines were commissioned will be addressed. It is important to note that these four aspects are all interrelated, but by focusing on each one, we can see how they are linked.

The Continuation of the Sino/U.S. Strategic Rivalry under Hu Jintao

While the 1990s witnessed multiple critical junctures in the Sino/U.S. rivalry, which generated direct calls for specific naval hardware, the first two decades of the 21st century have seen a gradual process of cumulative events, and points of moderate escalation that have justified a more powerful navy.[34] As is demonstrated in Table 4.2, the period after 2004 experienced many periods of rivalry maintenance and escalation that varied in salience by event. The culmination of these events kept threat perceptions very high in leadership circles. As will be discussed in detail next, the American 'Pivot' to Asia, formally announced towards the end of the Hu administration, caused considerable apprehension in Beijing.

The year 2004 was important for the transformation of the Chinese navy. As mentioned above, Hu Jintao took control of the Chinese military and, in addition to routine maintenance in the Sino/U.S. rivalry, the re-election of Taiwanese President Chen Shui-bian caused threat perceptions to increase in Beijing. Notably, during an expanded CMC meeting in December 2004, Hu gave a speech where he introduced a new military policy that defined the PLA's four 'new historic missions'. Of great relevance to this project, Hu called for the military to have the ability to develop powerful strategic support in order to safeguard national interests (Mulvenon 2009). At this meeting, Hu also encouraged the PLAN to start to venture out and conduct far seas operations and to develop power projection capabilities (Erickson et al. 2012). December of 2004 also witnessed the South Asian Tsunami, which devastated large sections of coastal Indonesia, Sri Lanka, and India. The fact that the PLAN did not have the ability to help in the humanitarian mission, while the USN dispatched an aircraft carrier was seen as a strategic liability in Beijing.[35] While the Tsunami did not drive the PLAN to develop a carrier, one argument in favour of justifying a carrier is its ability to perform a wide range of humanitarian activities. Incidentally, the apparent decision to push forward and actually start to refurbish the Varayag carrier was given in 2004 (Saunders and Scobell 2015).

From the early 2000s onward, the strategic rivalry between the U.S. and China did not experience any major points of escalation that

---

[34] Author's interviews with Chinese experts. Beijing. 2016–2017 academic year.
[35] Author's interviews with Chinese academics. Beijing. Spring 2017.

Table 4.2 Maintenance and Escalation in the Sino/American Strategic Rivalry: 1989–2020. (Events constituting critical junctures and major points of rivalry escalation in bold.)

(Author's database relying on multiple sources)[a]

Number	Year	Description of Dispute
1	1989	**American imposed sanctions on China in response to Tiananmen Square massacre. (Origin of the current strategic rivalry)**
2	1991	**Gulf War and quick American victory over Iraq.**
3	1991	**American Revolution in Military Affairs (RMA) and its impact on Chinese decision makers.**
4	1992	American Presidential Election: China becomes tool for Bill Clinton to attack George H.W. Bush. (Claims he 'coddled the butchers of Beijing'.)
5	1992	**Americans agree to sell Taiwan 150 F-16 fighter-bombers.**
6	1993	**Yinhe Incident: American Navy forces merchant Chinese ship to be boarded and searched.**
7	1994	Han attack submarine engaged by aircraft from the USN aircraft carrier Kitty Hawk in the Yellow Sea.
8	1995	Taiwanese leader Lee Tung-hui visits Cornell University.
9	1995	**Taiwan Strait Crisis: In response to PLA live fire exercises in the vicinity of Taiwan, American President Clinton orders the American aircraft carrier Nimitz to sail through the Taiwan Strait.**
10	1996	**Taiwan Strait Crisis: President Clinton orders two additional American aircraft carriers to sail off the east coast of Taiwan.**
11	1996–1997	USA reasserts its security relationship with Australia. Cause of concern to Beijing.
12	1997	Chinese argue that after the 1997 Asian financial crisis, Americans start to seek new bases in the region—viewed by Beijing as a new way to contain China.

Continued

Table 4.2 *Continued*

Number	Year	Description of Dispute
13	1997–1998	Under the Nye Initiative U.S., pushes Japan to jointly-develop theatre missile-defense systems.
14	1999	American led war in Kosovo.
15	1999	**Chinese Embassy in Belgrade is destroyed by American bombs**
16	1999, July	**July 9, Lee Teng-hui declares a special state-to-state relationship exists between Taiwan and the Mainland.**
17	2000	During the 2000 American Presidential Election, China is labelled a 'strategic competitor'.
18	2000	**Chen Shui-bian elected President of Taiwan on pro-independence ticket.**
19	2000s– present	Regular arms sales to Taiwan.
20	2000s	American bases in Central Asia, perceived by Chinese leaders as an attempt to 'contain' China.
21	2000s	South China Sea dispute escalates.
22	2000, April	U.S RC-135 reconnaissance aircraft intercepted by Chinese F-8 aircraft over the East China Sea.
23	2000, August	August, defence ties between Japan and India begin.
24	2001, March	PLAN frigate closely monitors the MSC survey ship the Bowditch- Bowditch leaves the area.
25	2001, April	**American EP-3 spy plane forced down on Hainan Island after mid-air collision with Chinese fighter-bomber. Chinese pilot Wang Wei killed.**
26	2001, May	USS Bowditch is 'buzzed' by PLA aircraft— even though the USS Cowpens is escorting it at the time.
27	2001	**American President George W. Bush vows to do 'whatever it takes to defend Taiwan'.**
28	2001, Post September 11	U.S. starts working more actively with Southeast Asian state, including the Philippines, Singapore and Thailand. China objects to this.
29	2001	Singapore upgrades (at its own expense) Changi naval base to accommodate American aircraft carriers.

Table 4.2 *Continued*

Number	Year	Description of Dispute
30	2002	American arms sales begin to India.
31	2002	Increasing incidents at sea between PLAN and USN.
32	2002, September	USS Bowditch is 'buzzed' by a PLA aircraft.
33	2002	U.S. Chairman of Joint Chiefs of Staff visits India to expand military relations—Renmin Ribao (People's Daily) sees this as America expanding in China's backyard.
34	2003	Chinese President Hu Jintao reportedly uses the phrase 'Malacca Dilemma'.[b]
35	2003	U.S. launches the second Iraq War- perceived by Beijing as concrete evidence of American hegemony.
36	2004–present	America internally balances against China—Units of B-52, B-1, and B-2 bombers put on cycles of four-month rotations that provided a constant presence of six bombers on Guam.
37	2004	American Global Posture Review of 2004 (GPR) seeks to dissuade China from challenging the existing power balance by revising the U.S. force posture in the region.
38	2004	**Taiwanese President Chen Shui-bian wins re-election in Taiwan**
39	2005	U.S. National Security Advisor Condoleezza Rice states that a USA/India relationship will cause China to play a more positive role in the region.
40	2005	U.S. and Singapore announce a Strategic Framework Agreement and upgrade their bi-lateral defence relationship to a 'major security-cooperation partnership'.
41	2005, June	**India and U.S. sign the New Framework for the Defense Relationship—lay out a 10-year programme for defence cooperation.**
42	2005–2006	**American Nuclear deal with India.**
43	2006	**American Quadrennial Defense Review (QDR) states goal to dissuade China from competing with the U.S. in the Asia-Pacific region.**
44	2006	**QDR calls for assigning 60 per cent of American submarines to the Pacific for engagement, presence, and deterrence.**

Continued

Table 4.2 *Continued*

Number	Year	Description of Dispute
45	2006	The word 'strategic' is added to Japan/India relations.
46	2006, June	US deploys an X-band radar to the Shariki base in Japan.
47	2006, October	Chinese SSK submarine surfaces eight kilometres from USS Kitty Hawk.
48	2006	The trilateral security dialogue among the U.S., Japan, and Australia is upgraded to the foreign and defense ministry level.
49	2007–2008	**Global financial crisis begins; China sees this as an enormous opportunity to enhance interests.**
50	2007, January	China conducts an anti-satellite test.
51	2007, April	Beijing protests Malabar exercises that include Japan, India, Singapore and Australia.
52	2007, August	Japan and India agree on a Roadmap for New Dimensions to the Strategic and Global partnership. This is based on democracy and other non-Chinese attributes.
53	2007	The U.S., Japan, and Australia hold military drills.
54	2007	American Cooperative Strategy for 21st Century Seapower (CS21), formally recognizes that the primary theatres for US naval combat forces are the Pacific Rim and the India Ocean.
55	2007, November	USS Kitty Hawk and two minesweepers denied permission on two separate occasions to make a port stop in Hong Kong.
56	2007	U.S. Maritime Strategy for the 21st Century released. Perceived by China as an American containment strategy.
57	2007	Beginnings of perceptions of an increasingly 'assertive China'.
58	2008	India and Japan sign an agreement on security cooperation only Japan's third such agreement.
59	2008	India announces plans for missile defence with US assistance- operational by 2011.

Table 4.2 *Continued*

Number	Year	Description of Dispute
60	2008–present	U.S. and Vietnam hold annual political, security and defence dialogue.
61	2008, October	More American arms sales to Taiwan.
62	2009, March	China acts aggressively towards the oceanographic ship the USS Victorious in the Yellow Sea and the USS Cowpens in the South China Sea.
63	2009	USS Impeccable harassed by Chinese vessels.
64	2009	PLAN submarine hits and damages a towed array from the USS John McCain in Subic Bay during an exercise.
65	2009	American F-22 fighter-bombers start operating from Guam.
66	2009, November	India and Australia complete a web of quadrilateral relations, encouraged by the U.S.
67	2009	Group of high-ranking Vietnamese defense officials board U.S. aircraft carrier for the first time.
68	2010, January	More American arms sales to Taiwan.
69	2010	**American AirSea Battle strategy linked to China.**
70	2010, July	'Two plus two', regular combined dialogues between the defense and foreign ministers begin between Japan and India.
71	2010, July	Secretary Clinton's remarks about U.S. interests in the South China Sea at the ASEAN Forum.
72	2010, August	U.S. and Vietnam begin annual defense policy dialogues.
73	2010	Vietnam officials flown to USS George Washington to observe its operations in the South China Sea.
74	2010	American Secretary of State Clinton and Vietnam Foreign Minister Pham Gia Khiem meet and Clinton reaffirms 'our shared interest in working toward a strategic partnership'.
75	2010	**U.S. and South Korea conduct naval exercises- loud Chinese protest.**

Continued

Table 4.2 *Continued*

Number	Year	Description of Dispute
76	2010	U.S. Secretary of State Clinton visits Hanoi twice, calls for U.S.- Vietnam 'Strategic Partnership'.
77	2010–2015	USN and Vietnam hold first engagement with Vietnam Navy- have annual exercises through 2015.
78	2010	U.S Secretary of Defense Robert Gates visits Vietnam.
79	2010	U.S. Secretary of State Clinton calls for collaborative and 'Multilateral' negotiations in the South China Sea.
80	2011	**American "Pivot" to Asia is announced.**
81	2011, January	Turning point in US/Philippine relations: In January the first ever 'bilateral strategic dialogue' takes place with talks on how to help the Philippines increase their maritime capacity.
82	2011, May	U.S. sells Philippines a decommissioned coast guard cutter—flagship of Philippine navy.
83	2011	American Secretary of State Clinton again calls for collaborative and 'Multilateral' negotiations in the South China Sea.
84	2011, July	U.S. and Vietnam hold naval drills and noncombat training exercises.
85	2011, July	U.S., Japan, and Australia hold drills in the South China Sea near Brunei.
86	2011, September	More American Arms sales to Taiwan.
87	2011	At the Shangri-La Dialogue in Singapore, American Secretary of Defense Robert Gates talked of the U.S. increasing its presence in Southeast Asia and spoke of future stationing of littoral combat ships in Singapore.
88	2011	President Obama gives a speech to the Australian Parliament. States American goals in region and says the reason for pivot is to play a larger and long-term role in shaping the region and its future.
89	2011, November	American Secretary of State Hillary Clinton calls the South China Sea the 'West Philippine Sea'.

Table 4.2 *Continued*

Number	Year	Description of Dispute
90	2012, January	Obama administration releases two new defense strategies and identifies China and Iran as two potential anti-access threats.
91	2012, March	U.S. seeks regional anti-missile system akin to that of the European system with Japan, South Korea, and Australia.
92	2012	American Defense Secretary Panetta says 60 per cent of the U.S. navy will be in the Pacific by 2020.
93	2012	Pentagon sees A2/AD strategy as a threat. Develops Air-Sea Battle where the navy and air force jointly attack and kill the enemy's 'kill chain' before it can attack American ships. In 2012, this was expanded to include all services under joint operations access concept.
94	2012	Guam hosts 5 SSGN (guided-missile submarines) at the same time.
95	2012, May	Chen Guangcheng (blind Chinese lawyer) incident.
96	2012, June	American Secretary of Defense Panetta announces in Singapore that the USN will shift from 55:45 Pacific/Atlantic division of ships to 60:40 in favour of the Pacific.
97	2012, June	**June US and South Korea hold largest military exercises since the Korean War.**
98	2012	India and Japan conduct first-ever bilateral naval exercises off Japan's east coast.
99	2012	American Secretary of Defense Panetta visits Cam Rahn Bay in Vietnam and speaks of 'tremendous potential' between Vietnam and the USA, and says access to this base for USN ships is a key component of the relationship.
100	2012	New approach to organizing American military power: Joint Operational Access Concept. (JOAC)—Secretary Panetta gives major speech on a strong American military commitment to Asia.
101	2012	U.S. Destroyer Squadron seven is deployed to Singapore.

Continued

Table 4.2 *Continued*

Number	Year	Description of Dispute
102	2013	Secretary Clinton reassures Japan about the American security umbrella and the disputed Diaoyu/Senkaku Islands.
103	2013	China establishes air-defense zone over east China Sea.
104	2013	India and Japan have naval exercises in Bay of Bengal.
105	2013, April 26	Chinese Ministry of Foreign Affairs says Diaoyu Islands are a matter of 'Core Interest'.
106	2013	First U.S. Littoral Combat Ships arrive in Singapore to patrol the South China Sea.
107	2013, December	PLAN warship nearly collides with USS Cowpens in the South China Sea.
108	2014	America accuses China of cyber spying in the U.S.
109	2014	U.S. deploys an X-band radar to the Kyogamisaki base in Japan.
110	2014	U.S. warns China not to establish an Air Defense Identification Zone (ADIZ) in the South China Sea- U.S. could adjust its 'presence and military posture'.
111	2014	India accepts Japanese participation in annual Indo-U.S. exercises designed to counter the PLAN's presence in IOR.
112	2014, April	President Obama signs a 10-year defense pact with Manila that allows an increased U.S. troop presence in the Philippines.
113	2014	**U.S. reaffirms three times that the US/Japan alliance covers the Diaoyu Islands. Obama also declares that the U.S.-Japan security treaty does apply to the Islands.**
114	2014	USN reveals it has access to Malaysian facilities for its anti-submarine warfare operation in the South China Sea.
115	2014	Chinese intercept of USN plane near Hainan.
116	2014	American Defense Secretary Chuck Hagel announces the 'Third Offset Strategy' designed to help the U.S. maintain an 'unfair competitive advantage' and 'unchallenged military superiority' by offsetting A2/AD.
117	2014	Calls in Vietnam's Central Committee to sign an alliance with the U.S.

Table 4.2 *Continued*

Number	Year	Description of Dispute
118	2014	Washington eases the arms embargo on Vietnam.
119	2015	U.S. Littoral Combat Ship docks in Danang, Vietnam for naval exercises.
120	2015	U.S. and Singapore sign a joint-defense enhancement agreement and station for the first time P-8 maritime surveillance aircraft in Singapore.
121	2015	More modern aircraft carrier USS Ronald Reagan replaces the USS George Washington at Yokosuka naval base in Japan Modernized guided missile cruisers USS Chancellorville and the Aegis-capable destroyer USS Benfold also join the carrier.
122	2015	Half of Vietnam's Politburo visits Washington.
123	2015	Six U.S. Cabinet- level officials visit Hanoi.
124	2015, May	American P-8 aircraft flies close to Fiery Cross Reef.
125	2015, July	Vietnam invites Obama's top Asia expert in the National Security Council to Vietnam.
126	2015, October	Destroyer USS Lassen transits within 12 nautical miles of 5 disputed maritime features near the Sprately Islands.
127	2016, January	Chinese authorities detain American official working in the American Consulate in Chengdu on suspicion of being a CIA officer.
128	2016, January	USS Curtis Wilbur conducts a freedom of navigation patrol in the South China Sea.
129	2016, March	Stennis Carrier Strike Group operates in the South China Sea.
130	2016, May	USS William P. Lawrence conducts a freedom of navigation patrol in the South China Sea.
131	2016, June/July	Stennis and Reagan Carrier strike groups patrol the South China Sea.
132	2016, October	USS Decatur conducts a freedom of navigation patrol in the South China Sea.
133	2016, December	President-elect Donald Trump speaks with Taiwanese President Tsai Ing-wen over the phone.

Continued

Table 4.2 *Continued*

Number	Year	Description of Dispute
134	2017, February	USS Carl Vinson carrier strike group conducts operations in the South China Sea.
135	2017, April	USS Stethem conducts operations in the South China Sea.
136	2017, May	USS Dewey conducts operations in the South China Sea.
137	2017	Indo-Pacific Strategy released.
138	2017	American National Security Strategy released. Perceived in China as 'anti-China'.
139	2017	**U.S. deploys the Terminal High-Altitude Area Defense missile system to South Korea. (THAAD)**
140	2017, July	Malabar exercises held in South China Sea between India, Japan and the U.S.
141	2017, July	USS Stethem conducts operations in the South China Sea.
142	2017, August	USS John McCain conducts patrols in the South China Sea.
143	2017, September	India, U.S. and Japan have a trilateral Foreign Ministers meeting to discuss maritime security and a free and open Indo-Pacific.
144	2017, October	USS Chafee conducts operations in the South China Sea.
145	2017, November	Revival of the 'QUAD' (Australia, Japan, U.S., and India) Perceived as an anti-China coalition.
146	2018, January	USS Hopper conducts operations in the South China Sea.
147	2018–present	American attempts to significantly curtail Huawei's business dealings.
148	2018–present	**President Trump's trade war with China.**
149	2018, March	USS Mustin conducts operations in the South China Sea.
150	2018, May	Due to trade war Chinese technology firm ZTE (Zhongxing) forced to temporarily cease major operating activities.
151	2018, July–present	American navy resumes the transit of warships through the Taiwan Strait. Had previously halted transits for a year.
152	2018, September	American DDG forced to make emergency manoeuvres after a Chinese warship comes within 40 meters of its bow in the South China Sea.

Table 4.2 *Continued*

Number	Year	Description of Dispute
153	2018, October	American Vice President Mike Pence gives a powerful speech critical of China at the Hudson Institute.
154	2018, November	U.S. and Australia announce plans to develop a naval base in Papua New Guinea.
155	2018, November	American Vice President Mike Pence tells leaders of ASEAN states that there is no place for 'empire and aggression in the Indo-Pacific'.
156	2018, December	Huawei CFO Meng Wanzhou arrested in Vancouver on American extradition request.
157	2018, December	President Trump signs Asia Reassurance Initiative Act (ARIA). Furthers American strategic aims in Asia.
158	2019, March	Taiwanese President Tsai stops in Hawaii.
159	2019, April	U.S. and Philippines practice storming a beech facing the South China Sea.
160	2019, May	Meeting of the 'Quad' in Bangkok.
161	2019, May	American, Indian, Japanese and Philippine navies conduct exercises in the South China Sea.
162	2019, August	President Trump calls Xi Jinping the 'enemy'.
163	2019, August	U.S. announces 8 billion dollar sale of up to 66 F-16 fighter bombers to Taiwan.
164	2019, September	U.S. expels two Chinese officials working at the Chinese Embassy in Washington on suspicion of being spies.
165	2019, September	Ministerial meeting at the rank of Foreign minister between the Quad's four members in New York.
166	2019, November	U.S. and Indian militaries conduct tri-service exercise 'Tiger Triumph'.
167	January 2020	American Navy conducts a freedom of navigation operation in the South China Sea.
168	February 2020	President Trump visits India.
169	2020	Onset of Covid-19, President Trump lashes out at China calling it the 'Chinese virus'. Leads to fierce Chinese pushback.
170	August 2020	USS Ronald Reagan and USS Nimitz aircraft carrier battle groups conduct operations and exercises in the South China Sea.

Continued

Table 4.2 *Continued*

Number	Year	Description of Dispute
171	August 2020.	U.S. secretary of Health and Human Services Alex Azar Visits Taiwan. Highest American official to visit Taiwan since 1979.
172	October 2020	U.S. and India sign the Basic Exchange and Cooperation Agreement for Geospatial Intelligence. (BECA)
173	November 2020	Maritime exercises conducted by Quad and include Australia.

[a]These sources were collected from a variety of avenues ranging from media publications in Chinese and English to scholarly books, to think tank publications. Through in-depth and focused interviews, the importance of these events was assessed.
[b]Never confirmed that he used this phrase, but accepted by security analysts as a major concern of Beijing.

brought the two states close to war, or at least a kinetic confrontation. However, as specified in the punctuated equilibrium model, once a rivalry is initiated, it enters a locked in stage where maintenance and occasional escalation are the norm. The critical junctures of the 1990s set the Chinese leadership on a path-dependent course where Washington was viewed as the enemy that must be countered. Episodes of rivalry maintenance during the Hu era reinforced negative Chinese perceptions of the U.S.

The continuing belief that the U.S. is determined to prevent China's rise and is carrying out a policy of containment is widespread on the Chinese mainland. Writing in the official magazine Liaowang, Chen Xiangyang speaks to Chinese fears of American containment in the quote:

U.S. global strategic focus has shifted from Europe to Asia, and has increased the strategic defense of the great powers, which is focusing on preventing China's rise ... The United States vigorously adjusts the alliance system in China's 'great periphery' region, aiming to take advantage of the U.S.-Japan, the U.S.-Australia, and the U.S. India alliance to prevent China's rise. (Chen 2006. Translated)

The 2006 American QDR, whose stated goal is to dissuade China from competing with the U.S. in the Asia-Pacific region was perceived as a prime example of American attempts to contain China (O'Rourke

2016).[36] In addition, the American Cooperative Strategy for 21st Century Seapower (CS21) formally declared that the primary theatres for U.S. naval forces are found in the Pacific Rim and the Indian Ocean (Holmes 2012). Many Chinese see the 2007 U.S. Maritime strategy 'A Cooperative Strategy for 21st Century Seapower' as an instrument of containment.[37] Chinese analyst Lu Rude views American actions as concrete evidence of American hegemonic thinking. He perceives the strategy as a pretext for 'implementing strategic encirclement of different kinds of maritime flashpoints and "potential enemy" through military deployment in Chokepoints of navigation and strategic nodes' (Holmes 2012).

Increasing ties between the U.S. and China's neighbours were also perceived by Beijing to be nefarious American attempts contain and encircle China. The warming of ties between New Delhi and Washington is viewed with suspicion by Beijing. Especially worrisome for China is the New Framework for the Defense Relationship, which laid out a 10-year programme for defence cooperation between India and the U.S. In addition, the Malabar naval exercises between India, the U.S., and various American allies and strategic partners further alienate the Chinese leadership. The 2005–2006 American nuclear deal with India, as well as the 2008 agreement between India and the U.S. to work on missile defence also increased threat perception in China. A highly regarded Beijing based Chinese scholar of security studies who specializes in South Asia stated that the September 2019 meeting between the foreign ministers of the 'Quad' (Quadrilateral Security Dialogue consisting of the Australia, Japan, India, and the U.S.) is a 'big concern' for China. This is seen as a cornerstone of the American 'containment' strategy towards China.[38] While some Chinese maritime security experts do not believe the Chinese government takes the Indian navy as seriously as it should, the combination of the Quad and the Indian navy is a concern, especially when Washington is perceived to be the driving force.[39] As mentioned above, concerns over Indo/U.S. security ties are so great that Beijing has

---

[36] Ibid.
[37] Nearly all American military policies in Asia were regarded by Chinese analysts and scholars as American attempts to contain China. Author's interviews in Beijing. 2016–2017.
[38] Author's interview with Chinese security scholar. Beijing 2018..
[39] Author's interview with a Beijing based scholar of maritime security. Beijing. 2018..

Table 4.3   Key American Bi-lateral Relationships with Indo-Pacific States (U.S. Department of State, 'US. Bilateral Relations Fact Sheets.')

Mutual Defense Treaty	
South Korea	Mutual Defense Treaty signed in 1953.
Japan	Treaty of Mutual Cooperation and Security signed in 1960.
Philippines	Manila Declaration Signed in 2011. This extended the U.S.-Philippines Mutual Defense Treaty of 1951.
Australia	In 1951, the 1951 ANZUS Security Treaty is signed.
Friends and Partners	
India	Growing defense and political ties. Multiple foundational defense agreements signed.
Vietnam	Expanding ties. In 2013, sign the U.S. Vietnam Comprehensive Partnership.
Singapore	American warships stationed in Singapore
Thailand	Thanat-Rusk communique of 1962 and the 2012 Joint Vision Statement for Thailand and U.S. defense alliance forms the foundation of American security commitments to Thailand.
Taiwan	The 1979 Taiwan Relations Act by law requires the United States to sell arms to Taiwan.

crafted a policy called the '1.5 war scenario', where a war with America and Japan would also require the PLAN to deal with India because of concerns that India might decide to shut down China's SLOCs in the IOR (You 2016). Table 4.3 depicts the American Mutual Defense Treaty partners and friends in the Asia Pacific.

Budding ties between Washington and New Delhi were encouraged in addition to strengthening ties between Washington and Hanoi and Manila. Beginning in the first decade of the 21st century, Washington started to move much closer to both states as concern over China's long-term ambitions, compounded by the territorial dispute in the South China Sea, brought decision makers together. These ties were in addition to America's continuing arms sales to Taiwan and the robust American military presence in Japan, South Korea, and the U.S. territory of Guam. The American military does have a relatively robust presence in East Asia. However, few Chinese commentators recognize potential threats emanating from North Korea as a possible cause of the American military presence in the region.[40]

Increasing Ties between the U.S. and India

The warming of ties between Washington and New Delhi has elicited various responses from Beijing. The 2005 nuclear agreement between the U.S. and India, where the George W. Bush administration sought to help India become a great power by assisting it with its nuclear energy programme, was a major milestone in Indo-American relations. This approach to India was spearheaded by Condoleezza Rice, who as Secretary of State pushed for stronger ties (Pant 2019). This was the first major agreement between the world's two largest democracies that would establish the foundation of a working political and security partnership designed to hedge against the uncertainty created by China's rise. As mentioned in the previous chapter, in the years that followed, Washington and New Delhi would deepen security ties by signing several foundational defence agreements, including the LEMOA in 2016, which was vital for military-to-military ties, and in 2018 the COMCASA. These agreements are crucial for the facilitation of defence ties and allow the sharing of intelligence and increased interoperability between the two militaries. In October 2020, the third foundational agreement, the Basic Exchange and Cooperation Agreement for Geospatial Intelligence (BECA) was signed. These agreements are in addition to the changing strategic environment that has seen the Trump Administration change the name of the 'Pacific Command' to the 'Indo-Pacific Command'. The latter name is designed to include India in Washington's emerging strategy vis-a-vis China.

While the working relationship between the U.S. and India is not yet a formal alliance, there appears to be a lack of agreement in Beijing on how to respond to this development (Colley 2020; Colley 2021B). Meng Qinglong has argued that the Indo-Pacific strategy is still in development stages and there are no clear signs that India has the same goals of the

---

[40] During the fieldwork stage, few Chinese experts pointed to the North Korean threat as a cause of America's military presence in Asia. Author's interviews in Beijing and Shanghai, 2016–2017.

U.S. (Meng 2018). Sun Xianpu believes that under Modi, India pursues a pragmatic policy towards China and is cautious in its dealings with Washington. Evidence of this can be found in India's support of the Asian Infrastructure Investment Bank and BRICS (Sun 2018). Cai Penghong is more concerned with the security ties between the U.S. and India and writes that the 2 + 2 dialogue between the two countries (where the heads of the military and foreign ministries meet) is a major problem for China. He warns that the signing of COMCASA is an important step for India to gradually enter the American defence circle, which poses a huge challenge to China (Cai 2018). One of China's leading authorities on maritime security believes that India is not prepared to join with the U.S. and is using Washington as a card to contain China. This scholar argued that the Chinese leadership does not take the IN seriously. Contrary to this another top Beijing based scholar of security studies, argued that Beijing is concerned about the strengthening ties between India and the U.S. and believed that the CPEC (China Pakistan Economic Corridor) is driving India much closer to the U.S.[41] Interestingly, in an analysis of the People's Daily and the Liberation Army News from the early 2000s until 2017, Korolev and Wu find a near complete absence of official discussion of an emerging China-U.S.-India strategic triangle (Korolev and Wu 2019).

At least in the public realm, Beijing does not appear to take India seriously. While India on its own does not pose a threat to the survival of the Chinese regime, when coupled with the U.S. in a security partnership, it represents a significant security challenge to China. Because China does not appear to be cognizant of how its behaviour is perceived in New Delhi this form of 'great power autism' (the inability of China to understand how its behaviour impacts other states) is a helpful approach towards understanding China's relations with India (Garver 2018). Simply put, Beijing seems oblivious to how China's increasing forays into the IOR and the BRI are perceived in India (Colley 2021B). From a purely logistical perspective, India holds a massive advantage in that it does not need to match the PLAN ton-for-ton, it just needs to take advantage of its geographical setting in any confrontation with the PLAN.

China does not regard India as a great power and Chinese South Asia scholars and analysts have perceived India as a secondary power and

---

[41] Author's interviews with Beijing based security scholars. 2018..

not a main concern (Ye 2020). However, as India moves closer to the U.S. some Chinese are taking note and are warning that Beijing must not push India into the arms of the Americans (Wang 2020). While others, notably Lin Minwang of Fudan University, see the signing of BECA as India officially becoming an American 'ally' and firmly tying itself in defence and security to the 'American chariot' (Lin 2020). Although Zhang Jiadong, also of Fudan, and the director of their Center for South Asian Studies, argues 'the current asymmetric and unbalanced US-India relationship is still qualitatively different from the alliance or quasi-alliance relationship. From India's perspective, it has not given up its strategic autonomy'. He further states that Washington is using India to 'contain China' (Zhang 2020).

Closer relations between America and Asian states are a form of rivalry maintenance and when combined with military manoeuvres, may be construed as a form of escalation. These bilateral ties were also accentuated by incidents at sea between the U.S. and China that constitute a more direct form of moderate rivalry escalation. While the dataset in Table 4.2 details periods of maintenance and escalation, several of these incidents stand out. The October 2006 surfacing of a Chinese SSK within eight kilometres of the USS aircraft carrier Kitty Hawk is perceived by the Americans to be a point of rivalry escalation in that the PLAN was attempting to test the American's anti-submarine warfare technology.[42] Three events in 2009 also stand out. In March of that year, China acted very aggressively towards the oceanographic ship USS Victorious in the Yellow Sea and the USS Cowpens and Impeccable in the South China Sea. In addition, a PLAN submarine hit and damaged a towed array from the USS John McCain in Subic Bay during an exercise (Bussert and Elleman 2011). These points of escalation are best explained as Chinese signals to the USN that they are encroaching into Chinese claimed waters as well as attempts to see how far the PLAN and various Chinese maritime agencies (acting with PLAN support and guidance) can push the USN.

---

[42] Author's discussions with American military personnel. Beijing 2010. Several American officers gave different accounts of this event. One stated that the anti-submarine systems were 'not turned on', and therefore the PLAN did not learn anything. Others mentioned that the U.S. Navy was aware of the SSK's presence.

The Pivot

From Beijing's perspective, one of the most important points of escalation in the rivalry with Washington has been the American 'Pivot to Asia'. This policy, which has its origins in the early months of the George W. Bush Administration, calls for rebalancing American military forces to the Asia-Pacific Region (Silove 2016). In particular, the American force structure would shift from a 55:45 Pacific/Atlantic division of ships, to a 60:40 division in favour of the Pacific (Green 2017). In her article, Silove traces the origins of the Pivot and demonstrates that it shares many similarities with the GPR of 2004. The GPR sought to dissuade China from challenging the existing power balance in the Asia-Pacific by revising the American military posture in the region. Importantly, the GPR and the subsequent Pivot sought to have American allies build interoperability with American forces and other allies military forces as a way to dissuade China from challenging American power. The American plan was to construct a network model that would connect the 'spokes' of each American friend, thus creating a web of defence relationships and interoperability between states, with the U.S. as the main power. The Pivot would 'move beyond the "hub and spokes" model of the past, toward a more networked architecture of cooperation among our allies and partners' (Silove 2016). The Pivot also signalled to China and America's Asian allies that the U.S. was actively moving away from the Middle East and Europe and would pay much greater attention to Asia. A key aspect of it would be strengthening American strategic and economic ties in the region. The Trans Pacific Partnership (TPP), a proposed regional free trade agreement, was considered a major cornerstone of the Pivot (Schiavenza 2013). Christensen argues that the U.S. never 'left' the Pacific and that many of the key features of the Pivot, such as increasing the number of F-22s in the region, the stationing of littoral combat ships, and nuclear-powered submarines and key features of the TPP, were in the works before Obama came to power. However, he does acknowledge that the Pivot raised considerable threat perceptions in China as concerns of 'American containment' were reinforced (Christensen 2015).

   Closely related to the Pivot is the AirSea Battle concept, which is about responding to advanced militaries, especially the rise of the Chinese military. Specifically, the AirSea Battle concept addresses anti-access and area-denial warfare. It calls for an in-depth attack across five key domains: air, land, sea, space, and cyberspace. The goal is to shape the A2/AD environment to allow for American power projection and freedom of action in the global commons (AirSea Battle 2013). It also needs to be noted that the Americans were balancing internally by building up forces in places such as Guam, where the numbers of heavy bombers and nuclear-powered submarine numbers were increased. Evidence of American external balancing is found in the stationing of American troops in Australia and carrying out exercises with Asian allies and partners (Bussert and Ellemaan 2011; Silove 2016). This 'Rebalancing Strategy' was initiated late in President Obama's first term in office. It is closely aligned with the Pivot, as it attempts to place greater emphasis on the Asia/Pacific and less attention on the Middle East. At its core, the 'Rebalancing Strategy' was an articulation of American security, economic, and political interests in Asia (Panda 2017).

Not surprisingly, Beijing viewed the Pivot as a major point of escalation in the rivalry. It also confirmed many suspicions that Washington was not only actively working to contain China, but it was working with China's neighbours to take part in the containment strategy. A well-respected scholar at a Chinese government run think-tank stated that China sees the Pivot as directing 60 per cent of the American navy at China, and that it is clear to Chinese leaders that the PLAN must combat this and develop its own capabilities to accomplish this.[43] A 2014 survey conducted by the American think-tank, the Center for International and Strategic Studies, found that 77 per cent of Chinese foreign policy experts believed the Pivot to be 'too confrontational towards China' (Green and Szechenyi 2014). It is important to note that the Pivot was a gradual event, Chinese planners knew about it for over a decade before it was officially announced; one Chinese security academic described it as a 'snowball effect', that was later clarified.[44] A very well placed scholar, who has briefed Hu Jintao, stated that the Pivot was such a big deal that during the 18th Party Congress in 2012, the development of the PLAN became 'a Party goal that was designed to counter the American Pivot'.[45] Lanxin Xiang

---

[43] Author's interview with Beijing based think-tank scholar. Beijing 2016–2017.
[44] Author's interview with Chinese security scholar. Beijing 2016–2017 academic year.
[45] Author's interview with China based security scholar. China 2016–2017 academic year.

has also argued that the American Pivot has prompted Hu Jintao to tell a PLA conference to 'speed up naval transformation' (Xiang 2012).

A Phantom Pivot?

Of potentially great significance is the fact that the publically available data from IISS does not support the belief that the U.S. has actually 'pivoted' its naval hardware to the Pacific. Chart 4.1 demonstrates that as of 2019 the American force structure in the Pacific had actually declined for many categories of warships. For example, the number of American frigates in the Pacific theatre declined from 15 in 2009, to just 9 in 2019. While the number of attack submarines decline from 31 in 2011, to 25 in 2019. The number of SSBNs has stayed at a relatively constant number of eight over the years examined. Notably, for much of the 2000s, six American aircraft carriers were stationed in the Pacific, by 2019 the number declined to four. The data depicted in Chart 4.1 show variation over a 22 year span, this guards against events such as the 11 September 2001 attacks and the drawing down of American forces after the major combat phase of the 2003 Iraq war, which could have a major influence on force structure in the region. Simply put, the empirical evidence from the Pacific does not support the argument that since 2011, the USN has shifted its force structure from a 55:45 Pacific/Atlantic division of ships, to a 60:40 division in favour of the Pacific. While it is possible, and perhaps likely, that Washington will eventually 'pivot' to Asia in the 2020s, so far its actions have not matched its words. Frustration with the lack of action on the Pivot has caused Phil Davidson, the commander of the U.S. Indo-Pacific Command to publically criticize the slow pace. He argued that the American navy is 'going to lose our quantitative edge' by 2025. He also stated that the day-to-day requirements for submarines are only slightly over half of what has been requested (Werner 2019). While the evidence may not support the pivot, in terms of the psychological dynamics of strategic rivalries, it is the perception in Chinese leader's minds that the USN is positioning its military assets close to China that really matters. These beliefs force China to respond with naval modernization.

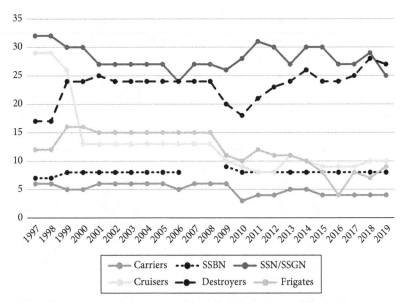

Chart 4.2 American Naval Force Structure in the Pacific. 1997–2019. (Number of Major Warships) (The Military Balance 1997–2019)

The Protection of Sea Lanes of Communication (SLOCS)

Directly related to China's rivalry with the U.S., and firmly embedded in the dynamics of the drivers of PLAN modernization, is the perceived need to protect maritime supply lines. SLOC protection has been a factor throughout the development of the PLAN, this section addresses this concern and discusses how it influences PLAN modernization. As China's dependence on foreign trade rapidly increased in the 21st century, the need to protect Chinese SLOCs became a concern for Beijing (You 2016). The key question is from whom would the PLAN need to protect China's SLOCs? Well informed scholars have argued that China benefits enormously from the role the USN plays in securing the high seas. They acknowledge that even though the Chinese leadership may not like the idea of depending on Washington to protect their SLOCs, China simply does not have the ability to secure them.[46] However, other Chinese scholars and commentators have voiced concern over both China's overall energy security (oil) as well as the PLANs inability to secure its own SLOCs (Zhang 2003; Zeng 2012; Hu 2020).

By the end of the Hu Jintao era, between 95 and 100 per cent of Chinese trade with Africa, the Middle East, and Europe flowed through the IOR (Erickson et al. 2012). In terms of energy security 80 per cent of China's imported oil passes through SLOCs that China does not control. Such as situation has caused an 'Indian Ocean Dilemma' for Chinese security planners (Zeng 2012). A well-respected American expert on the PLAN argued that Chinese SLOCs must be protected from the USA and that China now relies on the good will of the USA and finds this abhorrent. He pointed out that fear of interdiction of trade by the USN is a huge concern of Beijing and that the PLAN needs to be able to counter the American (and Indian) ability to block Chinese trade. This same source argued that China's fear is a key driver of the Sino/US strategic rivalry.[47] Map 4.2 depicts China's SLOCs, as well as some of the choke points Chinese maritime trade and PLAN vessels must transit.

Chinese frequently speak of China's 'Malacca Dilemma', which is the belief that the USN or an American ally could cut off the flow of trade and energy imports to China by simply blocking the narrow strip of water between Malaysia and Indonesia. There is a debate in China about how realistic this fear is. Several well-respected scholars of Chinese foreign economic policy and security cast doubt on the influence that such a 'dilemma' actually has on overall Chinese security. However, several did state that it is used by various interests as a justification for a much more powerful navy.[48] One scholar said that the dilemma 'does not exist, but it is powerful in policy circles because of fears over American containment.'[49]

In an interesting scholarly analysis of the bureaucratic factors driving the 'Malacca Dilemma', Wong argues that the real driver behind it is not the threat of the USN blocking the strait, but lower-level interests in Yunnan province. Wong points out that various PLA actors in Kunming have promoted an oil pipeline from Yunnan through Myanmar as a way

---

[46] Author's discussions with Chinese scholars. Beijing. 2007–2008 and 2017.
[47] Author's interview with American academic. Spring 2017.
[48] Author's interviews with Chinese scholars. Beijing. 2016–2017 academic year.
[49] Author's interview with Chinese Academic. Beijing. 2016–2017 academic year.

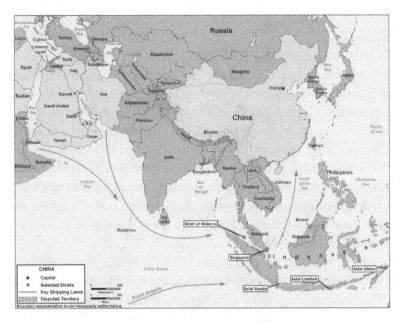

Map 4.2 China's IOR SLOCs (Annual Report to Congress 2008)

of bypassing the strait. The Yunnan government worked with the China National Petroleum Corporation (CNPC) to lobby for the pipeline. CNPC saw this as an opportunity to gain market share from its domestic rival SINOPEC, while the Yunnan government benefitted from increased investment in underdeveloped areas of the province, there were also plenty of opportunities for corruption. In other words, the Yunnan provincial government teamed up with CNPC and various officers in the PLA to promote the 'dilemma' in order to carry out a local initiative. Perhaps the most important takeaway from this case is the fact that the amount of oil transported through the pipeline is minuscule and inadequate for China's overall needs. In addition, the cost of transport vies the pipeline can double the price of oil. Wong argues that the pipeline is an example of 'the provinces interests kidnapping the center's interests' (Wong 2018. P 743).

Related to the role that SLOCs play in development of the PLAN is concerned over the protection of overseas Chinese nationals. High profile cases of the Chinese government rescuing Chinese nationals (and some foreigners) out of conflict zones, took place in Libya in 2011, and Yemen in 2015.[50] Additional rescues of Chinese nationals from 2006 to 2010 took place in Chad, Lebanon, Kyrgyzstan, Haiti, the Solomon Islands, Tonga, Thailand, and East Timor (Cole 2016). While the Chinese government clearly has significant overseas interests, the evacuation of civilians does not require submarines or advanced guided-missile destroyers. A similar logic exists for pirates. Somali pirates operating on speedboats do not call for SSBNs or aircraft carriers with extensive fix-wing fighter-bombers.

Bernard Cole sums up the role of the USN, and to a lesser extent its partners and allies, as the main driving force behind China's SLOC protection by stating, the PLA is perhaps most directly involved in China's search for energy security through the maritime role of securing the SLOCs and ocean-bed energy fields, and the U.S. is viewed as the likely force that will have to be countered (Cole 2016. P151).

You Ji argues that the protection of Chinese SLOCs from the USN is a vital concern for Chinese defence planners and that the PLA sees the U.S. as building 'containment belts' against Chinese SLOCs. This is a 'grave threat to China and if successful it will put the security of China's SLOCs at risk and could strangle China's economic lifeline' (You 2016. P 16).

Chinese protection of SLOCs in the IOR has led to a steady increase in PLAN port visits in the region over the past two decades. These visits, which have spiked in recent years, are charted in Chapter 3. Chinese security experts make clear that these forays are carried out with the American navy in mind. While these voyages are of enormous concern in New Delhi, few Chinese recognize the influence they have on Indian threat perceptions.[51] You Ji has written about the PLAN's 'two ocean strategy' in the Pacific and Indian Oceans, and how these are a response to the American naval presence in Asia. Specifically he argues that the PLAN must counter the American navy in the IOR and that the PLAN's activities in the South China Sea are a 'stepping stone into the Indian Ocean' (You 2016). While acknowledging that this may cause India to counter China on the naval front (thus the '1.5 war doctrines'), no

---

[50] For the Libya case, the Chinese navy played a very insignificant role, but took credit for rescuing thousands of Chinese nationals. According to Western military officials, Chinese commercial airlines controlled by the Chinese government, evacuated the vast majority of Chinese nationals. Author's discussions with NATO country defense Attaches in Beijing. 2011–2012.
[51] Author's interviews with Chinese and Indian security experts. Beijing and New Delhi. 2016–2017.

attention is devoted to how these activities are driving Indian fears and subsequent naval modernization.

As previously mentioned Beijing struggles to understand how its behaviour and expanding presence is causing concern in the region.[52] Of theoretical significance, the protections of SLOCS from the American navy constitutes a major linkage point between the Sino/U.S. rivalry and the Sino/Indian rivalry. As China's navy increases its ability to conduct blue water missions in defence of SLOCS, it is venturing into the IOR, thus causing Indian threat perceptions of China to rise.

Procurement under Hu Jintao

From 2004 until 2012, the PLAN, under Hu Jintao's leadership, became a force that was acquiring many of the signature vessels of a blue water navy. While this period did not witness a significant point of escalation, such as the 1995/1996 Taiwan Crisis, rivalry escalation was more gradual with a constant state of maintenance. As the contours of the American Pivot became clear, Chinese planners continued with their naval modernization.

Chinese Major General Luo Yuan argued in 2009 that China must speed up its naval modernization and accelerate the development of new weapons in order to counter the U.S. (Lin 2010). In December 2004, Hu Jintao breaking from past policy that called for the development of power projection capabilities with SSKs and smaller guided-missile ships gave the green light to an aircraft carrier programme. When he addressed the CMC in December of 2004, Hu Jintao specifically called for the development of power projection capabilities (Erickson et al. 2012). This was testament to this evolution of force structure and new strategic thinking on the part of Beijing. Notably, Jiang Zemin had opposed the idea of a carrier (Yung 2015). It is likely that by this time China's leaders were confident in their increasing ability to hold the USN at

---

[52] It was made clear to this author during fieldwork in New Delhi that the increasing PLAN forays into the Indian Ocean are an enormous concern to New Delhi. These voyages are the single most important driver of Indian naval modernization. Chinese experts also made it clear that PLAN modernization was caused by the USN in East Asia. However, not a single Chinese expert acknowledged that a more powerful PLAN might be viewed as threatening by China's neighbors. Author's interviews in Beijing and New Delhi. 2016–2017.

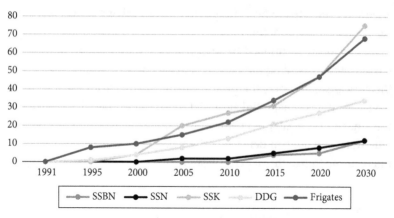

Chart 4.3 Increase of 'Modern' PLAN Hardware (Derived from Table 4.1)

bay in the event of a war over Taiwan. Even some of the more access-denial vessels were upgraded as Hu Jintao came to power. In 2004, the Wuhan shipyards launched the Yuan class SSK, which is widely considered a very quiet and effective diesel electric submarine (Cole 2016). The Yuan class is a significant upgrade from other SSKs in that it utilizes an 'air independent propulsion' system (AIP). An AIP system utilizes liquid oxygen to run the engine in a diesel submarine instead of being forced to snorkel to run the engines in order to charge the batteries of the submarine. Crucially, this allows the submarine to stay submerged for much longer periods of time (Erickson et al. 2017). The rapid development of the PLAN and the fixation on ASCMs led retired admiral Eric McVadon in 2007 to call the PLAN a 'modern cruise missile navy' (McVadon 2007).

Chart 4.3 depicts the rapid evolution of the PLAN during the Hu period. For example, when Hu first came to power the PLAN had only one semi-functioning SSBN, but by 2021, the PLAN was believed to have at least six such submarines equipped with up to 12 JL-2 strategic SLBMs (The Military Balance 2021). According to experts interviewed for this project, these submarines are directly driven by the rivalry with the U.S.[53] A fully operational SSBN gives China a nuclear second-strike capability.

---

[53] Author's interviews with Chinese academics. Beijing. 2016–2017 academic year.

In addition, American missile defences make a sea-based nuclear deterrent more attractive because they are able to fire their missiles from locations and trajectories where missile defences have poor coverage (Yoshihara 2007; Yoshihara 2014). Significant upgrades were also made in the DDG force. By 2005, of the PLANs 21 DDGs, only 40 per cent were considered 'modern', but by 2015, this percentage had climbed to 81 per cent.

A frequently overlooked aspect of PLAN modernization is the ability of the Chinese shipbuilding industry to carry out serial production. During the Hu era, the PLAN went from having their most advanced warships and submarines being of Russian origin, to being able to mass-produce their own platforms. (The last major Russian DDG delivery was in 2006.) For example, the modern 052 D Luyang III DDG, 054A Jiangkai II frigate, and 056 Jiangdao corvette have all entered serial production since 2008 (Murphy and Yoshihara 2015). The PLAN appears to have a very patient production and refinement process when it comes to indigenously produced hardware (Yoshihara and Holmes 2018). Many weapons systems are only produced in small quantities in order to study and test them on the high seas. Once problems have been identified and properly addressed, serial production can start. In the 1990s, only three DDGs were produced and the average production of DDGs and Frigates went from 1.6 per year from 2000 to 2004, to 4.2 per year from 2010 to 2014 (Fanell and Cheney-Peters 2017). After several decades the PLAN finally decided on the current 052D Luyang III class DDG (Cole 2016). As of 2021 the PLAN also appears to have started serial production of the 055 'Renhai' destroyer/cruiser. This ship when fully loaded displaces 13,000 tons and is one of the largest destroyers in the world. Although the PLAN calls it a destroyer, because of its size it is often classified as a cruiser by foreign military observers. The PLAN currently has three 055s in service and is expected to have five by 2023 (Joe 2021B). The 055 is also reportedly equipped with 136 missile cells of which 112 are vertically launched (The Military Balance 2021).

The extraordinary modernization of the PLAN needs to be viewed with caution. The Chinese defence budget has increased rapidly over the past two decades. However, as the PLAN's hardware starts to age, additional money will be needed for upgrades and repairs. Direct labour usually accounts for 30–50 per cent of a ship's acquisition cost, but in reality a ship is actually purchased three times over the course of its service life. The first cost is the initial acquisition price, but the second and third bills are for the operation and maintenance of the ships. A major reason for the prolonged expense is that modernization of a hull requires all of the old equipment to be removed so that the new equipment can be installed. For the PLAN significant maintenance costs are projected to begin in 2028 as many of the modern warships are due for their mid-life overhauls (Carlson 2020). How this factors into the modernization plans and costs of the PLAN is unknown, but this will certainly be a factor in future procurement and operational costs.

As noted before, the PLAN's hardware during the Hu era was not developed to defeat the USN, but was designed to deter the USN in areas beyond the first island chain. As can be seen in Map 4.2, the second island chain which extends well into the Pacific Ocean is the PLAN's next goal for the 2020s.

The idea of the 'risk fleet' is well supported in Chinese defence circles. A prominent security scholar stated that 'China does not want to attack the USA, but it wants to have the ability to cause harm to the American navy'.[54] By the time of the 18th Party Congress in the fall of 2012, the PLAN had been gradually transformed over the previous decade and a half from a green water force with virtually no power projection capability, to a force that was increasingly flexing its naval power. From exercises in the Gulf of Aden, to putting to sea China's first aircraft carrier, the beginning of the Xi Jinping era would see an increasingly confident PLAN with a Chinese leader who was committed to enhancing China's global power and image.

The Xi Jinping Era

We should enhance our capacity for exploiting marine resources, develop the marine economy, protect the marine ecological environment, resolutely safeguard China's maritime rights and interests, and build China into a maritime power ... We should

---

[54] Author's interview with Chinese security scholar. Beijing 2016-2017 academic year.

attach great importance to maritime security. (Hu Jintao quoted in Xinhua 2012)

The above quote calling for China to become a naval power comes from Chinese President Hu Jintao's report to the 18th Party Congress in November 2012. Prior to this speech the development of a powerful navy was a national goal, after this it became a goal of the CCP and was specifically designed to counter the American Pivot.[55] Under Xi Jinping, the PLAN has come to play a much more prominent role in China's embrace of the outside world. The 2012 launching of the aircraft carrier *Liaoning*, and the construction of future carriers has caught the world's attention. The PLAN has also been immune to the cuts in the number of service personnel in the Chinese military. By 2015, the PLAN had a force of 235,000 members of officers and men out of 2.3 million total military personnel. The precise budget of the PLAN and the percentage of the overall military budget is a state secret (Cole 2016). However, as mentioned above well-informed individuals believe it to occupy roughly 30 per cent of the overall military budget in 2015. This is up from 15–20 per cent in 2000.[56]

This section examines two aspects of naval modernization. First, the role of the continuing Sino/U.S. rivalry in modernization during the first seven years of the Xi administration. Second, how has Chinese naval strategy changed during the Xi era and related to this, what is the likely future trajectory of the PLAN?

Rivalry Maintenance

Under Xi Jinping, Beijing's rivalry has followed a path of stability with occasional episodes of maintenance and low to medium-level escalation. While the Table 4.2 provides a detailed breakdown of the rivalry, several events stand out as periods of escalation in Chinese minds. The clarification on two occasions by both Secretary of State Clinton and President Obama that the American security umbrella with Japan also covered the disputed Diaoyu/Senkaku Islands was further evidence in Chinese minds

---

[55] Author's interview with Chinese security scholar. Beijing 2016–2017 academic year.
[56] Author's phone interviews with security scholars. 2016–2017 academic year.

of American containment. Obama's 2014 trip to the Philippines where he unveiled a ten-year defence pact with Manila also irked Beijing. This was at a time of tense relations between Manila and Beijing as they were engaged in a heated dispute over islands in the South China Sea, which were geographically very close to the Philippines. A final significant point of rivalry maintenance were the increasingly warm ties between Vietnam and the U.S. and the various high level visits by top officials to each other's capitals. This was all taking place while anti-Chinese riots broke out in Vietnam over a Chinese offshore oil platform that was operating in disputed waters in the South China Sea. These events did not come as a shock to Chinese leaders who were already well accustomed to American actions and perceived slights to China. However, they did strengthen the hand of hardliners who advocated for a more powerful navy.

Naval Strategy under Xi Jinping

Chinese naval strategy has followed a clear path towards power projection under Xi. As the data in Table 4.1 demonstrates, at the beginning of 2021 the PLAN fielded 6 SSBNs, 6 SSNs, 2 aircraft carriers, and 31 DDGs (The Military Balance 2021). By 2030, these numbers, with the exception of the DDGs, are expected to almost double. This hardware amounts to a sizeable blue water naval force that will have the ability by the mid-2020s to place a significant amount of maritime power in either the Pacific, or Indian Oceans, and possibly even the Atlantic Ocean.

Less than a year into Xi's first term in power, the Academy of Military Sciences of the People's Liberation Army of China published the Science of Military Strategy. This document called for 'forward edge defense' and called for a strategic zone that covered the northern Indian Ocean and the western Pacific Ocean. This 'two oceans region' is extremely important to China's security (Science of Strategy 2013). When examining the increasing forays into the IOR since 2013, it is clear that this strategy is being fully operationalized by China's top decision makers.

The 2015 Chinese Defense White Paper is a crucial document that outlines Beijing's goals to become a 'maritime power', that has the ability to safeguard China's maritime interests. Specifically the document addresses the evolution of the PLAN from a force focused on access-denial, to a much more Mahanian inspired navy that has the ability to project power. The document states:

In line with the strategic requirement of offshore waters defence and open seas protection, the PLA Navy (PLAN) will gradually shift its focus from 'offshore waters defense' to the combination of 'offshore waters defense' with 'open seas protection', and build a combined, multi-functional, and efficient marine combat force structure. The PLAN will enhance its capabilities for strategic deterrence and counterattack, maritime manoeuvres, joint operations at sea, comprehensive defence, and comprehensive support (China's Military Strategy 2015).

The document makes direct and indirect references to the U.S. It mentions 'new threats from hegemonism, power politics, and neo-interventionism', as well as directly referencing the American Pivot, which it says is designed to enhance American military power in the region. These activities are causing 'grave concern' to countries (i.e. China) in the region. It goes on to further state: 'some external countries are also busy meddling in South China Sea affairs; a tiny few maintain constant close-in air and sea surveillance and reconnaissance against China. It is thus a long-standing task for China to safeguard its maritime rights and interests' (China's Military Strategy 2015).

The Sino/U.S. rivalry has a clear influence on the 2015 White Paper. The American Air-Sea Battle concept, now known as the 'Joint Concept for Access and Maneuver in the Global Commons' (JAM-GC), is viewed with deep suspicion in Beijing. The Chinese see this as both a concept and a mission (Cole 2016). As a well-informed scholar of Sino/U.S. relations stated, the deep 'strategic suspicion' between China and the U.S. is very difficult if not impossible to overcome.[57] China is clearly preparing for the possibility of a conflict with the U.S.

As China becomes more powerful and increases its naval power, it is starting to develop its own form of Monroe Doctrine, in many ways designed to keep the U.S. away from China's periphery, and to protect its interests further afield. According to a well-regarded Chinese scholar of maritime strategy, China is attempting to be the 'regional hegemon' in Asia with a chief goal of 'nudging the U.S. out of East Asia—coercively if necessary'.[58] A senior Asian security scholar working for the American

---

[57] Author's interview with Beijing based scholar. Beijing. 2016–2017 academic year.
[58] Ibid.

Pacific Command argued that the Maritime Silk Road Initiative (MSRI), which is part of China's broader 'Belt and Road Initiative', is part of a long-term strategy designed to assist China's blue water navy. This same scholar stated that currently China needs to rely on the USN for the protection of its SLOCs, and Beijing does not like this.[59] A Chinese scholar based at one of China's top government think-tanks argued that since the end of the Hu era, Xi Jinping has led a huge push in the development of the navy. Another scholar argued that this push is designed to deter the U.S., but in keeping with the concept of the risk fleet, China does not intend to use its naval power in a confrontation with the USN.[60] Interestingly, writing in *Peace and Development*, which has ties to the PLA, Meng Liang argues that with the BRI, the island states of the IOR can be used to prevent Japan, the U.S., and India from encircling China (Meng 2019).

According to Mahan, overseas bases are a cornerstone of a blue water fleet. Under Xi Jinping, China has made significant progress in establishing overseas bases/facilities for the PLAN. The December 2015 announcement of a Chinese naval base in Djibouti is empirical evidence that the PLAN is evolving into a blue water navy. In addition to the Djibouti facility, the PLAN is likely to set up similar facilities in other IOR states in the next decade. In fact, China's 13th Five Year Plan from 2016 to 2020 is very clear on Beijing's goals for access hubs in the IOR by stating, 'We will actively advance the construction of strategic maritime hubs along the 21st Century Maritime Silk Road' (The 13th Five Year Plan. P 148). A scholar of maritime security at a major Chinese government think-tank argues that there will likely be future bases in Sri Lanka, the Maldives, and or, Gwadar, Pakistan. On Gwadar, this scholar acknowledged the controversy this will likely cause with India, but said, 'of course Gwadar has a military purpose, it may be isolated, but some in China believe it is good for the PLAN'. The same scholar acknowledged that Indian perceptions of the Chinese using Sri Lanka for strategic purposes might be correct.[61] The PLAN has made extensive use of ports in Yemen and Port Salalah in Oman and was reportedly even offered a base in the Seychelles, but turned it down (Erickson 2014). Interestingly, the

---

[59] Author's interview with American Pacific Command Scholar. 2016–2017 academic year.
[60] Author's interviews with Chinese government scholars. Beijing 2016–2017 academic year.
[61] Author's interview with Chinese government think-tank scholar. 2016–2017 academic year.

Djibouti base and potential future bases in the IOR are not only causing India to modernize its navy, but of equal and perhaps greater concern to Beijing, they are pushing India closer to the U.S. and Japan in the political and military realms. The connection between increasing Chinese behaviour in the IOR and Indian naval modernization and outreach to other Chinese rivals (Vietnam, the U.S., Japan, and the resurrection of the 'Quad' is not fully understood in China). Chinese behaviour in some ways may bring about a self-fulfilling prophecy in that it claims that its strategic behaviour is designed to protect it from the U.S. and its allies and partners. However this very behaviour may be the cause of states working with Washington to counter China's rise (Colley 2021B).

A significant development of the Xi era has been the shift away from a strategy of preparing to fight regional wars in the Pacific Ocean, to one of possibly fighting two wars in the Indian and Pacific Oceans. In-line with the 'forward edge defense', the 2015 introduction of 'frontier defense', which calls for the PLAN to extend its ability to fight into the global commons, is a major development. While 'frontier defense' has been emerging since the early 2000s, by giving it a formal name, Beijing is signalling that it intends to be a great maritime power. Specifically, the concept incorporates the Indian Ocean as a normal region for the PLAN to conduct combat training exercises (You 2018). There is also renewed discussion about the need for the PLAN to erect a 'Pearl Chain' towards the IOR and beyond that would make use of the 'String of Pearls', but this would be strategic in nature and would assist in the projection of naval power (You 2016). Some of the experts interviewed for this project, who were adherents of realism, supported this perspective of China's current and future naval trajectory.[62] The PLAN under Xi is also deeply concerned with countering the USN in the Indo-Pacific. You Ji argues, 'breaking the U.S. stranglehold on the Indo-Pacific has been identified as the number one goal of the PLAN's Indo-Pacific strategy' (You 2016). In the post-2010 environment the PLAN seeks sea-control in parts of the IOR that are crucial to China's SLOCs, while ignoring the fact that this causes rivalry escalation with India. Raja Menon argues that Chinese SLOCs in the IOR are so important to Beijing that a permanent PLAN presence in the IOR is certain. He even argues that Chinese SLOCs may

---

[62] Author's interview with Chinese security scholars. Beijing, 2016–2017 academic year.

require PLAN bases in the South Indian Ocean around Mauritius and on the Tanzanian coast (Menon 2018).

The Foundation of a PLAN Indian Ocean Fleet?

High levels of strategic mistrust directed towards American intentions and capabilities in the IOR have led Chinese strategic planners to branch out into the IOR and to establish key partnerships with regional states. The rapid expansion of the PLAN has led some Chinese commentators to suggest that the PLAN should prepare an Indian Ocean fleet that will be able to protect China's interests from hostile powers (Colley 2021D). The PLA's 2013 document 'Science of Military Strategy' states that China needs to be able to control sections of the Indian Ocean: 'in the event of a loss of control of the circumstances, we implement operations with the main land and the coastal waters as the strategic inner line to deter, absorb, and control the Western Pacific Ocean and Northern Indian Ocean strategic outer line' (Science of Strategy. P 133).

While the PLAN currently has a force of 6–8 warships in the northern Indian Ocean at any given time, (mostly on anti-piracy patrol) according to a report from the U.S. Naval War College, it has over 100 vessels capable of blue water operations in the IOR and has the capacity to have 18 warships permanently stationed in the Indian Ocean (Becker 2020). Chinese academics with close ties to the Chinese government have also weighed in on the prospects of an Indian Ocean Fleet (Colley 2021D). Hu Bo, the director of the Center for Maritime Strategy Studies at Beijing University, has argued that China should deploy two ocean going fleets centred on carriers with one designated for the Indian Ocean (Hu 2020). The idea of Chinese carrier groups in the northern Indian and western Pacific Oceans is essential to Professor Hu who writes 'China must tirelessly strive to maintain an aircraft carrier combat group as well as several reconnaissance support and early warning positions in each of these two major regions, in order to realize effective power presence' (Hu 2020. P 13). The previously mentioned Chinese oceanographic research ships deployed in the IOR can provide crucial data to Chinese warships and submarines. In addition, China now has eight Type 903A (Fuchi) supply ships, which frequently accompany PLAN forays to the Gulf of Aden, and two new Type 901 Fuyu fast combat support ships designed to assist carriers (Becker 2020).

A Chain of Pearls?

With over 100 vessels capable of blue water missions, the PLAN clearly has the ability to maintain a constant presence in the Indian Ocean. However, a significant strategic liability (apart from the base in Djibouti) is the absence of permanent military installations in the region. The concept of foreign military bases has a negative historical connotation and legacy in Chinese political discourse as they are considered cornerstones of colonialism. Logistical facilities and potential bases are often called 'overseas strategic strong points' (Kennedy 2019). Cognizant of the potential political challenges that such facilities/bases may pose, several Chinese analysts from the Naval Academy of Military Science have argued that Chinese development of such outposts must be slow and cautious. They believe that Beijing should try to minimize the role of the military and avoid hegemonic behaviour so as to not raise concerns in India (Li et al. 2014). China's Science of Military Strategy is more direct and calls for these locations to be 'forward bases for the disposition of overseas military strengths, to bring about political and military influences on the relevant regions and form into a posture with the home land territory strategic layout that considers both the internal and external, links up the distant with the approximate, and mutually supporting' (Science of Military P 320. Translated).

The need to interlink these facilities so that they are 'mutually supporting' is of critical importance. Professor Hu writes that China will need to build 'dozens of overseas supply points, communication relay centers and comprehensive support bases around the world'. Specifically, Hu mentions a northern Indian Ocean supply line that is centred around Pakistan, Bangladesh, Myanmar, and Sri Lanka and a western Indian Ocean supply line that links up with the Seychelles and Madagascar. Such bases will provide the required support for 'China's overseas military activities' (Hu 2020. P 258).

A key question is whether the utility of such locations to be used as a 'pearl chain' is a potential Chinese grand strategy in the IOR. Gwadar is frequently cited by Indian security experts as a prime example of Chinese military ambitions in the Indian Ocean.[63] However, the evidence so far does not support such a strategy. Isaac Kardon of the U.S. Naval War College writes that the Strategic Strong Point model is not suited for the facilitation of high-end combat and they are better viewed as centres for logistics and intelligence collection (Kardon 2021). Security analysts frequently overlook the fact that the PLAN has never made a single port call at Gwadar. The port at Karachi, with its well-developed facilities and experience in logistics, has been the exclusive Pakistani destination for PLAN warships. In fact, cargo transiting through Gwadar's port relies on a government subsidy of 20 U.S. dollars per ton and oil passing through the pipeline is hit with a 42 per cent transport charge, compared to 2.5 per cent if transported by sea. This data calls into question the economic viability of the port and surrounding infrastructure (Kardon et al. 2020). Furthermore, Gwadar's first ever container ship arrived in March of 2018, but before this from 2007 to 2017 only 1.5 ships per month called at Gwadar (Thorne and Spevack 2018).

The Chinese base at Djibouti is a more viable strategic base. Reports that one of the six births at Djibouti's Doraleh multipurpose port is reserved for the PLAN and that Beijing built a new pier at its base to support a four ship PLAN flotilla has led to speculation that the PLAN seeks to be able to support a carrier battle group from the base (Becker 2020). However, the need to have bases or logistics facilities in between China and the Horn of Africa is a critical issue for any future PLAN Indian Ocean Fleet.

A Chinese Carrier Strike Force?

While China has not yet been able to master the technological and logistical challenges of aircraft carriers, they are likely to play a role in future power projection forays into the IOR.[64] There is wide speculation that the

---

[63] Author's interviews in New Delhi 2016.

[64] Even in 2015, the PLAN was struggling to make the carrier Liaoning fully operational. According to an American Air Force General, the PLAN is unable to launch aircraft with any real armaments and the jets that do take off from the carrier can only fly for 10–15 minutes before returning due to low levels of fuel. Author's interview with retired American Air Force General. China 2016–2017 academic year.

PLAN will have 4–6 aircraft carriers by the end of the 2020s. While these carriers on their own will not be of any strategic use against the U.S., as any PLAN carrier that engages the USN will have a lifespan measured in hours, they will certainly aid in projecting power (Bussert and Elleman 2011). There is very limited information on what would constitute a Chinese aircraft carrier battle group, but Fanell and Cheney-Peters state that it will include 4–6 DDGs and frigates, 1–2 attack submarines, and 1 supply ship. Each battle group could have at least 10 combatants (Fanell and Cheney-Peters 2017).

A final note on the limitations of the modern PLAN is called for. In the modern era, the PLAN has never been tested in battle or under conditions of high stress and uncertainty. Numerous naval attaches interviewed expressed doubt that all of their 'toys' would do what they are supposed to do in the event of a kinetic battle. Even the PLAN submarine fleet, which is the most feared branch of the PLAN, suffers from high levels of noise. PLAN nuclear-powered submarines have a long way to go before they can achieve the silence levels of American submarines. As one foreign military attaché remarked, they sound like 'someone turning on a clothes dryer full of ball bearings'.[65]

There are also significant questions as to the ability of the PLA and PLAN to carry out joint operations and coordinate battle plans. A serious impediment and limitation for the PLAN is in its inability to develop high-quality propulsion systems. According to Erickson, this liability is unlikely to improve in the near future (Erickson 2017A). The majority of the PLAN's vessels are powered by foreign-derived gas turbines (Erickson et al. 2017). The lack of transparency surrounding the modernization of the PLAN not only questions Beijing's claims that China will 'rise peacefully', but also make it difficult to ascertain the trajectory of the PLAN and how effective its various platforms are.

Overall, the current period of naval development under Xi Jinping has witnessed China taking a much more aggressive stance in the South China Sea and has seen the PLAN take major steps in its quest for power projection. While there are multiple drivers of this naval modernization, this chapter has demonstrated that China's strategic rivalry with the U.S. is the most important of them. The final section of this chapter

---

[65] Author's discussion with foreign defence attaché. Beijing. 2011.

examines each of the drivers and demonstrates their deficiencies as primary causes of China's naval modernization. In particular, we should be looking for evidence that demonstrates that these drivers are the central cause of modernization.

Part III: Competing Arguments for PLAN Modernization

Nationalism as a Driver of Chinese Naval Modernization

Nationalism can be a powerful force that has the ability to mobilize public support for military preparation and various sacrifices that accompany military modernization. Nationalism can also increase the power of the state by providing an opportunity to extract resources from society; these resources can be utilized for naval modernization (Schweller 2017). At times nationalism forces leaders to adopt certain programmes that may not be in a state's best interest. In regards to the China case study we are looking for evidence that nationalism is causing Chinese leaders to build or purchase specific naval hardware for national prestige, and to demonstrate to other states that China is a great power. Based on the extensive fieldwork interviews undertaken for this project, there was near universal agreement that nationalism was not the primary, or even the secondary driver of Chinese naval modernization. Multiple interviewees argued that nationalism is both created by, and controlled by, the Chinese government. Several experts pointed out that most Chinese 'stay silent' on issues related to nationalism and stressed that a relatively small group of 'angry youth', will not decide the strategic trajectory of China's maritime future.[66] Many of these scholars believe that the role of nationalism as a driver of Chinese strategic behaviour is inflated in the West by disproportionate coverage of relatively rare (and controlled) nationalistic protests.

Where nationalism does have a stronger causal role is in the development of China's aircraft carrier programme. There is wide agreement that for these platforms, nationalism does have a causal role. When this

---

[66] Author's interviewees with Chinese security experts. Beijing and Shanghai. 2016–2017 academic year.

author pointed out to a high ranking Chinese military official that aircraft carriers are considered by many in the U.S. to be 'obsolete', and 'super-fluous' (Turner 2006) the General stated that he agreed, but argued that 'the Chinese people want an aircraft carrier'.[67] The idea that carriers act as 'trophies' for the PLAN was also brought up in interviews. The Chinese word 'Mianzi' (loosely defined as face/prestige/honour) was frequently used to explain the rationale for the carrier programme. It was also re-ferred to as the 'bling of international status'. A prominent authority on Chinese security agreed that nationalism might be a driver of the carrier programme, but that the rest of the hardware was USA specific.[68] Pu and Schweller also argue that China's aircraft carrier programme is a form of 'status signaling' that demonstrates China's rise to the Chinese people (Pu and Schweller 2014).

Foreign scholars have also cast doubt on the power of nationalism. Several American scholars of Chinese security downplayed the role of nationalism as a driver. Alastair Ian Johnston has even argued that na-tionalism is actually declining in China. He states that perceptions of high levels of nationalism in contemporary China are the result of bi-ased media coverage, that cherry picks its case studies of nationalism (Johnston 2017). Even Liu Huaqing who was China's most eminent ad-vocate for an aircraft carrier and who believed that China could not be a great power without one was unable to capitalize on the rising tide of na-tionalism in the 1990s to fully start a carrier programme (Cole 2016). The inability of Liu to succeed will be addressed in the bureaucratic politics section below, but it is interesting that even in the 1990s when nation-alism coincided with several critical junctures in the Sino/U.S. rivalry, Liu was still not able to use nationalism to pursue his dream of a Chinese carrier.

Overall, nationalism has at best a limited influence on PLAN modern-ization. With the large exception of the aircraft carrier programme, na-tionalism in its present form in China does not have the leverage to force Chinese leaders into spending hundreds of billions of dollars on naval hardware. Chinese nationalists may be very skilled at making themselves heard, and at times, the government allows them a certain space to air

---

[67] Author's discussion with Chinese PLA General. China 2007–2008 academic year.
[68] Author's interview with Chinese security scholar. Beijing 2016–2017 academic year.

their grievances, but ultimately the Communist Party controls nationalism in China and has the ability to decide the direction that it takes.

The Security Dilemma as a Driver of Chinese Naval Modernization

There is limited evidence that the security dilemma provides an explanation for PLAN modernization. In order for the security dilemma to work we would have to find evidence that the Chinese navy is arming against the USN, and of equal importance, proof the USN is actively arming against China. While it is clear that China was arming against the U.S. during the period under review, it is much less certain the Americans were arming against China.

From 1991 until 2005, there is little evidence that the American navy was building naval platforms or submarines that were China specific. During this period the PLAN was largely reacting to the USN and the American's believed their forces were sufficient for any challenger. It is in the post-2005 environment that there is limited evidence that the USN was at least considering China in some (but certainly not all) weapons acquisitions. As O'Rourke has pointed out 'it is difficult for observers outside of DOD to know exactly how China's shipbuilding output or other aspects of its military maritime modernization effort have been affecting requirements for U.S. Navy capabilities' (O'Rourke 2017). The American Pivot to Asia and the Air-Sea Battle concept are related to China (and Iran in the latter case), but these deal with strategy and not procurement. During the Obama Administration, there was an internal gag order on DOD officials from identifying China as a threat to the U.S.[69] As mentioned above, the American government has also identified China as a challenger, specifically in the QDRs and reports by the Office of Naval Intelligence (The PLA Navy 2016). Like the Pivot, these documents speak to rivalry and threat perceptions, but they do not necessarily constitute concrete evidence that the USN is directly arming against the PLAN.

---

[69] Author's interview with American scholar of Chinese security. 2017.

The strongest publically available evidence that demonstrates some form of limited security dilemma is found in acquisitions of DDGs. The Navy's July 2008 announcement that it was restarting procurement of the Arleigh Burke-class DDG, and halting production of the Zumwalt-class DDG may be evidence of a partial security dilemma. The Arleigh Burke originally ceased production in 2005, but the Navy citing 'rapidly evolving threats' ordered more of these platforms. The Navy justified this decision by pointing out that the Arleigh Burke is cheaper than the Zumwalt-class and has the ability to counter ASCMs, conduct blue-water anti-submarine patrols, and protect against ballistic missiles. It is important to note that this decision may not be completely China centric. North Korea and Iran also have capabilities that are consistent with the Arleigh Burke's defensive capabilities (O'Rourke 2017). There have also been increasing calls to Congress to fund and procure more nuclear-powered attack submarines, in particular the Virginia-class SSN (Erickson 2013). Given China's weak anti-submarine warfare capabilities one would predict Washington to push for more of these vessels. However as demonstrated in Chart 4.4, the number of American SSNs is expected to decrease over the next decade before picking up again after the 2030s. This is a very important issue for not only the Navy, but also for the argument that the security dilemma best explains the relationship between the U.S. and China. If the security dilemma is present one would expect the Americans to rapidly increase their SSN force. Instead we see a sharp decline in the numbers of SSNs from 98 in 1987 to 51 in 2018. This number is scheduled to further fall to 42 by 2028. This decrease in the number of American SSNs has been noted by Beijing (Colley 2019A). While the numbers are forecasted to increase after 2030, the reduction in SSNs over the next decade casts doubt on the security dilemma as a tool to understand the Sino/American security dynamic. From a logical perspective the security dilemma would predict the USN to build as many SSNs as possible and to quickly reverse the declining numbers of these vessels. Considering that Washington has been concerned about the modernization of China's military, and in particular, the PLAN since the early 2000s, it is remarkable that the Navy's SSN force has been allowed to decline at such a rate.

One glaring deficiency in the American arsenal has been in the atrophy of ASCMs. The July 2017, announcement of a contract for the new

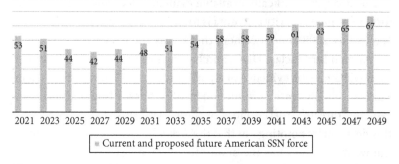

2021 2023 2025 2027 2029 2031 2033 2035 2037 2039 2041 2043 2045 2047 2049

Current and proposed future American SSN force

Chart 4.4 Projected American SSN Force 2021–2049 (Congressional Research Service 2019)

1,000 pound warhead LRASM (Long-range anti-ship missile), may also be heavily centred on countering the PLAN.[70] This missile is able to travel over 200 miles, a significant increase from the 70–150 miles range of the ageing Harpoon ASCM (Freedberg 2017). (Although the missile was unveiled in 2017, procurement would have been initiated several years earlier.)

The principal challenge with the security dilemma on the American side is that these DDGs and submarines are useful for dealing with the PLAN, but they are also important for other American security threats. Numerous officers and scholars argued that the American navy arms 'for everyone' and that China is just one of many factors. Increasing Russian assertiveness is also a consideration for the USN.[71]

Overall, there is limited evidence that the security dilemma holds as a solid explanation for naval modernization between China and the U.S. While it is clear that China is arming against the USN, the evidence of American procurement based solely on a Chinese contingency is extremely limited and while China may be the main cause of this limited modernization, it is too small to classify this as a full-scale security dilemma. As the PLAN continues to modernize and the Sino/U.S. rivalry

---

[70] A former high-level retired American defence official told this author that this weapon was developed with China in mind. Author's discussion with retired American defence official. 2017.

[71] Author's interviews with American active duty officers, military scholars, and retired officers. China. 2011–2012, 2016–2017.

continues, it is possible and perhaps likely that the American navy will devote significant resources to countering specific Chinese capabilities, however, for the period under review in this book, the available evidence is too limited and narrow to provide the security dilemma with a strong explanatory platform.

The Bureaucratic Politics Model as a Driver of China's Naval Modernization

The bureaucratic politics model can be very useful when trying to understand a state's behaviour. In the case of China, we should be looking for solid empirical evidence that naval modernization is heavily influenced by bureaucratic rivalries, and in particular that the PLAN has emerged as a major bureaucratic force that is able to substantially influence and even dictate the procurement process of naval hardware. There is little convincing evidence that the PLAN has this influence, in fact, there is overwhelming evidence that the PLAN is not a significant bureaucratic force and that it receives orders and does not give them.

As Fravel points out, there are two types of potential influence that we should be looking for. First, is the PLAN able to capture influence through lobbying and other independent actions outside of the normal bureaucratic channels? If this is the case, the PLAN should force the Chinese government to order specific platforms that government leaders do not want, and would not have otherwise ordered without pressure from the PLAN. Second, does the PLAN exert bureaucratic influence through normal bureaucratic channels? In the second scenario, the PLAN is one of many actors that are vying for influence with top decision makers (Fravel 2015).

There is powerful evidence that the PLAN fails in both of the above criteria. On the subject of formal levels of power, the PLAN (and the entire PLA) has been locked out of the PBSC since the retirement of Admiral Liu Huaqing in 1997 (Colley 2019B). The absence of a PLAN voice on the PBSC during a time a significant naval modernization raises important questions about the role of the PLAN as a lobbying group. Since 1997,

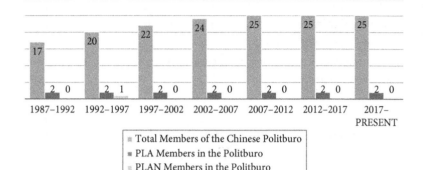

Graph 4.1 PLA and PLAN Representation in the Politburo 1987–Present (Author's Dataset; Colley 2019B)

the PLAN has also been absent from the second most powerful decision-making body in China, the Politburo. Perhaps the greatest challenge to the PLAN as an influential bureaucratic organization is found in the complete marginalization of the PLAN from the CMC. As Table 4.2 demonstrates, since the 1980s, the PLAN has never had more than one seat on the CMC. Surprisingly, even after the 1995/1996 Taiwan Crisis, the PLAN failed to have even one representative on the CMC from 1997 to 2002. From 2002 to 2017, the PLAN only garnered 1 of the 11 seats on the Commission. In addition, since 2007, the PLA has not been represented on the Secretariat, which is the most important body for the carrying out of PB and PBSC decisions. The Secretariat is made up of representatives of important state and party organizations and the absence of a PLA representative among its seven members is one more empirical example of its declining influence (Fewsmith 2018). Overall, this data makes it clear that at least in the formal levels of Chinese power, the PLAN not only is poorly represented, but it also struggles to get a seat at the table (Colley 2019B).

Further evidence of the lack of influence from the PLAN is found in the following three examples. First, China's aircraft carrier programme took several decades to develop, and Admiral Liu Huaqing was seen as a key lobbyist for the carrier. Since the 1980s, Liu was pressing for the PLAN to develop a carrier, but was repeatedly overruled by China's

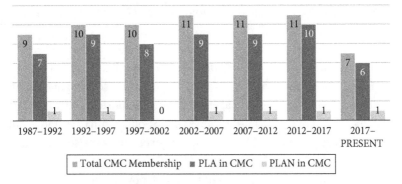

Graph 4.2   PLA and PLAN Representation in the Central Military
Commission 1987–Present (Author's Dataset; Colley 2019B)

top leaders. Vice Admiral Zhang Xusan also supported Liu, and as
Deputy Commander of the PLAN, also advocated for a carrier, but was
unsuccessful. Liu even held meetings with the PLA and brought in the
leadership of COSTIND (the General Staff Department's Armament
Department) as well as the General Logistics Department, and argued
that a carrier would support the CCP's goals. All of these efforts failed
to sway China's leaders, and it was only in 2004, seven years after Liu
stepped down from the PBSC, that Hu Jintao authorized China's carrier programme (Yung 2015). The failure by Liu and his allies to push
forward a carrier programme demonstrates the inability of the PLAN
to act as an interest group at both the formal and informal levels of
power. In the formal sense, Liu's position on the PBSC provided him
with direct contact with Jiang Zemin and other top leaders, he was also
on the PBSC during the 1995/1996 Taiwan Crisis. Informally, it shows
that the PLAN could not use back door channels to lobby for the carrier.
With a renewed interest in naval warfare and Jiang Zemin being careful
not to upset the PLA and allowing the PLA to have higher levels of influence, it is interesting that the carrier programme was not launched
(Garver 2016). Although several carriers were purchased by various
Chinese entities starting in 1985, the PLAN had to wait until 2004
for the programme to officially commence (Yung 2015). Kardon and
Saunders argue that the PLA should not even be labelled as an interest
group in 1996. They point out that China's military lacked autonomy,

coherence, and a voice that traditional interests groups have (Kardon and Saunders 2015).

Second, even in the Xi Jinping Era, the PLAN has not always been a significant bureaucratic organization. In 2013, the State Council created a unified government agency to oversee maritime sovereignty issues, which would not be a military agency. Of equal importance, the PLAN is China's backup in the various disputes in the South China Sea and is not the main force (Yung 2015). The Chinese government is also concerned with giving the PLAN significant power and therefore divides the PLAN into three different fleets to prevent too much power from developing in one unified fleet (Bussert and Elleman 2011). Third, from 2008 to 2009, the PLAN pushed for China to declare an Air Defense Identification Zone (ADIZ) in the East China Sea, this was overruled and it was not until 2013 under Xi Jinping that the ADIZ was announced (Fravel 2015). Scobell et al. argue that even though the PLAN is increasing in influence and its role as 'second rate' player is changing, especially since 2004, the Army and ground forces still have the most influence. The Air Force also competes with the PLAN and it has greater representation on the CMC with two seats held by Air Force generals (Scobell et al. 2015).

The fieldwork undertaken for this project also added strong support to the argument that the PLAN is not a significant bureaucratic entity. While acknowledging that the PLAN takes advantage of the rivalry with the U.S. by playing up the American threat, nearly every expert interviewed discounted the PLAN as a major cause of PLAN modernization. Most experts were very clear in pointing out that the PLAN and PLA, were the Party's military, and therefore take orders from the Party.[72] They emphasized that the Party does not take orders from the PLA, and much less the PLAN.[73] A retired high ranking American Navy officer with many years of experience working with the PLAN, said it has influence in other areas that may not be as sensitive or critical to China's long-term security. This individual stated that the PLAN pressured the CMC to allow it to go to the Gulf of Aden where they could learn how to operate on the high seas far away from homeports.[74]

---

[72] In China, the PLA takes orders from the CCP, not from the government.

[73] Author's interviews with Chinese security experts. Beijing and Shanghai 2016–2017 academic year.

[74] Author's interview with retired American Navy officer. 2017.

There was one noteworthy nuanced opinion of the PLAN as a bureaucratic force. A retired Chinese scholar of security studies stated that the PLAN had greater influence under Hu Jintao because 'Hu just signed papers, he did not have real control or input'. This source also claimed that Hu did not challenge appointments and argued that overall the PLA was much more aggressive under Hu and was also much more corrupt. This person, who asked not to be identified, also argued that under Hu, top PLA generals also wanted separation from Hu in order to control the PLA for themselves, apparently 'Hu could not control this, but this changed when Xi came to power'.[75] Another Chinese professor of international relations argued that the PLAN has not been as hard hit by the anti-corruption campaign, thus implying that it is being used to offset the Army by Xi Jinping.[76]

Overall, there is little evidence that the PLAN has been able to successfully transform itself into a potent lobbying group that is able to force China's leaders to support policies (and weapons systems) that the leadership is not in favour of. In fact, the available evidence demonstrates that the PLAN is an ineffective bureaucratic force that is firmly under the control of the CCP. Their noticeable absence in the top levels of formal power and military power provides strong evidence that they are not an effective lobbying force. Their inability to use back door channels also does not appear to demonstrate effective bureaucratic influence. Importantly, perceived assertive and belligerent behaviour by the PLA/PLAN and its staff does not mean that they exercise significant influence.

Why Strategic Rivalry Is the Best Explanation

As has been documented throughout this chapter, strategic rivalry is the most complete driver of PLAN modernization. The critical junctures that are embedded in the punctuated equilibrium model of rivalry maintenance and escalation have caused Chinese decision makers threat perceptions of the U.S. Navy to soar; as a result, they have decided

---

[75] Author's interview with retired Chinese security scholar. China 2016–2017 academic year.
[76] Author's interview with Chinese international relations scholar. Beijing 2016–2017 academic year.

to pursue naval modernization. In the first phase of modernization when the military and PLAN budgets were relatively low, the PLAN pursued a Corbettian naval strategy with the aim of keeping American naval forces out of the first island chain. As the Chinese economy expanded and more resources were available for the military, the PLANs budget increased and Chinese leaders embarked on building a more Mahanian blue water navy.

There is ample evidence that rivalry, while not being the only explanation, is the best one. The critical junctures of the 1990s led directly to calls from the Chinese leadership to develop 'assassin's mace' and anti-access naval hardware. Evidence in the form of published government documents, official memoirs, statements by leaders, western and Chinese scholarly research and extensive in-depth interviews that specifically sought the causes of PLAN modernization, all point to rivalry as the best explanation. Even after the PLAN was able to procure the hardware to keep the USN at a distance, the rivalry, or more precisely threat perceptions emanating from the rivalry, caused Chinese leaders to continue to build the navy to defend against the USN on the high seas. Box 4.1 highlights powerful evidence that Chinese leaders identified the U.S. as a critical rival that needed to be countered at sea. It also provides concrete examples of how certain events led to calls for naval modernization.

The timing of the PLAN's modernization is also important. Development of the navy is correlated with the resumption of the strategic rivalry. During the 1990s, the CCP was trying to maintain economic growth in the aftermath of the Tiananmen massacre and in the late 1990s, it was trying to avoid the 1997/1998 Asian financial crisis. Dedicating relatively scarce resources to the military was an impediment to economic growth. This also was discordant with the stated policy concept/strategy of 'Tao Guang Yang Hui', or 'keeping a low profile'. The key point here is that the rivalry with the U.S. acted as not only a driver, but also as an accelerator to the development to the PLAN.

The previous competing explanations put forward in this book do have some explanatory power, however on their own they fail in adequately explaining naval modernization. Many of them are either embedded in the strategic rivalry model or influence it in other ways. As long as the Sino/U.S. rivalry is maintained and experiences periods of

---

Box 4.1   Evidence of Chinese Identification of the U.S. as a Rival and Critical Junctures That Led to Naval Modernization

---

- 1991–1993: Chinese Admiral and PBSC Member Liu Huaqing chairs the 'Military Strategic Guidelines for a New Era'. This is a military modernization plan that is a direct response to the threat perceptions from the U.S.
- 1993: Yinhe incident leads to calls for the modernization of the PLAN. Nuclear powered submarines ordered after this.
- 1995/1996: Taiwan Crisis leads to calls for a modern navy. Directly leads to the purchase of naval hardware from Russia.
- Late 1990s: The CMC calls for warships that can directly counter the American Navy
- 1999: Bombing of the Chinese Embassy in Belgrade leads to calls for 'assassin's mace' programmes and robust naval modernization. Jiang Zemin calls the USA the 'enemy'.
- 1990s to present: Deeply rooted Chinese perceptions of American 'containment' of China drive naval modernization.
- 1990s to present: Statements by Chinese leaders and military officials that the PLAN must counter the American navy.
- 2000 to present: Chinese government White Papers directly and indirectly identify the U.S. as a rival that needs to be countered.
- 2010s: American 'Pivot to Asia' is cited as a major driver of PLAN modernization. At the 18th Party Congress in 2012, Chinese leaders call for a powerful PLAN.
- Widespread agreement in Chinese defence circles that a powerful PLAN is necessary to protect Chinese SLOCs from the American navy.

---

escalation, the PLAN will likely continue on its trajectory of blue water development. Crucially, for the rivalry argument to be discredited we would need to witness a prolonged period of a significant decrease in rivalry maintenance or outright termination, while still experiencing PLAN modernization. We could also see a reduction in naval modernization, while continuing to witness rivalry maintenance and escalation.

Implications for the Punctuated Equilibrium Model

As in the Sino/India case, the punctuated equilibrium model of rivalry maintenance and escalation provides a solid framework for analysing the Sino/U.S. rivalry. As the model predicts, Sino/American relations have experienced significant periods of rivalry escalation over the period analysed. As demonstrated in Table 4.2 over the last three decades there have been at least 170 important points of rivalry escalation and maintenance. What is most important for the argument of this book are the critical junctures, or the points of escalation that cause decision makers in Beijing to push for naval modernization. The period from 1989 to 2000 had at least five points of escalation that can be considered critical junctures. The sea change in relations between Beijing and Washington following the 1989 Tiananmen Square massacre was vital to reigniting the strategic rivalry. The 1993 Yinhe incident also played a major role. However, the most critical episode of rivalry escalation that supports the punctuated equilibrium model was the 1995/1996 Taiwan crisis. As was demonstrated above, this event was the most important driver of Chinese naval modernization. This event as well as the 1999 Belgrade Embassy bombing and the 2001 EP-3 spy plane incident also reinforce the model as they are considered major points of escalation.

While the post-2001 period has not experienced any events that brought Washington and Beijing close to war, there are still many points of escalation that support the model. For example, the 2010 Air-Sea Battle concept and the 2011 'Pivot to Asia' were perceived in Beijing as critical points of escalation. The coming to power of the Trump administration contained many points of escalation ranging from the trade war to sending high ranking officials to Taiwan. While these may not be directly linked to naval modernization, they reinforce Chinese decision maker's perceptions of American efforts to 'contain' China. This has significant influence on China's decision to pursue naval modernization. The punctuated equilibrium model predicts that once a rivalry is initiated it enters a 'lock in' period that regularly experiences periods of maintenance and escalation. The events depicted in Table 4.2 are powerful evidence of the model's utility in explaining the rivalry.

Conclusion

Over the period selected in this study the PLAN went from an obsolete force that was primarily designed to defend China's coast to a robust fleet that recently constructed its first overseas naval base in Djibouti. Crucial to the modernization of the PLAN has been the intense periods of rivalry escalation that dramatically altered Chinese decision makers' threat perceptions and caused them to build a navy to protect their interests from the U.S.

The long-term trajectory of the PLAN is unknown, but by 2049, the PLAN is projected to be a 'modern navy' (Cole 2016). The rise of the PLAN will likely be tied to the overall success of China as it attempts to become a superpower. The PLAN may have as many as six carrier battle groups by 2030. Of greater consequence to the USN is the level of technological sophistication in Chinese nuclear-powered submarines and smaller guided missile warships such as DDGs and corvettes. Such warships, including 36 DDGs, are fitted with the 'Dragon Eye' combat system, which is believed to be similar to the USN Aegis system (McDevitt 2020). If the PLAN continues on its current trajectory, the links between the Sino/U.S. rivalry and the Sino/Indian rivalries will become much greater. India is clearly responding to the PLAN with its own naval modernization, however, if PLAN visits in the IOR continue at their current pace, India will likely seek even greater cooperation with the U.S. and its allies. The prospects for a formal alliance between New Delhi and Washington are currently slim, but if China's 'Belt and Road Initiative' and PLAN forays continue, such an alliance may move closer to reality over the next one to two decades.

The Sino/U.S. rivalry shows no signs of abating, but over the past 20 years it has also largely avoided major political shocks that have brought the two states close to war. However, as stipulated in the punctuated equilibrium model, once a rivalry is initiated, it tends to enter a 'lock-in stage' that sets the rivalry up for the long-term. In all likelihood the 'strategic suspicion' that has characterized the bilateral relationship over the past quarter-century will continue indefinitely. Decision makers in both Beijing and Washington are unlikely to see each other as non-rivals. The Chinese leadership has convinced itself that the U.S. is a threat that must be countered. These threats are the driving force behind PLAN modernization.

5

Policy Recommendations and Conclusion

Policy Recommendations

This section provides theoretical informed policy recommendations for China, India, and the U. S. as they relate to this book. For each state I break the recommendations into three separate but related parts. First, I discuss recommendations for a more aggressive policy from the perspective of each state if they decide to counter their rival. This approach is consistent with behaviour that encourages rivalry maintenance and escalation and will likely exacerbate the existing rivalry. Second, I address actions that have the ability to reduce tensions and are more consistent with a policy of compromise and de-escalation in the rivalry. The third possible approach is a hybrid of the first two positions. Before I begin the policy recommendation section, it is necessary to address the issue of how a strategic rivalry can influence the policy process and how rivalries can be managed/terminated.

The Impact of Strategic Rivalry on the Policy Process

Strategic rivalries have the ability to heavily influence the decision-making process. Frequently, events related to rivalry maintenance and escalation are perceived in a negative light that hampers decision makers' ability to properly understand a situation or the context in which it is viewed. Leaders see what they want to see and may ignore evidence that contradicts their existing perceptions of their rivals. Of equal importance, as the punctuated equilibrium model demonstrates, rivalries tend to 'lock in' for the long-term and experience periods of relative stability

The Nexus of Naval Modernization in India and China. Christopher K. Colley, Oxford University Press. © Oxford University Press 2022. DOI: 10.1093/oso/9780192865595.003.0006

along with episodes of significant escalation. Considering the power of strategic rivalries to cloud decision maker's judgement on specific events, the development, and implementation of policy between the states in this book will be heavily influenced by the rivalries of each. For example, Multiple Chinese scholars have argued that China's Belt and Road Initiative (BRI) is heavily influenced by the American presence in East Asia, and such an initiative will help China counterbalance American global hegemony.[1]

In the Sino/U.S. case, it will be extremely difficult for Beijing to see any American military manoeuvre or relationship in the Indo-Pacific region as detached from the rivalry. For example, Chinese security specialists view American missile defence systems set up in South Korea as China specific, thus any justification based on North Korean attempts to threaten South Korea or the U.S. are conveniently ignored.[2] By viewing most acts as American attempts to 'contain' China, Chinese leaders will likely misinterpret American strategy in the region and may miss important opportunities for rivalry de-escalation.

In terms of the policy options, Chinese leaders and their bureaucracies may not be willing to take a more conciliatory approach towards the U.S. as this may be perceived as a sign of weakness. The initial Sino/U.S. rivalry was terminated when Chairman Mao and President Nixon decided to end it in order to counter the USSR. Unfortunately, no comparable situation exists today that would facilitate a termination in the Sino/U.S. rivalry. In fact, Washington's expanding ties with New Delhi will likely exacerbate the Sino/U.S. rivalry. Heath and Thompson examine the current and likely future trajectory of the U.S.-China strategic rivalry and the various means to manage it. Importantly for policy implications, the authors argue that the structural drivers of the rivalry are too deep to resolve through various forms of cooperation. Instead, they argue that leaders must try to manage the rivalry as best they can at lower levels. Crucially, they believe that the rivalry is now transforming from a regional to a global strategic rivalry. If policymakers just focus on issues such as Taiwan and the South China Sea, they will fail to address

---

[1] Author's interviews with Chinese foreign policy experts. Beijing 2016–2017.
[2] During the fieldwork for this book in China, many Chinese security experts believed that such missile defence systems were first and foremost about China. Author's interviews Beijing. 2016–2017.

the multi-level competition for leadership. The evolution of the rivalry to the global stage means that policy options are now determined by events beyond the maritime stage. Finally, they state that the best way to manage the rivalry is for Washington to discourage Beijing from challenging American global leadership. They also argue that the U.S. needs to bolster its technological lead over China (Heath and Thompson 2018).

As for the Sino/Indian strategic rivalry, it heavily influences New Delhi's perceptions of Beijing. The linkages between the Sino/U.S. rivalry and the Sino/Indian rivalry are increasing as PLAN activities in the IOR soar. With China's BRI showing no sign of slowing down, this will only exacerbate the rivalry and New Delhi will push for Indian naval modernization.[3] In the absence of a major shock or an extremely difficult diplomatic initiative that would settle the border dispute, it will be very difficult to reduce the rivalry. Frederic Grare has argued that India's Look East Policy has become New Delhi's preferred policy on how to deal with China and India is taking steps to prevent the emergence of a regional order dominated by Beijing (Grare 2017). Interestingly, Vietnam's policy choices also reflect concern over China's long-term intentions. Hanoi has ordered six Russian Kilo Class SSKs to hedge against the PLAN. Brantly Womack argues that Vietnam's increasing economic dependence on China has increased anxiety in Hanoi as they may be at the mercy of their much stronger rival (Womack 2011).

On the past management of the Sino/Indian strategic rivalry, Pardesi argues that there was a significant deterioration in mutual trust between China and India in 1959, which was a major cause of the 1962 war. His research finds no evidence that domestic factors were at play when the rivalry de-escalated in the late 1980s. Instead, he states that international level variables were the main cause of the reduction in tensions, specifically the loss of USSR support for India in the late 1980s, and the reduction of hostilities between China and the USSR during the same period (Pardesi 2011). Pardesi's findings may be important for the policy recommendations of this study as there is little chance of Beijing and Washington reducing their rivalry as New Delhi and Washington

---

[3] Indian security experts made very clear to this author the China's BRI was a major critical juncture in the Sino/Indian rivalry. In particular, the maritime dimension of the BRI was cited as a critical threat to India. Author's interviews in New Delhi. Summer 2016.

increase their security ties and show no signs of building greater strategic trust. While not China specific, Paul Kapur also casts doubt on the role of domestic factors in rivalry reduction. His study of India's rivalry with Pakistan argues that strategic variables are the best explanation for a reduction of tension from the early 1970s until the late 1980s. In addition, Kapur writes that after the 1971 Indo-Pakistani war, Pakistan could no longer challenge India. This changed when an insurgency erupted in Kashmir in the late 1980s, thus providing Pakistan an opportunity to again escalate the rivalry (Kapur 2011). While Kapur's work demonstrates that rivalry can be managed in effective ways, in the absence of a political shock, the dismemberment of Pakistan, or a significant insurgency, rivalries can be difficult to manage and resolve.

We know that rivalries can be dealt with effectively and, can be managed and are frequently terminated. For example, from 1816 to 2010, 139 rivalries were terminated. For the policy implications of this book, scholarly research has found two key pathways for rivalry termination. First, one or both sides lose their competitive status, which frequently occurs when a state has been defeated in war or both sides experience political or economic exhaustion. The onset of a civil war can also cause states to terminate rivalries. Of the 139 terminated rivalries, 48 of them ended by these means (Rasler et al. 2013).

The second main pathway happens when one or both states cease to perceive the other as an enemy. This is frequently facilitated by a change in the domestic leadership, or negotiations aimed at ending the rivalry, or a shift in priorities. Interestingly, 15 of the 139 rivalries were terminated this way, while the remaining 76 cases of rivalry termination were attributed to non-coercive causes. Crucially, the authors find that four factors frequently come together; these are shocks, expectation revision, reciprocity, and reinforcement (Rasler et al. 2013).

Whether or not these past instances offer a guide to successful management of the two rivalries under review, I argue that as of early 2022, the right conditions are not present. On the Sino/U.S. rivalry, both Beijing and Washington are not willing to go through a process of reciprocity that might alleviate the rivalry. In fact, the ongoing trade war and pandemic have deepened Chinese suspicion of the U.S., and the Biden administration does not appear to be willing to make significant changes to

U.S. China policy and work with Beijing on issues that might reduce tensions. Furthermore, Beijing has not given any indication that it is willing to meet the Americans halfway on issues that might lead to a reduction in tensions.

As for the Sino/Indian rivalry, as the PLAN continues to increase its presence in the IOR, New Delhi will continue to see China through the prism of strategic rivalry and will likely respond in a manner that will not reduce tensions. In fact, as the BRI continues to make headlines and inroads into the IOR, India will likely push back by increasing its military activities in South East Asia while working with other Chinese rivals such as Japan and the USA. We are already seeing this in the resurrection of the 'Quad', where India, Australia, Japan, and the U.S. carry out joint military exercises (Smith et al. 2018).

Ultimately, feasible policy options are determined by top leader's decisions, and President's Xi and Biden along with Prime Minister Modi do not appear to be willing to back down in each state's respective rivalries. Barring an unexpected shock, these rivalries will likely continue to follow the model that the punctuated equilibrium predicts.

Overall, rivalries go through various periods of maintenance and escalation. Unfortunately, for those seeking a reduction in rivalry escalation, or even termination, the required factors are not present, and will likely not be in place for the foreseeable future. As China continues to rise and increasingly challenges the U.S. in the region as well as spreading its influence in the IOR, both rivalries will be more difficult to manage as policymakers will view their rival's behaviour in the context of strategic rivalry.

Policy Recommendations for China

Anti-Rival (U.S.) Recommendations (Continuation of Rivalry Maintenance with Periods of Escalation)

In the post-2007–2008 financial crisis environment, China's behaviour has been perceived as becoming more aggressive and assertive. While some have questioned this argument (Johnston 2013), there is a general consensus in the diplomatic and security communities that the days of '*Tao guang yanghui*' (loosely translated as maintaining a low profile) are over and Beijing has taken on a much more aggressive international agenda (Zhao 2017; Swaine 2018).[4] As Xi Jinping continues to consolidate power and pursues a greater role for China in the international community, China is increasingly using coercion to get what it wants.[5] The following points are recommendations for Beijing if it wishes to continue this strategy. I argue that these policies would constitute a continuation of China's current trajectory and therefore are the most likely outcomes over the next 5–10 years. From a theoretical perspective, these policies are a continuation of rivalry maintenance and will likely produce points of escalation between both China and the U.S., and China and India as China's rivalry with the U.S. continues to spill over into its rivalry with India. This will cause further escalation in the Sino/Indian rivalry, thus justifying continuing Indian investment in naval modernization.

The PLAN will continue to pursue modernization and will likely meet the projections detailed in Table 4.1. This trajectory will place the PLAN as the world's second most powerful navy by 2030. Such a navy will have the ability to severely disrupt American surface operations within the second island chain. A PLAN complete with such a force structure will likely continue to build overseas naval bases as Beijing is actively courting Sri Lanka, Pakistan, the Maldives, the Seychelles, and possibly even Tanzania as potential locations for overseas bases. If the Chinese leadership pursues this course, the PLAN will have the ability to offer a credible deterrent/risk to any American or Indian attempts to disrupt China's IOR SLOCs.

Such a scenario will only increase the risk of conflict as it not only maintains the current rivalry, but additional bases in the IOR would constitute major points of rivalry escalation with New Delhi. This will lead to increasing threat perceptions of Chinese intentions, thus justifying a more powerful Indian navy. In this situation, rivalry escalation is not solely confined to PLAN bases or potential bases. Continued development of quieter nuclear-powered submarines as well as the possible phasing out of SSKs in favour of nuclear boats will alarm not only India, but also other regional states. While SSNs are feared by New Delhi, once the PLAN is able to put to sea a credible and reliable undersea

---

[4] Author's interviews with experts on Chinese foreign policy and members of the diplomatic and military communities in China. China and the U.S. 2008–2017.

[5] For example, China's behavior since 2010 in the South China Sea where it has ignored international law in its pursuit of regional hegemony.

nuclear-based deterrent centred on their SSBN programme, concerns will increase in Washington. In addition, threat perceptions will significantly rise if the PLAN is successful in developing indigenous propulsion systems that emit low levels of noise.

China's increasingly sophisticated anti-ship ballistic missile and anti-ship cruise missile programmes are also a cause of concern and a source of rivalry maintenance. While ostensibly these missiles are more defensive in nature, they can be used to intimidate American allies and Taiwan. As of mid-2021 the PLAN appears to have fielded a somewhat reliable SLBM housed in its Jin-class SSBM. By 2019 at least 48 of these were in operation, with each SSBN capable of carrying 12 missiles each. The most recent known tests of these missiles were in 2012, 2015, and 2019 (Missile Defense Project 2021; The Military Balance 2021). The 2019 tests reportedly utilized the JL-3 'Giant Wave' SLBM that is scheduled to be placed in the new 096 SSBN (Fanell 2020). While the Chinese aircraft carrier programme poses little to no risk to the U. S. and Japan, patrolling the IOR represents a significant point of escalation in China's rivalry with India. It is highly likely a Chinese carrier will make a patrol in the IOR in the next couple of years. Beijing appears to be tone-deaf when it comes to Indian sensitivities. The presence of the *Liaoning* or another future PLAN carrier in the IOR would lead New Delhi to speed up its development and/ or purchase of missiles that could cripple or destroy a Chinese carrier from afar. It would also likely lead to a self-fulfilling prophecy by Beijing. Beijing believes that the U.S. is determined to 'contain' and 'surround' China, thus a more technologically sophisticated Chinese carrier with electro-magnetic catapults capable of launching fully loaded warplanes would lead to expanded ties between the American and Indian militaries.

Short of war, Beijing's increasing artificial island-building projects and improving force structure have enabled it to consolidate control over the entire South China Sea and pose a potentially serious challenge/threat to American friends and allies in the region. If Beijing continues its current behaviour of pushing claims in the East and South China Seas, while ignoring international opinion and court rulings, it will likely lead to an even stronger push back from the hedging strategy that many regional states are currently pursuing. (It is important to note that China has not yet published the precise geographic coordinates of the 'Nine Dash Line' in the South China Sea, thus refusing to clarify what it claims is 'Chinese territory.) Beijing's attempts to cultivate (with political and economic incentives) pliable regional states to support China's maritime goals and strategy may be successful in some areas, but not others. Finally, increasing pressure on Taiwan to agree to a unification that is more on Beijing's terms is likely to fail, and may lead to more friction and escalation between Beijing and Washington.

Potential Consequences

If Beijing continues its current assertive trajectory, the likely consequences of such rivalry maintenance and escalation will manifest themselves in multiple ways. Regional states will likely pursue policies that call for both internal and external balancing not only with China's neighbours, but also with its rivals (India and the U.S.).[6] States may also hedge against the rise of China. Even though their economies are heavily dependent on China, which necessitates working with China, at the same time these states are actively building military capabilities that have the ability to defend against the PLA/PLAN. Interestingly, while China's neighbours have increased the lethality of their naval platforms and submarines, over the last 25 years, they have not increased their military budgets as a percentage of their GDP (Kang 2017). However, regional states have made significant increases in their submarines and surface ships, and fighter-bombers (Beckley 2017). Nevertheless, a continuation of Chinese assertiveness could cause these figures to rise.

A potentially significant consequence for China will be if neighbouring states continue to increase the interoperability of their militaries. This is already happening as India, Australia, Japan, and the U.S. have resurrected the 'Quad', which is a security arrangement designed to act as a hedge against a rising China (Valencia 2017). A continuation of aggressive Chinese policies would be a gift to hawks in places such as Washington, New Delhi, and Tokyo who would justify a more muscular approach to

---

[6] As for India, this is more the case of East Asian states such as Japan and Vietnam working with New Delhi against China, and not South Asian states joining with New Delhi against China.

China based on real and perceived assertiveness. In addition, challenges with Taiwan are likely to persist and intensify as Beijing's heavy-handed approach to Hong Kong and the rapid erosion of democratic institutions and norms there has sent a clear message to Taiwan that it cannot trust the Mainland to honour any agreement that would 'guarantee' Taiwanese self-determination in any future 'One-Country, Two Systems' format. This situation will likely perpetuate the 'Taiwan question', and thus Sino/American mistrust emanating from this challenge.

I argue that this is the most likely outcome over the next decade. The Chinese leadership believes it is China's turn (again) to become a great power, and Xi Jinping has made this a cornerstone of his foreign policy and his overall rule and legitimacy. Beijing appears to be tone-deaf to how its behaviour is perceived outside of the Mainland. While the Chinese government may at times have justifiable concerns about American strategic plans for China, the top leadership is frequently unable to consider how Chinese behaviour raises threat perceptions in other states.

Compromise/Accommodation
Policy Recommendations

If Beijing seeks to reduce rivalry escalation with both the U.S. and regional states, it must make considerable progress in allaying its neighbour's fears. It is possible now that Xi Jinping has appeared to have consolidated power, he may be more open to reducing apprehensions about China's rise. This would be the best course of action in order to secure China's long-term security and to help prevent a loose coalition of states from hedging against China's rise with the assistance of the U.S. In order for China to do this, it should adhere to the following recommendations.

A common complaint of officials who deal with the Chinese military (and the Chinese government in general) is the lack of information about Chinese intentions. Beijing should allow for greater transparency of the PLA and especially the PLAN. This would include making public the PLAN's annual budget. Not every PLAN activity has to be viewed through the lens of strategic rivalry. Chinese leaders should also build on the progress of the Gulf of Aden (SHADE) patrols and extend this to other parts of the world where China can show that it is a 'responsible stakeholder'. The American proposed 'Operation Sentinel', designed to protect the free passage of ships through the Strait of Hormuz is one such opportunity. However, given China's strong ties to Iran, it is unlikely to take part in such a mission (Colley 2019C). In addition, the PLAN should actively take part in exercises such as RIMPAC, and not just send surveillance ships that sit on the sidelines and spy on the other participants.[7]

Of crucial importance would be some sort of Chinese initiated de-escalation of tensions in the South China Sea. Beijing would be wise to back down on claims there and immediately halt any continuing construction. China has a commendable record in compromising on territorial disputes (Fravel 2008), and this should be extended to the case of the South China Sea. Directly related to this issue is the 2016 court ruling in The Hague on the South China Sea that ruled against Chinese claims. This was a diplomatic disaster for Beijing. If China is seen as stepping back, it would be helpful in reducing regional concerns. Such a move would entail dismantling any military facilities on the artificially constructed islands in the South China Sea.

In China's border disputes with India, Beijing should push hard for a border 'swap' by following in the footsteps of previous negotiations that attempted to settle the dispute based on the current status quo.[8] China should also address Indian fears regarding the China Pakistan Economic Corridor (CPEC) and directly consult with New Delhi on the BRI. While the PLAN will continue to carry out forays into the IOR, Beijing should publicly declare that the PLAN does not have any ambition to establish military bases in Sri Lanka, Pakistan, the Maldives, or the Seychelles. With Taiwan, Beijing should attempt to move away from its increasingly coercive policies, and return to the relatively stable ties that categorized much of the 2008–2016 period. Importantly, China should be willing to reciprocate any positive action by a rival.

---

[7] In 2015, the PLAN was invited to RIMPAC, but the two ships that were sent to Hawaii did not take part in the exercises and instead spied on the other participants from afar. Author's interview with American General. 2016–2017 academic year.

[8] The border 'swap' entails China keeping Aksai Chin and India holding on to Arunachal Pradesh. This is also the current status quo.

Hybrid Approach to Policy Recommendations

It is unlikely that Beijing will follow the advice in the second part of these recommendations. However, a hybrid approach between the first and second approaches might be more politically feasible and would reduce the likelihood of rivalry escalation. The following are recommendations that try to fuse the two.

Beijing can continue to develop a powerful navy while building on SHADE and taking part in other confidence-building exercises. This would also entail increasing transparency of the PLA/PLAN through such acts as publishing the PLAN's budget. China could show its confidence on the South China Sea by pledging to halt the construction of new islands, while attempting to work in a multi-lateral negotiating environment with all of the claimants. (Not just on a bilateral basis.)[9] A pledge to keep Chinese nuclear-powered submarines out of the IOR and abiding by UNCLOS rules in the South China Sea would undoubtedly help to reduce tensions. One possible face-saving mechanism to resolving maritime disputes is to call for some form of joint ownership of disputed maritime territory. Other important steps would be the halting of military manoeuvres around the East China Sea and ceasing to act as an impediment to India's aspirations for a permanent seat on the UN Security Council.

Policy Recommendations for India

Anti-Rival (China) Recommendations

As India seeks to counter China's rise and the increasing PLAN forays into the IOR, it has multiple options. These will certainly antagonize Beijing and will likely lead to rivalry escalation. A key aspect of this strategy would be to overcome domestic opposition to increasing ties with the U.S. The following are possible policies New Delhi could follow if it seeks a more assertive relationship with China.

New Delhi can continue its embrace of Washington and deepen existing security ties. This would involve additional purchases of advanced American

---

[9] Many may ignore the diplomatic benefits of this and argue that this is not a sign of confidence, but a demonstration of weakness.

technology and the possibility of a major trophy platform such as the acquisition of former American warships.[10] India can continue to work with and conduct exercises with East Asian states such as Japan and Vietnam while also irritating China by holding these exercises in East Asian waters instead of the Indian Ocean. Rivalry maintenance will be sustained with regular IN warship voyages into the South China Sea and the potential for escalation exists if India's new SSBNs and SSNs are sent into East Asian waters.

On the diplomatic front, New Delhi can pressure regional states to reject a greater Chinese influence in the IOR, while at the same time provide incentives for these states to work with India. In addition, India can refuse to compromises on the disputed border, while also maintaining the boycott of China's BRI. The Indian military can limit Pakistan and China's ability from creating a potential 'Hormuz Dilemma' where India would not be able to access the Persian Gulf, by increasing Chinese concerns over a 'Malacca Dilemma'. This would require a visible surface warship presence as well as an undersea presence in the form of advanced submarines. While some Chinese strategists are concerned with the American navy's ability to disrupt China's SLOCs, concern over India's ability to threaten Beijing in a similar manner is emerging as a significant fear in Chinese defence circles. India should capitalize on its evolving undersea warfare capability and allow its advanced SSKs and emerging nuclear-powered submarines to surface in the Strait of Malacca when PLAN flotillas are transiting into the IOR.

Compromise/Accommodation Policy Recommendations

If New Delhi seeks to prevent future instances of rivalry escalation with China, it can pursue policies that seek greater accommodation with Beijing. However, this approach could have major domestic challenges as rival political parties could claim that a leader is either 'selling India out', or is engaging in 'appeasement'. Nehru addressed this when he stated

---

[10] During discussions with Indian security experts several mentioned the possibility of the IN obtaining the American carrier. Author's discussions with Indian security experts. 2016–2017 academic year.

that had he negotiated with China on the border, he would no longer be Prime Minister of India (Garver 2001). It is this author's opinion that the following recommendations are the best options for India's long-term security. However, if they are not met with an equal form of reciprocity from the Chinese side, India should opt for the first set of recommendations. In addition, the fallout from the Covid-19 pandemic, which tore through India in the spring of 2021, may make it even more difficult for Indian leaders to compromise with China.

A key component of a more accommodative Indian relationship with China could be found in a change of policy on the BRI. Beijing's failure to consult New Delhi on CPEC made it politically impossible for the Indian government to take part in the BRI. India has much to gain from greater connectivity with the region and if the Chinese are willing to help facilitate the development of physical infrastructure, this could prove to be enormously beneficial for India in the long run. New Delhi should press Beijing to de-couple CPEC from BRI, thus providing political cover for India to work with the initiative. Beijing should be aware of Indian sensitivities and make it clear that CPEC and the BRI are not connected. (Beijing is keenly aware of how territorial disputes influence such situations. China is very clear about its 'One China Policy' when it comes to Taiwan. India should more forcibly push a 'One Kashmir Policy' with Beijing.) Overall, while the BRI certainly has a strong political (and geostrategic) rationale, it also has the potential to transform the region's poor infrastructure, thus helping India to alleviate a core developmental constraint; the lack of quality infrastructure.

As pointed out in the China section, India and China need to resolve their festering territorial dispute. India should push for a border swap and signal to Beijing that it would be open to such a deal that would recognize the existing status quo. While this has the potential to be a political liability for any government bold (or foolish) enough to attempt such a compromise, in the absence of an agreement, periods of significant rivalry escalation will perpetually plague Sino/Indian relations. The deadly violence between Indian and Chinese troops along the Ladakh border in the summer of 2020 was a stark reminder that no matter how many meetings Chinese and Indian negotiators have over the border issues, the territorial dispute has not been solved and always has the potential to escalate into serious violence.

New Delhi should play a less hegemonic role in the region, which would reduce the incentive of smaller regional states to reach out to China. India could also focus on trade and less on security. While India's Act East Policy is about increasing trade with East Asian states, it also has a strong security component of which Beijing is keenly aware. In accordance with this, Indian leaders should realize that manoeuvres with states such as Vietnam and Japan increase Chinese concerns of being surrounded and should either hold such exercises in the Indian Ocean, or invite China to take part. (This happens with RIMPAC exercises in Hawaii.) Such a policy would require reciprocity from Beijing to keep its distance from IOR states such as the Maldives. Importantly, India should maintain a respectable distance from the U.S. on political, and especially security issues. The warming of ties between the two is the cause of significant anxiety in Beijing.

Hybrid Approach to Policy Recommendations

The first two sections for policy recommendations may be unrealistic, however a hybrid approach may be more conceivable, and is also more of a continuation of the current status quo. Such an approach would aim to reduce, but not eliminate, future periods of significant rivalry escalation. While the rivalry would continue to exist, it would be more manageable.

A hybrid approach would see India continue to work with the U.S. in the economic realm, but would make clear that India will not become enmeshed in American strategic plans for the region. This approach would also see India take part in the BRI, while clearly conveying to Beijing that in its current form, CPEC is unacceptable. New Delhi would also tell Beijing that Chinese bases in the IOR will only push New Delhi closer to China's rivals and, especially, the U.S. The two sides would have to reach some sort of understanding that acknowledges the status quo in the Himalayas. While domestic politics in each country may prevent a formal acknowledgement of a border swap, having a robust agreement on the border, such as a 'zone of peace' where military personnel on each side are not allowed within 50 kilometres of the border, may help to reduce tension, and thus rivalry escalation on the land border. Finally, New

Delhi could reduce the IN's increasing activities in East Asia, while expecting PLAN reciprocity in the IOR.

Policy Recommendations for the U.S.

Anti-Rival (China) Recommendations

Since the turn of the century, Washington has conducted a policy of hedging against China's rise. On the one hand, the U.S. has played a critical role in China's development as American companies have invested hundreds of billions of dollars into the Chinese economy, while trillions of dollars' worth of Chinese manufactured goods have arrived in the U.S. In addition, hundreds of thousands of Chinese students have studied or are studying at American institutions of higher education. Thomas Christensen has even argued that since 1978, no country has done more to make China stronger economically and diplomatically than the U.S. (Christensen 2006). On the other hand, Washington continues to sell arms to Taiwan, reinforce its strategic ties in the region and has openly stated in the form of 'The Pivot', its intentions to move a majority of its naval hardware to the Asia-Pacific region, which all contribute to rivalry escalation.

A more assertive stance by the U.S. in the region would reinforce the American led order that has underpinned the last half-century of economic development in East Asia. Washington should also seek to capitalize on regional anxieties of China's rise. One area where this could be accomplished is in assisting American allies and friends in their development of A2/AD capabilities (Beckely 2017). While China has pursued these with great concern, Washington should promote similar strategies with states such as Vietnam, the Philippines, Taiwan, and Japan. The following policy recommendations are in some ways a continuation of the status quo, but they differ slightly in a few important areas. Critically, they would further entrench the rivalry and would open the door to potential shocks that would cause points of rivalry escalation.

If it chooses to pursue the status quo, Washington should not only aggressively revitalize The Pivot to Asia, but also actively reinforce it by providing incentives and technical help to assist American allies and partners in overcoming the challenges of interoperability in their respective defence systems. This would facilitate both internal and external balancing in regional states that are fearful of China's rise as well as its future ambitions. The Pentagon should also continue to move strategic American assets such as nuclear-powered submarines, DDGs, stealth warplanes, and carrier battle groups into permanent positions in the region (Guam would be useful). If China decides to establish an ADIZ in the South China Sea, Washington must not recognize it and openly flout it while also encouraging and assisting other states to do the same. The decision to fly B-52 heavy bombers through the Chinese declared ADIZ in the East China Sea is an example worth repeating. In terms of American naval procurement, the navy should receive at least three SSNs (Virginia-class) per year and develop more lethal and hypersonic ASCMs.

On America's allies and friends in the region, Washington should move to reassure these states of American resolve and assist them in ways that enhance American strategic aims. The hasty American withdrawal from Afghanistan in the summer of 2021 needs to be explained clearly to American allies in the Pacific as a necessary decision that terminated a never-ending war, and is not viewed as evidence of America shirking its perceived responsibilities. The possibility of an alliance with Vietnam should be explored and the USN should slowly increase joint patrols in the South China Sea with other claimants. Part of this would involve assisting regional states with capabilities to resist Chinese island-building activities in disputed waters. This could take multiple forms, but one area where the PLAN has seriously neglected in its modernization drive is its ability to carry out anti-submarine operations. Just as the IN is training Vietnamese Kilo-class submarine crews, the USN should offer its assistance. The U.S. should also have a consistent policy on China that does not vary significantly from one administration to another and should focus on a broad range of strategic issues, not just a single issue such as North Korea.

A key pillar of American 21st-century Asia policy should be on building strong ties with India. While the U.S. and India may not be natural allies, they face similar security challenges with the rise of China. Washington should continue to increase security and political ties with India, while attempting to allay various Indian concerns about American motives in the region. The U.S. should offer New Delhi trophy systems, such as a decommissioned aircraft carrier and increase technical help such as assisting the Indian aircraft carrier programme in setting up electro-magnetic catapult systems (Hall 2019).[11]

Washington must not compromise with China on security issues, such as the South China Sea or fail to back Japan in its territorial disputes with China. Most importantly, America needs to realize that many in China believe that the USA is a declining power. Washington must work hard to not only preserve the institutions of international order, but must also reinforce them. The Biden Administration should join the Comprehensive and Progressive Agreement for Trans-Pacific Partnership (CPTPP) (formally the Trans Pacific Partnership (TPP)) and realize that the initial rejection of this was a strategic mistake that only enhances Beijing's real or perceived influence. Congress should also ratify the United Nations Convention on the Law of the Sea. Finally, America needs to take advantage of the fact that China does not have any real formal allies.[12]

All of the above recommendations would increase Chinese perceptions of American designs to contain China, but they would also potentially limit Chinese room to disrupt the American led security order. If China is in fact playing a 'long game' where over several decades it seeks to displace the U.S. as the leading world power, Washington needs to act in a pro-active manner that seeks to prevent such a power transition (Doshi 2021). Under these circumstances, the rivalry would be perpetuated and could experience several potentially dangerous periods of escalation. American security commitments have served the region well for the past 70 years. While the U.S. should not shoulder a disproportionate share of the costs of maintaining stability and other states need to increase their defence budgets, Washington needs to be firm and clear with Beijing that it is not going anywhere. This requires American leaders to point out to China that China benefits enormously from the security that the American military provides. Ultimately the Chinese are probing the U.S. for weakness, and Washington needs to be resolute in its security guarantees. Finally, American leaders need to work with other states. The Trump Administration's failure to work with American

---

[11] The American military assists the Indian navy with aircraft carrier technology.
[12] China's relations with North Korea and Pakistan are increasingly perceived as strategic liabilities. Author's interviews in Beijing 2008–2017.

allies and partners in the Trade War with China was an enormous strategic mistake that dramatically reduced American leverage. With the vast majority of the world's advanced economies sharing similar grievances towards China's economic policies, President Trump failed to take advantage of this great opportunity. As of the beginning of 2022, the continuing fallout from the Covid-19 pandemic has created a situation where China is on the defensive over its initial handling of the virus, thus presenting the Biden administration with multiple diplomatic and strategic paths to counter China in both Asia and beyond.

Compromise/Accommodation Policy Recommendations

Washington has the option of working with Beijing to alleviate many Chinese concerns. This may help reduce tension in the strategic rivalry, but could also be perceived as allowing Chinese domination over East Asia. Goldstein has developed what he refers to as 'cooperation spirals', where China and the U.S. scale down their rivalry in a step-by-step process that reduces Beijing's fears, while gradually limiting Washington's influence. One powerful criticism of this (which Goldstein openly acknowledges) is that it can be interpreted as 'appeasement' by American allies, but more crucially by Beijing (Goldstein 2015). As previously stated China does have a solid record of compromise in its territorial disputes, however, the vast majority of its concessions took place at times of internal unrest and weakness (Fravel 2008). A much more powerful China, led by a man who openly calls for China to return to its past glory, may not be willing to reciprocate with a state that he perceives to be an extra-regional power meddling in China's neighbourhood. Furthermore, an American compromise could lead to a greatly diminished U.S. role in East Asia and would likely facilitate Chinese hegemony over the region. This could also lead to full-scale arms races as states prepare for an unknown future of Chinese dominance and a rapidly developing Chinese Monroe Doctrine. From a theoretical perspective, this approach would reduce points of friction between the U.S. and China, and while not terminating the rivalry, it would reduce the chances of escalatory spikes, which can be extremely harmful to bilateral relations. If the U.S. opts for this course of action, they could follow these recommendations.

Washington could limit support for regional Chinese rivals. This would require a reduced American naval footprint in the region as well as a scaling back of American troops and hardware from places such as South Korea and Japan. Washington can also continue to work with the PLAN using SHADE and RIMPAC exercises as a template. (This would also require a substantial effort on the part of Beijing.) Importantly, in the event of a North Korean collapse, a guarantee of no American troops in North Korea could be provided to Beijing.

On the Taiwan issue, Washington could limit support for Taipei and gradually reduce arms sales to Taipei. (This would be difficult due to U.S. law.) Even with this, Taiwan would still pose a significant obstacle, especially considering that the precedent of Beijing's current Hong Kong policy has been counterproductive for future 'reunification' talks. However, Washington could pick up from Jiang Zemin's 'Eight Points' and try to work from there (Shirk 2007).

A compromise/accommodation policy may actually work in Washington's favour. There is a strong possibility that China's rise will be curtailed by structural impediments that are internal to China. These range from challenges associated with demographics, to corruption, to long-term economic liabilities, to environmental degradation (Beckley 2011; Krober 2016; Naughton 2016; Bekkevold and Ross 2016). If this transpires, an American policy that seeks to accommodate China may find that China's assertive behaviour on the international stage is short-lived as the structural challenges begin to consume Chinese leaders attention and energy.

It is important to note that China spends more money on its internal security than it does on external security. In other words, for all of the hype surrounding yearly increases in the PLA budget, few take the time to point out that the CCP is more concerned about threats from its *own people*, than threats from foreign rivals (Fang 2016). A similar situation in the U.S. would see the FBI's annual budget soar to over 700 billion dollars. A state that is preoccupied with internal security and that faces significant unrest in the western half of the country is not a state that is ready to dominate the global stage.

China is punching well above its weight on the international stage, and the perceived isolationist stance by the departed Trump Administration allowed China, and, in particular, Xi Jinping, to act as the guardian of the global economic order, while also pretending that China is an easy place to conduct business and trade in a fair manner. Fortunately, the Biden administration has ceased this flirtation with isolationism and bigotry and appears to be embracing globalization.

Washington needs to realize that a state/government that is terrified by the likes of Google, Facebook, and the *New York Times,* and that frequently locks up lawyers who defend the rule of law/the Chinese Constitution, is not a state that is ready to pose a significant structural challenge to the international order. The U.S. must capitalize on these enormous deficiencies that are embedded in Chinese political culture and permeate the Chinese political system. By taking a more standoffish approach towards the rise of China, the U.S. would reduce tensions with Beijing, while being able to use a reduced American military presence as a major bargaining chip. The rivalry shows no sign of terminating, but the potential for it to be significantly reduced and, most importantly, avoid major points of escalation does exist.

Hybrid Approach to Policy Recommendations

As China continues to rise and its naval power increases, the U.S. has the option to both work with China and to resist its increasing hegemonic behaviour. In many ways, this is a fusion of the previous two approaches. For a hybrid approach to work, both China and the U.S. would have to make substantial changes in their policies and crucially, in their perceptions of each other. Reciprocity would be difficult but essential. Importantly, in this approach as with the compromise approach, the U.S. would be accepting the demise and eventually end of American military hegemony in East Asia. This may also entail the abandonment of American allies. If China's true intentions are indeed 'peaceful', this policy may work out well, but if China continues on its current path of the pursuit of regional hegemony, it will likely lead to the increased militarization of East Asia. Combined with territorial disputes, it will increase the likelihood of significant rivalry escalation and possible war.

An agreement by the U.S. to gradually decrease behaviour that China finds objectionable, such as spy plane activities close to China and maritime surveillance ships in disputed waters, would require China to reciprocate and cease spying on American entities as well as agree to solve many of its territorial disputes in a diplomatic manner. (This is unlikely.) Equally unlikely it would need an American acknowledgement of Chinese power and de-facto hegemony in East Asia. The issue of Taiwan would have to be addressed and the situation that prevailed from 2008 to 2016 would have to be restored with Beijing's full agreement. The U.S. could help nudge Taiwan closer to the Mainland, but Beijing would have to renounce the use of force as a tool of reunification.

Both China and the U.S. would need to pursue some form of Goldstein's 'cooperation spirals', where trust and cooperation are forged over time through small and reciprocal steps that eventually lead to more significant compromises (Goldstein 2015). In addition, the U.S would have to move away from security ties with regional states, and place more emphasis on economic ties. Importantly, clearly designated red lines would have to be drawn for both states. (Ex- invasion of Taiwan, further construction, and militarization in the South China Sea.)

Impact of Covid-19

A final note is in order on the impact of the Covid-19 pandemic on the rivalry. As of early 2022, the pandemic is far from over and the prevalence of Covid-19 may become a constant for the foreseeable future. The overall impact of the pandemic has been severe, but with the advent of powerful vaccines and a steady distribution of them, the structural impact of the pandemic may not be as debilitating and long-lasting as originally feared, especially on national economies. However, the political consequences will be longer-lasting and are related to the rivalry.

China's initial mishandling of the pandemic was partially rectified by Beijing by imposing a massive and successful lockdown throughout large parts of China. However, Beijing's refusal to allow an independent and unfettered investigation into China to study the origins of the virus has caused significant mistrust and alienation both worldwide and in neighbouring states (Silver et al. 2021; The World Needs 2021). While China's vaccine diplomacy is laudable, questions about the efficacy of Chinese vaccines have led numerous states to opt for Western vaccines that have performed better in both clinical and real-world trials (Wee and Myers

2021). Beijing's increasing aggressive 'wolf warrior' diplomacy has not helped China's image. A key question is how will the pandemic be perceived outside of China? As of June 2021, majorities in 15 of 17 Western countries hold negative views of China that are near historic highs. Importantly, 76 per cent of Americans view China 'unfavourably', while 88 per cent of Japanese and 78 per cent of Australians (both Quad members) also hold negative views (Silver et al. 2021).

Whether growing animosity towards China translates into rivalry escalation, has yet to be determined. However, if large numbers of bureaucrats and the general public in states engaged in a rivalry with China blame Beijing for Covid-19, this will harden public mistrust of China and will likely cause them to support a tougher stance on China. Such a situation, combined with an assertive China that believes its time has arrived to join the great power club, will almost certainly lead to escalation in China's various rivalries.

Policy Recommendations Conclusion

Overall, there are various measures China, India, and the U.S. can take in mitigating their strategic rivalries. The key issue, at least for the next decade and a half, is how will India and the U.S. respond to an increasingly stronger and assertive China? While China has many structural deficiencies that will begin to manifest themselves over the next couple of years and decades, the same is certainly true of India (Ganguly and Thompson 2017). A key question of international relations in the next half-century is how will China deal with its newfound power? American and Indian policy needs to be able to account for both an aggressive China that seeks to avenge what it perceives to be past indemnities, and a more liberal China that is primarily occupied with solving internal contradictions while openly embracing the international order. While pushing for the later, Indian and American policymakers are well-advised to hope for the best, but prepare for the worst.

Conclusion

The core puzzle that this book has sought to answer is what is driving naval modernization in contemporary China and India. Developing blue water naval power is a rare event as the requisite hardware costs tens, if not hundreds of billions of dollars and takes decades to come to fruition. Some states (increasingly Great Britain and France) opt for token platforms that have the ability to show the flag at distant ports and can take part in international naval exercises. Many states that were maritime powers are actively downsizing their navies and instead are maintaining just a few warships that can project power. China and India are different in this regard, as they are actively building blue water fleets and have plans for obtaining powerful platforms and submarines over the next 10–15 years. Given the strategic importance of these developments, it is surprising that there are very few studies on what is driving this process. Many scholars and analysts have offered explanations ranging from nationalism, to the security dilemma as drivers. Notably, they acknowledge that rivalry is present, but take it for granted and never specify what they mean by rivalry. Even fewer studies have attempted to dig into the details of modernization and offer a thorough account of this process. It was this gap in the literature that this project has attempted to fill. By providing a granular account of the dynamics of strategic rivalry this project has demonstrated that there are multiple drivers of this process, however rivalry is the most complete explanation.

Strategic rivalries have the ability to influence how decision makers view their enemies. Once a rivalry is initiated, it is difficult to terminate. Bureaucracies are also heavily influenced by rivalries and they tend to adopt worst-case scenario planning in order to protect their state from a rival. Bureaucratic actors can also play an important role in perpetuating a rivalry. This study has utilized the punctuated equilibrium model of rivalry maintenance and escalation. The model stipulates that once a rivalry commences it enters a 'lock in stage' that experiences relative periods of stability. These stable periods are occasionally ruptured by rivalry shocks, or critical junctures, which are crucial to understanding why decision makers decide on certain policies. The junctures dramatically increase threat perceptions of the rival and cause leaders to opt for specific policies. For the India case there are clear linkages between the Sino/U.S. rivalry and the Sino/Indian rivalry. In this configuration, Chinese naval modernization, which is a response to Chinese maritime rivalry escalation with the American navy, drives Indian naval modernization. As the PLAN rapidly modernizes and increases its forays into the IOR,

China's strategic rivalry with India experiences periods of escalation, thus causing Indian naval modernization. As Model 5.1 demonstrates, in the two cases under review, critical junctures and their accompanying increases in threat perceptions were a major, and in some cases, the primary cause of naval modernization.

Importantly, the maritime dimensions of these two rivalries did not just happen by chance. Both of the rivalries under review were originally spatial rivalries. The Sino/Indian rivalry was largely centred on the various territorial disputes between China and India on their shared Himalayan border, while the Sino/U.S. rivalry was heavily influenced by the status of Taiwan. As the rivalries evolved and as the states increased their power and influence, the contests developed into positional rivalries, while also retaining the spatial aspects of each rivalry. This book has traced the process of these disputes evolving into positional rivalries. The steady increase in rivalry escalation in the maritime domain was the leading cause of both naval modernization in the two cases, and the emergence of the positional rivalry.

The findings in this project also reinforce earlier scholarship that argues that past conflicts increase the chances of future conflict (Hensel 1999; Colaresi and Thompson 2002). In addition, in both rivalries I find evidence that the belief systems of the relevant bureaucracies have hardened, thus both perpetuating the rivalry and playing a contributing bureaucratic role as a driver of naval modernization. This evidence is also in line with McGinnis and Williams' argument that the history of a rivalry

Model 5.1 Rivalry Escalation and critical junctures in the Punctuated Equilibrium Model[a]

[a]The majority of critical junctures take place at sea, but they can take place in other areas.

to date serves as a driver of both maintenance and escalation (McGinnis and Williams 2001).

This project has not been a mechanical attempt to place naval modernization into a rivalry model. While many experts assumed that rivalry was a major cause of naval modernization in the two cases, no scholarly work had sought to prove this assumption. Through scrutiny of available resources and extensive fieldwork, which included in-depth focused interviews in multiple countries with some of the world's leading authorities on the Chinese and Indian navies, I found powerful evidence in support of the rivalry explanation.

India

Indian naval modernization is not on a par with the PLAN, but as demonstrated in the table on Indian naval hardware, it is making substantial progress in its ability to project power, and in increasing the lethality of its weapons systems. Interestingly, the IN is attempting to 'leap frog' from a coastal force to a blue water navy (Colley 2021B). The evidence presented in the India chapter casts significant doubt on counter-arguments such as nationalism, bureaucratic politics, and the security dilemma as primary drivers of the IN's push to the open ocean. In the India case the available evidence strongly points to the rivalry with China as the principal cause of IN modernization.

During the 1990s, naval development was a gradual effort that really did not take off until the end of the decade. However, as China's rise continued and it developed a navy capable of deterring the American navy, and as the Sino/Indian strategic rivalry experienced periodic points of rivalry escalation (primarily in the maritime domain), decision makers in New Delhi started to increase funding to the IN. This initiated a sustained effort to build a navy that would be able to increase the PLAN's vulnerability in the IOR. The force structure of the IN has evolved quickly into a navy that now boasts an aircraft carrier (with another one under construction), and over a dozen DDG's, frigates, and corvettes. In addition, the IN's undersea warfare programme is becoming increasingly sophisticated with the acquisition of advanced SSKs and an emerging nuclear submarine programme. While India may be punching above its weight considering its level of development, in terms of the lethality of its navy, it is the most powerful naval power in the IOR.[13]

The linkages between the two rivalries are clear. As the PLAN modernized and started to conduct patrols in the IOR, this significantly increased fears in India of 'Chinese encirclement'. These concerns, which constituted episodes of rivalry maintenance and escalation, are the driving force behind Indian naval modernization. As PLAN activities in the IOR have expanded enormously since 2005, and as the BRI gathers momentum, the Sino/Indian rivalry will likely remain firmly in place with regular periods of escalation. This will only increase calls for a more powerful and lethal Indian navy.

This project has also constructed a rivalry maintenance and escalation dataset between China and India for the years 1991–2020. This set tracks points of escalation and through interviews and examination of open-source materials has demonstrated how these events were perceived by decision makers in New Delhi. In the absence of a rivalry with China, the IN might still be engaged in some limited form of naval modernization, but the force structure would be different. India's traditional rival Pakistan is a land-based threat, and even the extremely limited maritime capabilities that the Pakistani navy, or terrorist groups supported by the Pakistani security apparatus do not justify the kinds of vessels the IN is commissioning. As made clear in the interview process, many of India's major naval purchases are China specific. In the absence of a critical (and visible) threat, it would be difficult for the Indian government to justify the billions of dollars necessary for the purchase and construction of nuclear-powered submarines and increasingly sophisticated surface combatants.

China

The PLAN has developed much faster than the IN, but in the early 1990s, it was also primarily a green water fleet with a large percentage of its hardware dating to the 1950s. Chinese naval modernization benefits from

---

[13] This would obviously not include the American navy.

much greater scholarly attention. However, as is the case with the IN, most writings on the PLAN have been policy-based, or has only briefly touched on the drivers of modernization. Arguments in favour of the security dilemma, bureaucratic politics, and nationalism have been put forward, but fail to fully explain modernization. Rivalry is almost always assumed, but never specified, and no scholarly work has attempted to dig into the history of China's rivalry with the U.S. and trace the process of naval modernization as it relates to the U.S.

This project has demonstrated that rivalry is the key driver of the PLAN. In the absence of a perceived critical threat emanating from the USN, the trajectory of the PLAN would be very different. Scholars of Sino/U.S. relations are well aware of the periods of intense rivalry escalation between the two states; however, few have closely examined how these shocks have influenced the development of the PLAN.

Based on a close study of open-source material and dozens of focused interviews with scholars of Chinese security and current and retired government officials, this project has found that arguments that compete with rivalry are at best only partial explanations.[14] Rivalry is the key driving force behind the PLAN evolution in force structure. In the absence of the Sino/U.S. rivalry, the PLAN would likely experience some form of modernization, but the force structure would be dramatically different. For example, the heavy investment in SSKs would be unnecessary in a security environment where access denial is not a pressing security issue. The development of SSBNs and SSNs is also closely linked to the rivalry.

Through a detailed dataset of rivalry maintenance and escalation, I have shown that certain episodes of rivalry escalation were instrumental in moulding decision maker's perceptions of the U.S. These were crucial in determining naval procurement. For example, the 1995/96 Taiwan Crisis was a critical juncture that shaped the Chinese leaderships views on the U.S., and more importantly, how they must deal with the Americans. Subsequent events such as the Belgrade embassy bombing and the announcement of 'The Pivot', only confirmed Chinese suspicions

---

[14] These interviews and discussions cover the period from 2006 to 2018. Interviews and discussions conducted from 2006 to 2008 were from this author's Master's Thesis at Renmin University of China.

of American attempts to contain China. This narrative has influenced some of the other partial drivers such as bureaucratic politics and nationalism, but the key explanatory variable is rivalry.

Comparison to Other Cases

The development of powerful naval power is a rare event. Even rarer is the development of a navy that has the ability to project power in the open ocean. The German navy of the late 19th and early 20th centuries does share certain characteristics with my cases. The Germans developed their fleet both to defend the German coast and to cause the British to hesitate when considering attacking Germany in the maritime domain. The primary goal of this strategy was to construct a powerful enough fleet that would be able to inflict significant damage on a rival's navy, thus dissuading the rival from attacking in the first place. Both China and India have followed this logic, and have recently expanded their fleets into more blue water capable platforms and submarines.

The experience of the USSR is also interesting to take into account. The 1962 Cuban missile crisis was a critical juncture in Moscow's rivalry with the U.S. This event was a major catalyst for the development of the Soviet navy's efforts at projecting power (Kurth 2007). The critical junctures in the Sino/U.S. rivalry in the 1990s played a similar role in Beijing's decision to build and purchase a powerful navy. By the 2000s, this started to take the form of Chinese naval power projection. While there was no Taiwan incident or Cuban Missile Crisis in India's rivalry with China, the 1962 war and the increasing instances of PLAN forays into the IOR as well as significant rivalry escalation at sea with China, led to similar calls in New Delhi to construct a powerful navy.

The cases of Germany and the USSR have a key difference with India and China. Both Germany and the USSR were land powers that continued to face threats emanating from land. The Germans had to worry about the rest of Europe, as well as the British fleet, while the Soviets had to deal with Europe and from the early 1960s until close to the demise of the USSR, the threat posed by China. While both China and India face land threats from each other, their traditional threats from other land powers have been greatly diminished. For India, Pakistan is more of an irritant in terms of its ability to seriously threaten India in a conventional land war. For China, the threat from Russia is also greatly reduced. What this means is that both China and India have the ability to invest far greater resources into their respective navies than did Germany or the USSR. In addition, the USSR struggled to finance a powerful blue water navy. This does not mean that the cases of China and India are unique, but it does support the argument that their forms of naval modernization are rare.

Limitations of This Study

This study utilized multiple methodological approaches to the study of naval modernization. Open-source material ranging from government White Papers, to Office of Naval Intelligence reports were scrutinized to help establish causality. I also relied on the scholarly community for their academic research in both theoretical and area-specific publications. Many of these books and articles were extremely helpful to this project. I also relied on speeches by government officials to assist in my research. Frequently these speeches either directly or indirectly called out a rival as a driver of naval modernization. Perhaps the greatest asset to this project is the in-depth focused interviews with a wide range of experts. Unfortunately, I am unable to name them, but many of these individuals have deep knowledge of how decision makers perceive their rivals, and more importantly, how leaders decide to counter them. Multiple people interviewed for this project had direct knowledge of the decision-making process.

While I was able to access influential individuals and speak with them, there are many unknowns in this project. Crucially, the subject matter of this project is of a sensitive nature. While it is not always considered secret, much of the decision-making process that goes into procurement of naval hardware is not publically available. This is true even in open democracies such as the U.S. In the case of China, this is even more difficult to uncover. During the fieldwork stage in China, dozens of people approached for interviews did not even respond to enquiries. Many of these scholars and think-tank experts have very detailed knowledge of the procurement process of naval platforms. With the exceptions of brief encounters at conferences, I was not able to speak with a single active duty PLAN officer. However, I was able to have many conversations with members of the foreign military attaché corp. I overcame some of these obstacles by interviewing people with direct knowledge of naval acquisition and many of their analyses were congruent. Over the course of this project I found that many Chinese language sources referenced in various English language publications were no longer publically available. Because of this several citations make reference to the original source while acknowledging the English language publication where it was cited.

The fine details of procurement in India, and especially China, may never be known. However, this book has helped to shed light on one of the more important security developments of the 21st century. Understanding precisely why China and India are building powerful navies demands more than an assumption of rivalry, or the security dilemma. It demands a deep and comprehensive examination of various explanations and a careful analysis of each argument.

Contribution

This book has contributed to the field in multiple ways. In terms of the rivalry research programme, it extends the explanatory power of rivalries to the maritime domain by arguing they are a major cause of naval modernization. This is done through the utilization of the punctuated equilibrium model, which shows how rivalries evolve and how major points of escalation can cause threat perceptions to soar, thus driving naval modernization. Importantly, for the two cases under review, rivalry was assumed a driver, however, no study had ever investigated whether rivalry was a major driver. I have also constructed two original data sets that track rivalry maintenance and escalation between India and China and between China and the U.S. These datasets not only list specific events with brief descriptions between 1991 and 2020, but of equal importance, they identify which events are viewed as critical junctures for the push for naval modernization. In addition, this book demonstrates the interconnectedness of the Sino/U.S. rivalry to the Sino/Indian rivalry, it shows that the two rivalries do not exist in a vacuum and that events in one rivalry frequently have a significant influence on another rivalry.

In the area studies literature I also make several contributions. For both China and India I take the drivers beyond the assumptions of rivalry and investigate why rivalry matters. In both states I examined the main arguments and found that in the absence of a rivalry, naval modernization was much less likely to go forward in the form that we are witnessing. For the China case, I debunk nationalism as a primary driver. Little evidence supported perceptions of Chinese leaders building a navy because they are beholden to a nationalistic public. Of equal importance, scant evidence was found to support the 'Mianzi' (face) argument that naval procurement is the result of demonstrating to neighbouring states that China is a great power. These findings challenge the argument that nationalism is a powerful guiding force in China's foreign and security affairs.

I also question the utility of theoretical arguments based on the security dilemma and the bureaucratic politics models in both cases. As demonstrated, the security dilemma is difficult to prove and in the India/China case there is scant evidence of its existence, while in the China/U.S. case there is limited (but increasing) evidence that this is present. I also debunk bureaucratic politics approaches by showing that the military, and especially the naval bureaucracy in India, has little influence at the top levels of power. In the China case, I show a similar situation where the PLAN has largely been locked out of the formal top levels of power. Ultimately, this book goes beyond the assumptions and delivers a detailed account of naval modernization in the two states under review.

An Emerging Triangle?

A final note is required on the prospects of an emerging strategic triangle. There is a possibility of this transpiring, and if it does, it will open up some very interesting theoretical insights into rivalry dynamics as well as strategic hedging and balancing. As mentioned above, it is premature to label the evolving dynamic between China, the U.S., and India as a triangle. However, if Beijing continues to escalate the rivalry with India (from India's perspective), various domestic constituencies in India may drop their apprehension of joining with Washington to form some form of partnership designed to counter Chinese influence in the region. Large political and ideological obstacles would have to be overcome for this to happen, but if China's BRI continues to raise concerns in New Delhi, and the PLAN's forays keep increasing in the IOR, this could become a more realistic possibility in the future.

In addition, the possibility of these contests transitioning into ideological rivalries is not currently feasible. For such a rivalry to emerge it would need to be contested over different belief systems that are based on economic, political, societal, or even religious activities (Colaresi et al 2007). While there is speculation that the 'China model' is a rival to the West, there is little evidence that such a model actually exists (Kennedy 2010). The story of China's economic rise does not resemble in any consistent form a linear systematic process that has been articulated and executed (Huang 2008; Kroeber 2016). Instead, it is best seen as a process of trial and error, or as Deng Xiaoping pointed out, it is 'crossing the river by feeling the stones'. In other words, there is scant evidence that there is an actual model that is capable of being emulated by other states.

Overall, naval modernization does not happen by chance. It requires an enormous amount of political and economic capital as well as a long-term ambition and dedication to be able to project power to distant parts of the world. This book has demonstrated that in the absence of a rivalry naval modernization is less likely. In the absence of a strategic threat, states are not inclined to invest the massive amount of resources that modernization requires. Given the current geopolitical trends and the increasing power of China and India, the study of naval power and maritime rivalry will continue to occupy scholars and policymakers.

APPENDIX

General Questions during Interviews

Fieldwork Information

1. What do you see as the main driver/drivers of Chinese/Indian naval modernization?
2. Do you see nationalism or bureaucratic politics as a main driver?
3. What events over the past 25 years do you see as major points of escalation in your rivalry with the other state? Does this contribute to naval modernization?
4. Are specific platforms being developed to oppose your rival?
5. Where do you see your state's navy in the next 5–10 years?

These questions were helpful to advance the conversation and frequently led to a more fine-grained discussion on the topic. Importantly, and especially for the China case, no interview was conducted with more than one person physically present. For the fieldwork in New Delhi, only one interview consisted of two people. For interviews with American experts, some interviews were conducted over the phone. Below is a breakdown of where the fieldwork and interviews took place.

Fieldwork

New Delhi: (Primary research May and June 2016. As well as brief visits afterwards) Interviews were conducted in New Delhi where I was based at the Observer Research Foundation's (ORF) New Delhi office. I made extensive use of ORF's contacts and resources as well as their resident experts. Interviewees consisted of New Delhi based academics who specialize in security and China, think-tank analysts, former Indian Ambassadors, active duty and retired military personnel, as well foreign experts in New Delhi.

China: (Primary research 2016– 2018) I was based in Beijing and conducted in-depth interviews with actors including Chinese academics, Chinese think-tank scholars, and journalists who cover security issues. Apart from Chinese sources, I spoke with and interviewed current and retired members of the foreign military attaché corps, foreign diplomats, and long-term foreign journalists who cover issues related to Chinese security. These retired attachés included naval captains and generals from the American military.[1] I was able to access people in China through both my personal connections from my living and working in China (2002–2012) as

---

[1] Please see below for a description of interviewees.

well as help from my host institution and the use of snowball sampling from people I interviewed.

It needs to be mentioned that access was at times difficult in Beijing. Many individuals I approached told me they could not speak on the topic to a foreigner. I was able to contact several former PLAN admirals over the phone who were happy to speak with me as long as I received permission from the Ministry of Defense. The process of selecting Chinese experts and the difficulty of finding ones willing to talk to a foreigner is an important methodological challenge. Many of those who did speak with me have spent significant time overseas and are accustomed to speaking to foreigners about security issues. It is possible that they were deliberately providing me with misinformation; however, I do not believe this to be the case. What they told me was very similar to what other experts outside of China said and is in many ways congruent with official government statements.

Works Cited

1. Admiral Sunil Lanba. Comments at the 2019 Raisina Dialogue. January 9, 2019. New Delhi. India.
2. 'AirSea Battle.' United States Department of Defense. Washington D.C. May 2013. Accessed on January 25, 2018. https://www.defense.gov/Portals/1/Documents/pubs/ASB-ConceptImplementation-Summary-May-2013.pdf
3. Allen, Kenneth. Saunders, Philip C. Chen, John. 'Chinese Military Diplomacy, 2003–2016: Trends and Implications.' China Strategic Perspectives 11. National Defense University Press. Series Editor: Phillip C. Saunders. Washington D.C. July 17, 2017. Accessed on May 26, 2018. 1–96. http://ndupress.ndu.edu/Media/News/Article/1249864/chinese-military-diplomacy-20032016-trends-and-implications/
4. Allison, Graham. Zelikow, Philip. *Essence of Decision*. New York. Pearson. 1999.
5. Annual Report to Congress. 'Military Power of the People's Republic of China 2008.' Office of the Secretary of Defense. United States' Government. Washington D.C. Accessed on August 27, 2021. 1–66. chrome-extension://oemmndcbldboiebfnladdacbdfmadadm/https://nuke.fas.org/guide/china/dod-2008.pdf
6. Annual Report to Congress. Military and Security Developments Involving the People's Republic of China. Office of the Secretary of Defense. United States Department of Defense. Washington D.C. May 15, 2017. 100–106. Accessed on March 5, 2020. https://dod.defense.gov/Portals/1/Documents/pubs/2017_China_Military_Power_Report.PDF
7. Bajpal, Kanti. 'Narendra Modi's Pakistan and China Policy: Assertive Bilateral Diplomacy, Active Coalition Diplomacy.' *International Affairs*. Vol. 93. No. I. 2017. 69–91.
8. Baum, Matthew A. Potter, Philip. 'The Relationships between Mass Media, Public Opinion, and Foreign Policy: Toward a Theoretical Synthesis.' *Annual Review of Political Science*. Vol. 11. June 2008. 39–65.
9. Baum, Richard. 'From "Strategic Partners," to "Strategic Competitors": George W. Bush and the Politics of U.S. China Policy.' *Journal of East Asian Studies*. Vol. 1. No. 2. August 2001. 191–200.
10. Beasley, Ryan. 'Collective Interpretations: How Problem Representations Aggregate in Foreign Policy Groups.' In the Donald A. Sylvan and James F. Voss ed. *Problem Representation in Foreign Policy Decision Making*. New York. Cambridge University Press. 1998. 80–115.
11. Becker, Jeffrey. 'China Maritime Report No. 11: Securing China's Lifelines across the Indian Ocean.' China Maritime Studies Institute. U.S. Naval War College. CMSI China Maritime Reports. Newport RI. December 2020. Accessed on March 16, 2021. 1–17. chrome-extension://oemmndcbldboiebfnladdacbdfmadadm/https://digital-commons.usnwc.edu/cgi/viewcontent.cgi?article=1010&context=cmsi-maritime-reports

12. Beckley, Michael. 'China's Century? Why America's Edge Will Endure.' *International Security*. Vol. 36. No. 3. Winter 2011–2012. 41–78.

13. Beckley, Michael. 'The Emerging Military Balance in East Asia.' *International Security*. Vol. 42. No 2. Fall 2017. 78–119.

14. Bekkevold, Jo Inge. Ross, Robert S. 'New Leaders, Stronger China, Harder Choices.' In the Robert S. Ross and Jo Inge Bekkevold ed. *China in the Era of Xi Jinping*. Washington D.C. Georgetown University Press. 2016. 265–278.

15. Bhaskar, Uday C. 'The Navy as an Instrument of Foreign Policy: The Indian Experience.' In the Harsh Pant ed, *The Rise of the Indian Navy*. New York. Routledge. 2012. 41–54.

16. Bickford, Thomas J. 'The Chinese Military and Its Business Operations: The PLA as Entrepreneur.' *Asian Survey*. May 1994. Vol. 34. No. 5. 460–474.

17. Blasko, Dennis J. 'The 2015 Chinese Defense White Paper on Strategy Perspective.' *The Jamestown Foundation*. Vol. XV. No. 12. June 19, 2015.

18. Brewster, David. 'India and China at Sea.' *Asia Policy*. No. 22. Seattle. National Bureau of Asian Research. July 2016. 4–10.

19. Bussert, James C. Elleman, Bruce A. *People's Liberation Army Navy*. Annapolis. Naval Institute Press. 2011.

20. Cai, Penghong. 'The Impact and Challenges of the "2+2" Dialogue and Security Cooperation between the United States and India.' *Contemporary World*. No. 11. 2018. 38–42. 蔡鹏鸿. "美印"2+2"对话和安全合作对印太安全的影响和挑战." 当代世界.2018年第11期. 38-42.

21. Capoccia, Giovanni R. Kelemen, Daniel. 'The Study of Critical Junctures: Theory Narrative and Counterfactuals in Historical Intuitionalism.' *World Politics*. Vol. 59. No. 3. April 2007. 341–369.

22. Carlson, Christopher P. 'PLAN Force Structure Projection Concept.' China Maritime Studies Institute. China Maritime Report No. 10. U.S. Naval War College. Newport RI. November 2020. Accessed on June 23, 2021. 1–15. https://digital-commons.usnwc.edu/cmsi-maritime-reports/10/

23. Carlson, Christopher P. Bainchi, Jack. 'Warfare Drivers.' In the Andrew Erickson ed. *Chinese Naval Shipbuilding*. Annapolis Md. Naval Institute Press. 2017. 19–40.

24. Chellany, Brahma. 'India Needs to Build Sufficient Naval Prowess in the Indian Ocean.' *Hindustan Times*. March 12, 2015. Accessed on June 13, 2017. http://www.hindustantimes.com/ht-view/india-needs-to-build-sufficient-naval-prowess-in-indian-ocean/story-EDq0qtVSMZz86lKRFEiLMO.html

25. Chen Xiangyang. 'Draw Up New Greater Periphery' Strategy as Soon as Possible,' *Liaowang*, 29 July 17, 2006. 64. 陈向阳. "尽快制定新的"大周边"战略." 瞭望新闻周刊 29 2006. 64.

26. Cheung, Tai Ming. *Fortifying China*. Ithaca. Cornell University Press. 2009.

27. Cheung, Tai Ming. 'The Riddle in the Middle: China's Central Military Commission in the Twenty-first Century.' In the Philip C Saunders and Andrew Scobell eds. *PLA Influence on China's National Security Policymaking*. Stanford, California. Stanford University Press. 2015. 84–119.

28. 'China's Military Strategy 2015.' *Xinhua*. Information Office of the State Council of the People's Republic of China. Beijing. Accessed on March 5, 2020. http://english.www.gov.cn/archive/white_paper/2015/05/27/content_281475115610833.htm

29. 'China's National Defense in 2000.' Information Office of the State Council of the People's Republic of China. Beijing. October 2000. Accessed on March 5, 2020. http://china.org.cn/e-white/2000/index.htm

30. 'China's National Defense in 2002.' Information Office of the State Council of the People's Republic of China. Beijing. October 2002. Accessed on March 5, 2020. http://china.org.cn/e-white/20021209/index.htm

31. 'China's National Defense in 2004.' Information Office of the State Council of the People's Republic of China. Beijing. October 2004. Accessed on March 5, 2020. http://www.china.org.cn/e-white/20041227/

32. 'Chinese naval fleets escort 3,400 foreign ships over past 10 years.' *XinhuaNet*. January 1, 2019. Accessed on November 24, 2019. http://www.xinhuanet.com/english/2019-01/01/c_137712892.htm

33. Christensen, Thomas J. 'Fostering Stability of Creating a Monster? The Rise of China and U.S. Policy toward East Asia.' *International Security*, Vol. 31. No. 1. Summer 2006. 81–126.

34. Christensen, Thomas J. 'Obama and Asia.' *Foreign Affairs*. September/October 2015. Accessed on January 25, 2018. https://www.foreignaffairs.com/articles/asia/obama-and-asia

35. Cohen, Stephen. Dasgupta, Sunil. *Arming Without Aiming*. Washington D.C. Brookings Press. 2010.

36. Cohen, Warren. *America's Response to China*. New York. Columbia University Press. 2010.

37. Colaresi, Michael. Thompson, William. 'Hot Spots or Hot Hands? Serial Crisis Behavior, Escalating Risks, and Rivalry.' *The Journal of Politics*. Vol. 64. No. 4. November 2002. 1175–1198.

38. Colaresi, Michael P. Rasler, Karen. Thompson, William. *Strategic Rivalries in World Politics*. Cambridge. Cambridge University Press. 2007.

39. Cole, Bernard. *Asian Maritime Strategies*. Annapolis. Md. Naval Institute Press. 2013.

40. Cole, Bernard. *China's Quest for Great Power*. Annapolis Md. Naval Institute Press. 2016.

41. Colley, Christopher. 'A Future Chinese Indian Ocean Fleet?' *War on the Rocks*. April 2, 2021D. Accessed August 24, 2021. https://warontherocks.com/2021/04/a-future-chinese-indian-ocean-fleet/

42. Colley, Christopher K. 'China's Ongoing Debates about India and the United States.' *Asia Dispatches*. June 30, 2020. Accessed on January 6, 2021. https://www.wilsoncenter.org/blog-post/chinas-ongoing-debates-about-india-and-united-states

43. Colley, Christopher K. 'How Politically Influential Is China's Military?' *The Diplomat*. April 27, 2019B. Accessed on November 19, 2019. https://thediplomat.com/2019/04/how-politically-influential-is-chinas-military/

44. Colley, Christopher K. 'Is America Now Directly Arming Against China?' *The Diplomat*. August 2, 2019A. Accessed on November 19, 2019. https://thediplomat.com/2019/08/is-america-now-directly-arming-against-china/

45. Colley, Christopher K. 'The Emerging Great Power Triangle: China, India and the United States in the Indian Ocean Region. In the Abraham Denmark and Lucas Myers ed. "Essays on the Rise of China and Its Implications". *The*

Wilson Center. Washington D.C. 2021B. 66–86. Accessed on August 20, 2021. https://www.wilsoncenter.org/publication/2020-21-wilson-china-fellowship-essays-rise-china-and-its-implications

46. Colley, Christopher K. 'The Transformation of the Indo-China Rivalry in the Twenty-First Century.' In the Aparna Apande ed. *Routledge Handbook on South Asian Foreign Policy.* Routledge. New York. 2021A. 267–280.

47. Colley, Christopher K. 'Why China's PLA Will Not Replace the Americans in the Middle East.' *The Diplomat.* November 1, 2019C. Accessed on November 24, 2019. https://thediplomat.com/2019/11/why-chinas-pla-will-not-replace-the-americans-in-the-middle-east/

48. Colley, Christopher K. Hosur Suhas, Prashant. 'India-China and Their War Making Capabilities.' *Journal of Asian Security and International Affairs.* Vol. 8. No. 1. 33–61. February 28, 2021.

49. Colley, Christopher K. Ganguly, Sumit. 'The Evolution of India's Look East Policy and China's Maritime Silk Road Initiative.' In the Jean-Marc F. Blanchard ed. *China's Maritime Silk Road Initiative and Southeast Asia.* Palgrave Macmillan. Singapore. 2019. 219–246.

50. Congressional Research Service. 'Navy Virginia (SSN-774) Class Attack Submarine Procurement: Background and Issues for Congress.' Washington D.C. November 13, 2019. Accessed on November 19, 2019. https://fas.org/sgp/crs/weapons/RL32418.pdf

51. Corbett, Sir Julian. *Some Principles of Maritime Strategy.* Annapolis Md. Naval Institute Press. 1988.

52. Cordner, Lee. 'Progressing Maritime Security Cooperation in the Indian Ocean.' *Naval War College Review.* Vol. 64. No. 4. Autumn 2011. 68–88.

53. Diehl, Paul. Goertz, Gary. *War and Peace in International Rivalry.* Ann Arbor. University of Michigan Press. 2000.

54. Dittmer, Lowell. 'The Strategic Triangle.' *World Politics.* Vol. 33. No. 4. July 1981. 485–515.

55. 'Djibouti Base: Don't Underestimate or Overestimate It.' *The Global Times.* July 7, 2017. '吉布提基地: 莫小视也别夸大它.' 环球时报. Accessed on January 28, 2018. http://opinion.huanqiu.com/editorial/2017-07/10966656.html

56. Doshi, Rush. *The Long Game.* Oxford University Press. New York. 2021.

57. Dutta, Prabash K. 'Chinese Military Drill in Indian Ocean: Much Ado about Nothing.' *India Today.* February 22, 2018. Accessed on September 13, 2019. https://www.indiatoday.in/india/story/chinese-military-drill-in-indian-ocean-much-ado-about-nothing-1175417-2018-02-22

58. *Ensuring Secure Seas: Indian Maritime Security Strategy.* Integrated Headquarters Ministry of Defense. New Delhi. 2015 Accessed on February 16, 2020. https://www.indiannavy.nic.in/sites/default/files/Indian_Maritime_Security_Strategy_Document_25Jan16.pdf

59. Erickson, Andrew S. Denmark, Abrham M. Collins, Gabriel. 'Beijing's Starter Carrier and Future Steps.' *Naval War College Review.* Winter 2012. Vol. 65. No. 1. 15–54.

60. Erickson, Andrew S. Ray, Jonathan. Forte, Robert T. 'Underpowered.' In the Andrew Erickson ed. *Chinese Naval Shipbuilding.* Annapolis. Md. Naval Institute Press. 2017. 238–248.

61. Erickson, Andrew S. Goldstein, Lyle J. Murry, William S. Wilson, Andrew R. 'Introduction.' In the Andrew Erickson, Lyle Goldstein, William S. Murry, and Andrew R. Wilson eds. *China's Future Nuclear Submarine Force*. Annapolis Md. Naval Institute Press. 2007. ix–xvi.

62. Erickson, Andrew S. 'China's Naval Modernization: Implications and Recommendations.' *Congressional Testimony*. December 11, 2013. Accessed on December 5, 2017. 1–15. http://docs.house.gov/meetings/AS/AS28/20131211/101579/HHRG-113-AS28-Wstate-EricksonA-20131211.pdf

63. Erickson, Andrew. 'Exhibit 0-2. China's Primary Naval Order of Battle (Major Combatants), 1985–2030.' In the Andrew Erickson ed. *Chinese Naval Shipbuilding*. Annapolis Md. Naval Institute Press. Annapolis 2017B. XVI–XVII.

64. Erickson, Andrew. 'Introduction.' In the Andrew Erickson ed. *Chinese Naval Shipbuilding*. Annapolis Md. Naval Institute Press. Annapolis Md. 2017A. 1–16.

65. Erickson, Andrew. 'Rising Tide, Dispersing Waves: Opportunities and Challenges for Chinese Seapower Development.' *Journal of Strategic Studies*. Volume 37, Issue 3. May 2014. 372–402.

66. Erickson, Andrew. Collins, Gabriel. 'Dragon Tracks: Emerging Chinese Access Points in the Indian Ocean Region.' Center for Strategic and International Studies. June 18, 2015. Accessed on June 7, 2017. https://amti.csis.org/dragon-tracks-emerging-chinese-access-points-in-the-indian-ocean-region/

67. Erickson, Andrew. Goldstein, Lyle. 'China's Future Nuclear Submarine Force.' In the Andrew Erickson, Lyle J. Goldstein, William S Murry, and Andrew Wilson eds. *China's Future Nuclear Submarine Force*. Annapolis Md. Naval Institute Press. 2007. 182–211.

68. Erickson, Andrew. Wilson, Andrew R. 'China's Aircraft Carrier Dilemma.' In the Andrew Erickson, Lyle J. Goldstein, William S Murry, and Andrew Wilson eds. *China's Future Nuclear Submarine Force*. Annapolis Md. Naval Institute Press. 2007. 229–269.

69. Fanell, James E. 'Strike Groups with Chinese Characteristics.' *Proceedings*. Vol. 146/3/1,405. March 2020. Accessed on January 19, 2021. https://www.usni.org/magazines/proceedings/2020/march/strike-groups-chinese-characteristics

70. Fanell, James E. Cheney-Peters, Scott. 'Maximal Scenario.' In the Andrew Erickson ed. *Chinese Naval Shipbuilding*. Annapolis Md. Naval Institute Press. 2017. 261–273.

71. Fang, Frank. 'China Continues Vast Spending on Domestic Security.' *Epoch Times*. March 6, 2016. Accessed on December 31, 2017. https://m-news.theepochtimes.com/china-continues-vast-spending-on-domestic-security_1984944.html

72. Farmer, Ben. 'Royal navy has "woefully low" number of warships that risk leaving Britain vulnerable, MPs warn.' *The Telegraph*. November 21, 2016. Accessed on March 24, 2017. http://www.telegraph.co.uk/news/2016/11/21/royal-navy-has-woefully-low-number-of-warships-that-risks-leavin/

73. Fewsmith, Joseph. 'The 19th Party Congress: Ringing in Xi Jinping's New Age.' *The China Leadership Monitor*. Winter 2018. No. 55. 1–22 Accessed on February 4, 2018. https://www.hoover.org/sites/default/files/research/docs/clm55-jf-final.pdf
http://www.tandfonline.com/doi/pdf/10.1080/01402390500088627?needAccess=true

74. Gady, Franz-Stefan. 'India's New Attack Subs to Be Fitted with Imported Air Independent Propulsion System.' *The Diplomat*. December 5, 2019. Accessed on December 9, 2019. https://thediplomat.com/2019/12/indias-new-attack-subs-to-be-fitted-with-imported-air-independent-propulsion-system/

75. Fravel, Taylor. *Active Defense*. Princeton. Princeton University Press. 2019.

76. Fravel, Taylor M. 'Stability in a Secondary Strategic Direction.' In the Kanti, Bajpai. Selina Ho, and Manjari Chatterjee Miller eds. *Routledge Handbook of China-India Relations*. New York. Routledge. 2020. 169–179.

77. Fravel, Taylor. *Strong Border, Secure Nation*. Princeton. Princeton University Press. 2008.

78. Fravel, Taylor. 'The PLA and the National Security Decision making: Insights from China's Territorial and Maritime Disputes.' In Philip Saunders and Andrew Scobell eds. *PLA Influence on China's National Security Policymaking*. Stanford. Stanford University Press. 2015. 249–273.

79. Freedberg, Sydney J. 'Navy Warships Get New Heavy Missile: 2,500 LB LRASM.' *Breaking Defense*. July, 26, 2017. Accessed on December 9, 2017. https://breakingdefense.com/2017/07/navy-warships-get-new-heavy-missile-2500-lb-lrasm/

80. Ganguly, Rajat. 'India's Military: Evolution, Modernization and Transformation.' *India Quarterly*. Vol. 71. No. 3. 2015. 187–205.

81. Ganguly, Sumit. Mason, Chris M. 'An Unnatural Partnership? The Future of U.S.-India Strategic Cooperation.' U.S. Army War College Press. Carlisle Pennsylvania. May 2019.

82. Ganguly, Sumit. Thompson, William. *Ascending India and Its State Capacity: Extraction, Violence and Legitimacy*. New Haven. Yale University Press. 2017.

83. Garver, John. Wang, Feiling. 'China's Anti-encirclement Struggle.' *Asian Security*. Vol. 6. No. 3. 2010. 238–261.

84. Garver, John. *China's Quest*. New York. Oxford University Press. 2016.

85. Garver, John W. 'China's Rise and the Eurasian Transportation Revolution.' In the Jean-Marc F. Blanchard ed. *China's Maritime Silk Road Initiative and South Asia*. Singapore. Palgrave. 2018. 33–54.

86. Garver, John. 'Limitations on China's Ability to Understand Indian Apprehensions about China's Rise as a Naval Power.' In the David Brewster ed. *India and China at Sea*. New Delhi. Oxford University Press. 2018. 75–89.

87. Garver, John. *The Protracted Contest*. Seattle. University of Washington Press. 2001.

88. Gilboy, George. Heginbotham, Eric. *Chinese and Indian Strategic Behavior*. New York. Cambridge University Press. 2012.

89. Glaser, Bonnie S. 'The PLA Role in China's Taiwan Policymaking.' In the Philip C Saunders and Andrew Scobell eds. *PLA Influence on China's National Security Policymaking*. Stanford CA. Stanford University Press. 2015. 166–197.

90. Glosny, Michael A. Saunders, Philip C. 'Debating China's Naval Nationalism.' *International Security*. Vol. 35. No. 2. Fall 2010. 161–175.

91. Glosny, Michael A. 'Strangulation from Sea.' *International Security*. Vol. 28. No. 4. Spring 2004. 125–160.

92. Goertz, Gary. Jones, Bradford. Diehl, Paul. 'Maintenance Processes in International Rivalries.' *Journal of Conflict Resolution*. Vol. 49. No. 5. 2005. 742–769.

93. Goldstein, Lyle. *Meeting China Halfway*. Washington D.C. Georgetown University Press. 2015.

94. Goldstein, Lyle. Murry, William. 'Undersea Dragons.' *International Security*. Vol. 28. No. 4. Spring 2004. 161–196.

95. Grare, Frederic. *India Turns East*. New York. Oxford University Press. 2017.

96. Green, Michael. *By More Than Providence*. New York. Columbia University Press. 2017.

97. Green, Michael. Szechenyi, Nicholas. 'Power and Order in Asia.' The Center for Strategic and International Studies. New York. Rowman and Littlefield. July 2014. Accessed on December 2, 2017. https://csis-prod.s3.amazonaws.com/s3fs-public/legacy_files/files/publication/140605_Green_PowerandOrder_WEB.pdf

98. Gries, Peter Hays. *China's New Nationalism*. University of California Press. Berkeley. 2004.

99. Gurang, Shaurya Karanbir. '14 Chinese Navy Ships Spotted in Indian Ocean, Indian Navy Monitoring Locations.' *The Economic Times*. July 12, 2018. Accessed on November 11, 2019. https://economictimes.indiatimes.com/news/defence/14-chinese-navy-ships-spotted-in-indian-ocean-indian-navy-monitoring-locations/articleshow/61882634.cms?from=mdr

100. Hall, Ian. *Modi and the Reinvention of Indian Foreign Policy*. Bristol University Press. Bristol. 2019.

101. Hamilton, C.I. *Anglo-French Naval Rivalry, 1840–1870*. Oxford. Clarendon Press. 1993.

102. Haokip, Thongkholal. 'India's Look East Policy: Its Evolution and Approach.' *South Asian Survey*. Vol. 18. No. 2. 2011. 239–257.

103. Heath, Timothy R. Thompson, William. 'Avoiding U.S.-China Competition in Futile: Why the Best Option Is to Manage Strategic Rivalry.' *Asia Policy*. Vol. 13. No. 2. April 2018. 91–120.

104. Hensel, Paul. 'An Evolutionary Approach to the Study of Interstate Rivalry.' *Conflict Management and Peace Science*. Vol. 17. No. 2. 1999. 175–206.

105. Hersh, Seymour M. 'The Online Threat.' *The New Yorker*. November 1, 2010. Accessed on January 25, 2018. https://www.newyorker.com/magazine/2010/11/01/the-online-threat

106. Herwig, Holger H. 'Imperial Germany: Continental Titan, Global Aspirant.' In the Andrew S. Erickson, Lyle L. Goldstein and Carnes Lord eds. *China Goes to Sea*. Annapolis. Naval Institute Press. 2009. 170–198.

107. Holmes, James R. 'The State of The U.S.-China Competition.' In the Thomas G. Mahnken ed. *Competitive Strategies for the 21st Century*. Stanford. Stanford University Press. 2012. 131–146.

108. Holmes, James R. Yoshihara, Toshi. 'China's Naval Ambitions in the Indian Ocean.' *The Journal of Strategic Studies*. Vol. 31. No. 3, June 2008. 367–394.

109. Holmes, James R. Yoshihara, Toshi. 'China's Navy: A Turn to Corbett?' *Proceedings Magazine*. December 2010. Volume 136/12/1,294

110. Holmes, James R. Yoshihara, Toshi. 'Redlines for Sino-Indian Naval Rivalry.' In the John Garofano and Andrew J. Dew eds. *Deep Currents and Rising Tides. Georgetown University Press. Washington DC.* 2013. 185–209.

111. Holmes, James R. Yoshihara, Toshi. 'Strongman, Constable, or Free-Rider? India's "Monroe Doctrine" and Indian Naval Strategy.' *Comparative Strategy.* Vol. 28. No. 4. 2009. 332–348.

112. Holslag, Jonathan. *China and India.* New York. Columbia University Press. 2010.

113. Holzman, Franklyn D. 'Are the Soviets Really Outspending the U.S. on Defense?' *International Security.* Vol. 4. No. 4. Spring 1980. 86–104.

114. Huang, Yasheng. *Capitalism with Chinese Characteristics.* New York. Cambridge University Press. 2008.

115. Hu, Bo. *Chinese Maritime Power in the 21st Century.* Routledge. New York. 2020.

116. Hudson, Valerie. *Foreign Policy Analysis.* Plymouth, United Kingdom. Rowman and Littlefield. 2014.

117. 'India and China Have Their First Deadly Clashes in 45 Years.' *The Economist.* June 18, 2020. Accessed on December 22, 2020. https://www.economist.com/asia/2020/06/18/india-and-china-have-their-first-deadly-clashes-in-45-years

118. 'India's Armed Forces Get Their Biggest Shake-up in Decades.' *The Economist.* January 18, 2020. Accessed on February 6, 2020. https://www.economist.com/asia/2020/01/18/indias-armed-forces-get-their-biggest-shake-up-in-decades

119. 'Indian Maritime Doctrine 2009.' Integrated Headquarters, Ministry of Defence. New Delhi. Accessed on February 16, 2020. 1–188https://www.indiannavy.nic.in/sites/default/files/Indian-Maritime-Doctrine-2009-Updated-12Feb16.pdf

120. 'Indian Navy Aiming at 200-ship Fleet by 2027.' *The Economic Times.* July 14, 2018. Accessed on November 11, 2019. https://economictimes.indiatimes.com/news/defence/indian-navy-aiming-at-200-ship-fleet-by-2027/articleshow/48072917.cms?from=mdr

121. 'India's Upping Antennae in Bay of Bengal to Counter China.' *Zeenews.* November 14, 2007. Accessed on June 13, 2017 http://zeenews.india.com/news/nation/india-upping-antennae-in-bay-of-bengal-to-counter-china_407387.html

122. Institute for Defense Studies and Analyses in New Delhi. 'Yearly Indian Defense Budget Analyses.' Years from 1990–2021. http://www.idsa.in/

123. Jaffrelot, Christophe. *Hindu Nationalism: A Reader.* Princeton. Princeton University Press. 2007.

124. Jaffrelot, Christophe. *Religion, Caste and Politics in India.* New York. Oxford University Press. 2011.

125. Jaishankar, Druva. 'Survey of India's Strategic Community.' Brookings India IMPACT Series No. 032019-01. March 2019. Accessed on November 13, 2019. 1–30. https://www.brookings.edu/wp-content/uploads/2019/03/Survey-of-India%E2%80%99s-Strategic-Community.pdf

126. Janardhan, N. Colley, Christopher K. 'Flag Follows Trade.' In the N Janardhan ed. *The Arab Gulf's Pivot to Asia.* Hamburg. Gerlach Press. 2020. 193–209.

127. Jervis, Robert. 'Cooperation under the Security Dilemma.' *World Politics.* Vol. 30. No 2. 1978. 167–214.

128. Joe, Rick. 'A Tale of 2 Navies: India and China's Current Carrier and Escort Procurement.' *The Diplomat.* August 4, 2021B. Accessed on August 17, 2021. https://

thediplomat.com/2021/08/a-tale-of-2-navies-india-and-chinas-current-carrier-and-escort-procurement/

129. Joe, Rick. 'A Tale of 2 Navies: Reviewing India and China's Aircraft Carrier Procurement.' *The Diplomat*. July 3, 2021A. Accessed on August 24, 2021. https://thediplomat.com/2021/07/a-tale-of-2-navies-reviewing-india-and-chinas-aircraft-carrier-procurement/

130. Johnston, Alastair Ian. 'How New and Assertive Is China's New Assertiveness?' *International Security*. Vol. 37. No. 4. Spring 2013. 7–48.

131. Johnston, Alastair Iain. 'Is Chinese Nationalism Rising?' *International Security*. Vol. 41, No. 3. Winter 2016/2017. 7–43.

132. Joshi, Manoj. 'Building upon the American Connection.' *The Observer Research Foundation*. October 28, 2020. Accessed on November 8, 2020. https://www.orfonline.org/expert-speak/building-upon-the-american-connection/

133. Joshi, Saurabh. 'India-China Military Gap—"too Wide to Bridge" Navy Chief.' *Strat Post*. August 10, 2009. Accessed on June 13, 2017. http://www.stratpost.com/india-china-military-gap-%E2%80%98too-wide-to-bridge%E2%80%99-navy-chief/

134. Joshi, Yogesh. Mukherjee, Anit. 'From Denial to Punishment: The Security Dilemma and Changes in India's Military Strategy towards China.' *Asian Security*. Volume 15, Issue 1. November 9, 2018. 1–19.

135. Joshi, Yogesh. O'Donnel, Frank. *India and Nuclear Asia*. Georgetown University Press. Washington D.C. 2019.

136. Kang, David. *American Grand Strategy and East Asian Security*. New York. Cambridge University Press. 2017.

137. Kannan, Saikiran. 'Exclusive: As Chinese Survey Ships Map Indian Ocean, Experts Raise Defence Alarm.' *India Today*. January 24, 2021. Accessed on August 17, 2021. https://www.indiatoday.in/india/story/exclusive-as-chinese-survey-ships-map-indian-ocean-experts-raise-defence-alarm-1761945-2021-01-23

138. Kanwal, Gurmeet. 'India's Military Modernization: Plans and Strategic Underpinnings.' *The National Bureau of Asian Research*. September 24, 2012. Accessed on August 29, 2021. https://www.nbr.org/publication/indias-military-modernization-plans-and-strategic-underpinnings/

139. Kapur, Paul S. 'Peace and Conflict in the Indo-Pakistani Rivalry: Domestic and Strategic Causes.' In the Sumit Ganguly and William Thompson eds. *Asian Rivalries*. Stanford. Stanford University Press. 2011. 61–78.

140. Kardon, Isaac. 'Research and Debate—Pier Competitor: Testimony on China's Global Ports.' *Naval War College Review*. Vol. 74. No. 1. Winter 2021. 1–26. Accessed on June 23, 2021. https://digital-commons.usnwc.edu/nwc-review/vol74/iss1/11/

141. Kardon, Isaac B. Kennedy, Conor M. Dutton, Peter A. 'Gwadar.' China Maritime Studies Institute. *China Maritime Report No. 7*. U.S. Naval War College. August 2020. 1–63. Accessed on June 23, 2021. https://digital-commons.usnwc.edu/cmsi-maritime-reports/7/

142. Kardon, Isaac B. Saunders, Phillip. 'Reconsidering the PLA as an Interest Group.' In the Philip C Saunders and Andrew Scobell eds. *PLA Influence on*

China's National Security Policymaking. Stanford. Stanford University Press. 2015. 33–57.

143. Kennan, George. 'X. The Sources of Soviet Conduct.' *Foreign Affairs.* Vol. 25. No. 4. July 1947. 1–10.

144. Kennedy, Conor. 'Strategic Strong Points and Chinese Naval Strategy.' *China Brief.* The Jamestown Foundation. March 22, 2019. Accessed on March 16, 2021. https://jamestown.org/program/strategic-strong-points-and-chinese-naval-strategy/#:~:text=Strategic%20strong%20points%20will%20improve,and%20s afeguarding%20China's%20overseas%20interests.

145. Kennedy, Paul. *Strategy and Diplomacy 1870–1945.* Boston. Fontana Press. 1984.

146. Kennedy, Scott. 'The Myth of the Beijing Consensus.' *The Journal of Contemporary China.* Vol. 19. No. 65. 2010. 461–477.

147. Khurana, Gurpreet S. 'India's as a Challenge to China's Belt and Road Initiative.' *Asia Policy.* Vol. 14. No. 2. April 2019. 27–33.

148. Khurana, Gurpreet. 'India's Maritime Strategy: What "the West" Should Know.' *IAPSDialogue.* April 3, 2017. Accessed on August 29, 2021. https://theasiadialogue.com/2017/04/03/indias-maritime-strategy-what-the-west-should-know/

149. Kirchberger, Sarah. 'Evaluating Maritime Power: The Example of China.' In the John Hall ed. *Power in the 21st Century.* Malden MA. Polity Press. 2011. 151–175.

150. Kliman, Daniel. Rehman, Iskander. Lee, Kristine. Fitt, Joshua. 'Imbalance of Power.' Center for a New American Security. October 23, 2019. Accessed on January 24, 2020. https://www.cnas.org/publications/reports/imbalance-of-power

151. Koh, Collin Swee Lean. 'China-India Rivalry at Sea: Capability, Trends and Challenges.' *Asian Security.* Volume 15, Issue 1. November 1, 2018. 1–20.

152. Koh, Swee Lean. Collin. ' "New Normal" in the Indo-Pacific.' In the Raja Mohan and Anit Mukherjee eds. *India's Naval Strategy and Asia Security.* New York. Routledge. 2016. 136–165.

153. Kolnogorov, Vadim. 'To Be or Not to Be: The Development of Soviet Deck Aviation.' *Journal of Strategic Studies.* Vol. 28. No. 2. 2007. 339–359.

154. Kondapalli, Srikanth. 'China's Evolving Naval Presence in the Indian Ocean Region: An Indian Perspective.' In the David Brewster ed. *India and China at Sea.* New Delhi. Oxford University Press. 2018. 111–124.

155. Korolev, Alexander. Wu, Fengshi. 'Is There a U.S.-China-India triangle?— Beijing's Official Views.' *India Review.* Vol. 18. No. 4. October 22, 2019. 437–456.

156. Kroeber, Arthur R. *China's Economy.* New York. Oxford University Press. 2016.

157. Kurth, Ronald. 'Gorshkov's Gambit.' *Journal of Strategic Studies.* Vol. 28. No. 2. 2007. 261–280.

158. Ladwig, Walter. 'Drivers of Indian Naval Expansion.' In the Harsh V Pant ed. *The Rise of the Indian Navy: Internal Vulnerabilities, External Challenges.* London. Routledge. 2012. 19–40.

159. Latif, Asad-ul Iqbal. 'Three Sides in Search of a Triangle. Institute of South East Asian Studies.' Singapore. Singapore. 2009.

160. Levy, Jack. Thompson, William. *The Causes of War.* Malden Ma. Wiley-Blackwell. 2010.

161. Li, Jian. Chen, Wenwen. Jin, Jing. 'Indian Ocean Sea Power Pattern and China Sea Power: Indian Ocean Expansion.' *Pacific Journal*. Vol. 22. No. 5. May 2014. 68–76. 李剑，陈文文，金晶，"印度洋海权格局与中国海权的印度洋拓展." 太平洋学报，2014年第5期 68-76. http://www.cnki.com.cn/Article/CJFDTotal-TPYX201405009.htm

162. Liff, Adam P. 'China and the US Alliance System.' *The China Quarterly*, 233, March 2018. 137–165.

163. Liff, Adam P. Erickson, Andrew S. 'Demystifying China's Defense Spending: Less Mysterious in the Aggregate.' *The China Quarterly*. Vol. 216. December 2013. 805–830.

164. Liff, Adam P. Ikenberry, John G. 'Racing toward Tragedy?: China's Rise, Military Competition in the Asia Pacific, and the Security Dilemma.' *International Security*. Vol. 39. No. 2. October 2014. 52–91.

165. Lim, Yves-Heng. 'China's Rising Naval Ambitions in the Indian Ocean: Aligning Ends, Ways and Means.' *Asian Security*. Volume 16, Issue 2. January 26, 2020. 1–17.

166. Lin, Jian. 'Major General Luo Yuan: Make the U.S. Feel Some Pain over arms Sales to Taiwan.' *International Pioneer Guide*. January 18, 2010. 林建. "对台军售,要让美国知道疼." 国际先驱导报. 2010年1月18日.

167. Lin, Minwang. 'India Has Chosen a High-risk Strategic Path.' *South Asian Studies Communication Time*. October 27, 2020. 林民旺：印度选择了一条高风险战略路径：来源：南亚研究通讯时间：2020-10-27 https://www.essra.org.cn/view-1000-1375.aspx

168. Liu Jianfei. 'The Tendency of the Transformation of the U.S. Strategy towards China.' *World Economics and Politics*. No 2. February 2005. 30–36. 刘建飞. "美国对华战略的转变趋向." 世界经济与政治第二期. 2005. 30-36.

169. Mahan, Alfred Thayer. *The Influence of Sea Power Upon History, 1660–1783*. New York. Dover. 1987.

170. Mahnken, Thomas. 'Arms Races and Long Term Competition.' In the Thomas Mahnken and Dan Blumenthal eds. *Strategy in Asia*. Stanford. Stanford University Press. 2014. 225–240.

171. Mahoney, James. 'Regime Change: Central America in Comparative Perspective.' *Studies in Comparative International Development*. Spring 2001. Springer Link. Vol. 36. No. 1. 111–141.

172. Mann, James. *About Face*. New York. Alfred A. Knopf, Inc. 1999.

173. Mansour, Imad. Thompson, William. 'Introduction.' In the Imad Mansour and William Thompson eds. *Shocks and Rivalries in the Middle East and North Africa*. Washington D.C. George Town University Press. 2020. 1–12.

174. Martinson, Ryan D. Dutton, Peter A. 'China's Distant-Ocean Survey Activities: Implications for U.S. National Security.' *China Maritime Studies Institute*. *China Maritime Report No. 3. U.S. Naval War College*. November 2018. Accessed on June 23, 2021. https://digital-commons.usnwc.edu/cmsi-maritime-reports/3/

175. Mason, Chris M. 'Less than Meets the Eye: A Critical Assessment of the Military-to-military Dimension of the U.S.-India Security Partnership.' In the Sumit Ganguly and Chris M. Mason eds. *The Future of U.S.-India Security Cooperation*. Manchester. Manchester University Press. 2021. 19–37.

176. Mathew, Thomas. 'Mighty Dragon in the Sea.' *Hindustan Times*. June 23, 2009. Accessed on June 13, 2017. http://www.hindustantimes.com/india/mighty-dragon-in-the-sea/story-4z564DnnvoQkfiq0GIduqN.html

177. McDevitt, Michael. *China as a Twenty-First-Century Naval Power*. Annapolis Maryland. Naval Institute Press. 2020.

178. McDevitt, Michael. 'Sea Denial with Chinese Characteristics.' In the Andrew S. Erickson, Lyle, Goldstein, William S. Murry, and Andrew R. Wilson eds. *China's Future Nuclear Submarine Force*. Annapolis. Naval Institute Press. Annapolis. 2007. 359–372.

179. McGinnis, Michael. Williams, John. *Compound Dilemmas: Democracy, Collective Action, and Superpower Rivalry*. Ann Arbor. University of Michigan Press. 2001.

180. McVadon, Eric A. 'China's Maturing Navy.' In the Andrew Erickson, Lyle J. Goldstein, William S Murry, and Andrew Wilson eds. *China's Future Nuclear Submarine Force*. *Naval Institute Press*. Annapolis. Naval Institute Press. 2007. 1–21.

181. Medeiros, Evan S. *Reluctant Restraint*. Stanford. Stanford University Press. 2009.

182. Mehta, Sureesh. 'India's National Security Challenges.' *Outlook*, August 9, 2009. Accessed on February 22, 2016. http://www.outlookindia.com/website/story/indias-national-security-challenges/261738

183. Meng, Liang. 'Development and Obstacles of "One Belt One Road".' In the Core Island Countries in the Indian Ocean. *Peace and Development*. No. 2. 2019. 101–116. 孟亮."一带一路"倡议在印度洋核心岛国的进展及阻力. 和平与发展. 2019年第2期. 101–116.

184. Meng, Qianlong. 'Looking at the Prospects of Indo-Pacific Strategy from the Perspective of US-Indian Relations.' *Frontiers*. No. 3 2018. 26–37. 孟庆龙."从美印关系看印太战略的前景." 学术前沿. 2018年第8期. 26–37.

185. Menon, Raja. 'Scenarios for China's Naval Development in the Indian Ocean and India's Naval Response.' In the David Brewster ed. *India and China at Sea*. New Delhi. Oxford University Press. 2018. 125–136.

186. Menon, Raja K. 'Technology and the Indian Navy.' In the Harsh Pant ed. *The Rise of the Indian Navy*. New York. Routledge. 2012. 81–95.

187. 'Missile Defense Project. "JL-2," Missile Threat, Center for Strategic and International Studies.' August 12, 2016, last modified July 31, 2021. Accessed on August 29, 2021. https://missilethreat.csis.org/missile/jl-2/

188. Modelski, George. William, Thompson. *Seapower in Global Politics, 1494–1993*. Seattle. University of Washington Press. 1988.

189. Mohan, Raja. *Samudra Manthan: Sino-Indian Rivalry in the Indo-Pacific*. Washington DC. Carnegie Endowment for International Peace. 2012.

190. Mukherjee, Anit. 'The Great Churning: Modi's Transformation of the Indian Military.' *War on the Rocks*. May 5, 2021. Accessed on August 17, 2021. https://warontherocks.com/2021/05/the-great-churning-modis-transformation-of-the-indian-military/

191. Mukherjee, Anit. 'The Unsinkable Aircraft Carrier.' In the Raja Mohan and C. Anit Mukherjee eds. *India's Naval Strategy and Asian Security*. New York. Routledge. 2015. 89–105.

192. Mukherji, Rahul. 'India's Foreign Economic Policies.' In the Sumit Ganguly ed. *Engaging the World: Indian Foreign Policy since 1947*. New Delhi: Oxford University Press, 2016. 470–495.

193. Mulvenon, James. 'Chairman Hu and the PLA's New Historic Missions.' *The China Leadership Monitor*. No. 27. Friday January 9, 2009. 1–11. http://media. hoover.org/sites/default/files/documents/CLM27JM.pdf

194. Murphy, Martin N. Yoshihara, Toshi. 'Fighting the Naval Hegemon.' *Naval War College Review*. Summer 2015. Vol. 68. No 3. 13–39.

195. Nathan, Andrew. Scobell, Andrew. *China's Search for Security*. New York. Columbia University Press. 2012.

196. Naughton, Barry. 'The Challenges of Economic Growth and Reform.' In the Robert S. Ross and Jo Inge Bekkevold eds. *China in the Era of Xi Jinping*. Washington D.C. Georgetown University Press. 2016. 66–91.

197. O'Donnell, Frank. Bollfrass, Alex. 'The Strategic Postures of China and India.' Belfer Center. Harvard Kennedy School. March 2020. Accessed on August 17, 2021. chrome-extension://oemmndcbldboiebfnladdacbdfmadadm/https:// www.belfercenter.org/sites/default/files/2020-03/india-china-postures/ China%20India%20Postures.pdf

198. O'Rourke, Ronald. 'China Naval Modernization: Implications for U.S. Navy Capabilities- Background and Issues for Congress.' *Congress Research Service*. May 31, 2016. 1–109.

199. O'Rourke, Ronald. 'How China's Shipbuilding Output Might Affect Requirements for U.S. Naval Capabilities.' In the Andrew Erickson ed. *Chinese Naval Shipbuilding*. Annapolis. Naval Institute Press. 2017. 317–331.

200. Page, Benjamin. Xie, Tao. *Living with the Dragon*. New York. Columbia University Press. 2010.

201. Panda, Ankit. 'India's Defense Budget: How to Escape Stagnation?' *The Diplomat*. February 4, 2020. Accessed on February 6, 2020. https://thediplomat. com/2020/02/indias-defense-budget-how-to-escape-stagnation/

202. Panda, Ankit. 'Strait from the US State Department: The "Pivot" to Asia Is Over." *The Diplomat*. March 14, 2017. Accessed on January 25, 2018. https:// thediplomat.com/2017/03/straight-from-the-us-state-department-the-pivot-to-asia-is-over/

203. Pant, Harsh. Joshi, Yogesh. 'The American "Pivot" and the Indian Way.' *Naval War College Review*. Vol. 68. No 1. Winter 2015. 1–23.

204. Pant, Harsh. 'India in the Indian Ocean: Growing Mismatch between Ambitions and Capabilities.' *Pacific Affairs*. Vol. 82. No. 2 Summer 2009. Pages 279–297.

205. Pant, Harsh V. 'Introduction.' In the Harsh Pant ed. *The Rise of the Indian Navy*. New York. Routledge. 2012. Pages 1–15.

206. Pant, Harsh V. 'The India-US-China Triangle from New Delhi: Overcoming the "hesitations of history." ' *India Review*. Vol. 18. No. 4. October 22, 2019. 386–406.

207. Pardesi, Manjeet S. 'Instability in Tibet and the Sino-Indian Strategic Rivalry.' In the Sumit Ganguly and William Thompson eds. *Asian Rivalries*. Stanford. Stanford University Press. 2011. 79–117.

208. Pardesi, Manjeet S. 'Managing the 1986-87 Sino-Indian Sumdorong Chu Crisis.' *India Review*. Vol. 18. No. 5. 2019. 534–551.

209. Parpiani, Kashish. Singh, Angad. 'Third India-US 2+2 Dialogue: Breaking the Model on Post-war Model of Bilateral Ties.' *Observer Research Foundation.* October 26, 2020. Accessed on November 8, 2020. https://www.orfonline.org/expert-speak/third-india-us-22-dialogue-breaking-the-mould-on-post-war-model-of-bilateral-ties/

210. Pattanaik, Smruti S. 'India's Policy Response to China's Investment and Aid to Nepal, Sri Lanka and Maldives: Challenges and Prospects.' *Strategic Analysis.* Vol. 43. No. 3. June 3, 2019. 240–259.

211. Pehrson, Christopher. 'String of Pearls: Meeting the Challenge of China's Rising Power Across the Asian Littoral.' *Strategic Studies Institute.* July 2006. 1–26. http://www.strategicstudiesinstitute.army.mil/pdffiles/PUB721.pdf

212. Peri, Dinakar. 'Amid China's maritime expansion, Naval budget for modernization gets massive boost.' The Hindu. February 3, 2022. Accessed on March 20, 2022. https://www.thehindu.com/news/national/maritime-capacity-building-modernisation-in-focus-in-defence-budget/article38368553.ece?homepage=true

213. Pierson, Paul. *Politics in Time.* Princeton. Princeton University Press. 2004.

214. Pu, Xiaoyu. Schweller, Randall L. 'Status Signaling, Multiple Audiences, and China's Blue Water Naval Ambition.' In the Deborah Welch Larson, T.V. Paul, and William C. Wohlworth eds. *Status in World Politics.* New York. Cambridge University Press. 2014. 141–160.

215. Rajagopalan, Rajejwari Pillai. 'India's Maritime Strategy.' In the Raja Mohan and Anit Mukherjee eds. *India's Naval Strategy and Asia Security.* New York. Routledge. 2016. 29–58.

216. Rawat, Manoj. 'Quad 2.0 Is Off to a Good Start—It Must Keep Going.' *The Diplomat.* November 23, 2020. Accessed on December 22, 2020. https://thediplomat.com/2020/11/quad-2-0-is-off-to-a-good-start-it-must-keep-going/

217. Raska, Michael. Bitzinger, Richard A. 'Capacity for Innovation: Technological Drivers of China's Future Military Modernization.' In the Roy Kamphausen and David Lai eds. *The PLA in the 2025,* Carlisle, PA: Strategic Studies Institute, 2014. 129–161.

218. Rasler, Karen. Thompson, William. Ganguly, Sumit. *How Rivalries End.* Philadelphia. University of Pennsylvania Press. 2013.

219. Rehman, Iskander. 'India's Aspirational Naval Doctrine.' In the Harsh Pant ed. *The Rise of the Indian Navy.* New York. Routledge. 2012. 55–79.

220. Rehman, Iskander. 'Tomorrow or Yesterday's Fleet?' In the Raja Mohan and Anit Mukherjee eds. *India's Naval Strategy and Asia Security.* New York. Routledge. 2016. 1–28.

221. Reuters Staff. 'Wary of China, India to Boost Eastern Naval Fleet.' *Reuters.* November 15, 2007. Accessed on August 16, 2021. https://www.reuters.com/article/idINIndia-30499920071115

222. Reuveny, Rafael. Thompson, William. 'Observation on the North-South Divide.' In the Rafael Reuveny and William Thompson eds. *North and South in the World Political Economy.* Malden Ma. Blackwell Publishing. 2008. 1–16.

223. Rider, Toby. Findley, Michael. Diehl, Paul. 'Just Part of the Game? Arms Races, Rivalry, and War.' *Journal of Peace Research.* Vol. 48. No. 1. 2011. 85–100.

224. Ross, Robert. 'China's Naval Nationalism: Sources, Prospects, and the U.S. Response.' *International Security.* Vol. 34. No. 2. Fall 2009. 46–81.
225. Sanger, David E. 'U.S. Would Defend Taiwan, Bush Says.' *The New York Times.* April 26, 2001. http://www.nytimes.com/2001/04/26/world/us-would-defend-taiwan-bush-says.html
226. Saunders, Philip. Scobell, Andrew. 'PLA Influence on China's National Security Policymaking.' In the Philip C Saunders and Andrew Scobell eds. *PLA Influence on China's National Security Policymaking.* Stanford. Stanford University Press. 2015. Pages 1–30.
227. Sawhney, Ashok. 'The Navy in India's Socio-economic Growth and Development.' In the Rajash Basrur, Ajaya Kumar Das, and Manjeet S. Pardesi eds. *India's Military Modernization.* New Delhi. Oxford University Press. 2014. 22–54.
228. Schiavenza, Matt. 'What Exactly Does It Mean That the U.S. Is Pivoting to Asia.' *The Atlantic.* April 15, 2013. Accessed on January 25, 2018. https://www.theatlantic.com/china/archive/2013/04/what-exactly-does-it-mean-that-the-us-is-pivoting-to-asia/274936/
229. Schweller, Randall. 'Domestic Politics and Nationalism in East Asian Security.' In the Robert S. Ross and Oystein Tunsjo eds. *Strategic Adjustment and the Rise of China.* Ithaca. Cornell University Press. 2017. 15–40.
230. Schweller, Randall L. 'The Logic and Illogic of the Security Dilemma and Contemporary Realism: A Response to Wagner's Critique.' *International Theory.* Vol. 2. No. 2. July 2010. 288–305.
231. 'Science of Strategy.' Academy of Military Science Military Strategy Department. Military Science Press. Beijing, China. December 2013. Translated by China Aerospace Studies Institute. Air University. Montgomery Alabama. Accessed on August 22, 2021. chrome-extension://oemmndcbldboiebfnladdacbdfmadad m/https://www.airuniversity.af.edu/Portals/10/CASI/documents/Translations/2021-02-08%20Chinese%20Military%20Thoughts-%20In%20their%20 own%20words%20Science%20of%20Military%20Strategy%202013.pdf?ver= NxAWg4BPw_NylEjxaha8Aw%3d%3d
232. Scobell, Andrew. McMahon, Michael. Cooper, Cortez A III. 'China's Aircraft Carrier Program.' *Naval War College Review.* Vol. 68. No 4. Autumn 2015. 65–79.
233. Scott, David. 'India's Aspirations and Strategy for the Indian Ocean—Securing the Waves?' *Journal of Strategic Studies.* Vol. 36. No. 4. February 2013. 485–511.
234. Scott, David. 'India's Drive for a "Blue Water" Navy.' *Journal of Military and Strategic Studies.* Vol. 10. No. 2. Winter 2007–2008. 1–42.
235. Scott, David. 'India's Grand Strategy for the Indian Ocean.' *Asia-Pacific Review.* Vol. 13. No. 2, November 28, 2006. 97–129.
236. Sense, Paul D. Vasquez, John A. *The Steps to War: An Empirical Study.* Princeton New Jersey. University Press. 2008.
237. Shambaugh, David. *Modernizing China's Military.* Berkley. University of California Press. 2002.
238. Shankar, Mahesh. 'Territory and the China-India Competition.' In the T.V. Paul ed. *The China-India Rivalry in the Globalization Era.* Washington D.C. Georgetown University Press. 2018. 27–53.

239. Shi, Hongyuan. 'India's Perception and Response to China's Entry into the Indian Ocean.' November 4, 2012. 时宏远，印度对中国进入印度洋的认知与反应，南亚研究，2012年第4期　http://www.cnki.com.cn/Article/CJFDTOTAL-LAYA201204005.htm

240. Shim, Elizabeth. 'India to Add 56 Warships, Six Submarines to Naval Fleet.' *UPI*. December 4, 2018. Accessed on November 11, 2019. https://www.upi.com/Top_News/World-News/2018/12/04/India-to-add-56-warships-six-submarines-to-naval-fleet/2151543950800/

241. Shirk, Susan. *China Fragile Superpower*. New York. Oxford University Press. 2007.

242. Shirk, Susan. 'One-Sided Rivalry: China's Perceptions and Policies Toward India.' In the Francine Frankel and Harry Harding eds. *The India–China Relationship: What the U.S. Needs to Know*. Washington D.C. Woodrow Wilson Center Press. 2004. 75–100.

243. Silove, Nina. 'The Pivot before the Pivot: U.S. Strategy to Preserve the Power Balance in Asia.' *International Security*. Vol. 40. No. 4. Spring 2016. 45–88.

244. Silver, Laura. Devlin, Cat. Huang, Christine. 'Large Majorities Say China Does Not Respect the Personal Freedoms of Its People.' *Pew Research Center*. June 30, 2021. Accessed on August 24, 2021. https://www.pewresearch.org/global/2021/06/30/large-majorities-say-china-does-not-respect-the-personal-freedoms-of-its-people/

245. Silver, Laura. Devlin, Cat. Huang, Christine. 'Unfavorable Views of China Reach Historic Highs in Many Countries.' *Pew Research Center*. October 6, 2020. Accessed on December 14, 2020. https://www.pewresearch.org/global/2020/10/06/unfavorable-views-of-china-reach-historic-highs-in-many-countries/

246. Silver, Neil E. 'The United States, Japan, and China: Setting the Course.' *The Council on Foreign Relations*. 2000. Accessed on January 25, 2018. https://www.cfr.org/report/united-states-japan-and-china

247. Singh, Abhijit. 'An Indian Maritime Strategy for an Era of Geopolitical Uncertainty.' *Journal of Defense Studies*. Vol. 9. No. 4. October–December 2015. 7–19.

248. Singh, Abhijit. 'Sino-Indian Dynamics in Littoral Asia—The View from New Delhi.' *Strategic Analysis*. Vol. 43. No. 3. June 3, 2019. 199–213.

249. Singh, Rahul. 'India No Match for China: Navy Chief.' August 11, 2009. *Hindustan Times*. Accessed on August 17, 2021. https://www.hindustantimes.com/india/india-no-match-for-china-navy-chief/story-OYkJQjfLtOR9rOjmrECJ4H.html

250. Smith, Jeff M. Tatsumi, Yuki. Rajagopalan, Rajeswari Pillai. Medcalf, Rory. Brewster, David. 'Return of the Quad.' *The Diplomat*. No. 42. May 2018. Accessed on March 8, 2020. https://magazine.thediplomat.com/#/issues/-LAWCg2zSGAbYVn-2Qr2/read

251. Special Correspondent. 'Aw, India Is Less Macho Now-Candid Navy Chief: Military No Match for China's Might.' *The Telegraph*. August 10, 2009. Accessed on June 8, 2017. https://www.telegraphindia.com/1090811/jsp/frontpage/story_11346512.jsp

252. Stockholm International Peace Research Institute. 'SIPRI Yearbook 2016.' Accessed on March 24, 2017. https://www.sipri.org/sites/default/files/Milex-constant-USD.pdf

253. Stockholm International Peace Research Institute. 'SIPRI Arms Transfers Database- Methodology.' Accessed on June 13, 2017 https://www.sipri.org/databases/armstransfers/background

254. Sun, Xianpu. 'Modi Government's Diplomatic Strategy Adjustment and Its Impact on China.' *Contemporary World and Socialism*. No. 4. 2018. 158–166. 孙现朴，"印度莫迪政府外交战略调整及对中国的影响."当代世界与社会主义. 2018年第4期. 158–166.

255. Swaine, Michael D. 'Chinese Views of Foreign Policy in the 19th Party Congress.' *The China Leadership Monitor*. No. 55. Winter 2018. 1–13. Accessed on February 4, 2018. https://www.hoover.org/sites/default/files/research/docs/clm55-ms-final.pdf

256. Tang, Shiping. 'The Security Dilemma: A Conceptual Analysis.' *Journal of Security Studies*. Vol. 18. No. 3. 2009. 587–623.

257. Tang, Wenfang. Darr, Benjamin. 'Chinese Nationalism and Its Political and Social Origins. *Journal of Contemporary China*. Volume 21, Issue 77. 2012. 1–17.

258. Tangredi, Sam J. *Anti-Access Warfare*. Annapolis. Naval Institute Press. 2013.

259. Tham, Engen. Blanchard, Ben. Wang, Jing. 'Chinese Warships Enter East Indian Ocean amid Maldives Tensions.' *Reuters*. February 20, 2018. Accessed on September 13, 2019. https://www.reuters.com/article/us-maldives-politics-china/chinese-warships-enter-east-indian-ocean-amid-maldives-tensions-idUSKCN1G40V9

260. 'The 13th Five Year Plan for Economic and Social Development of the People's Republic of China: 2016–2020.' Translated by Compilation and Translation Bureau, Central Committee of the Communist Party of China. Central Compilation and Translation Press. Beijing, China. 2016. Accessed on February 8, 2020. https://en.ndrc.gov.cn/newsrelease_8232/201612/P020191101481868235378.pdf

261. 'The Carrier Strike Group.' United States Department of Navy. Accessed on January 25, 2018. http://www.navy.mil/navydata/ships/carriers/powerhouse/cvbg.asp

262. 'The Military Balance.' The International Institute for Strategic Studies. Book Series. Routledge. Years 1991–2021. Accessed on August 27, 2021. https://www.routledge.com/The-Military-Balance/book-series/MB

263. 'The Military Balance.' The International Institute for Strategic Studies. Book Series. Routledge. 1991.

264. 'The Military Balance.' The International Institute for Strategic Studies. Book Series. Routledge. 1998.

265. 'The Military Balance.' The International Institute for Strategic Studies. Book Series. Routledge. 2004.

266. 'The Military Balance.' The International Institute for Strategic Studies. Book Series. Routledge. 2015.

267. 'The Military Balance.' The International Institute for Strategic Studies. Book Series. Routledge. 2019.

268. 'The Military Balance.' The International Institute for Strategic Studies. Book Series. Routledge. 2021.

269. 'The PLA Navy.' Office of Naval Intelligence. Washington D.C. 2015. Accessed on February 20, 2016. http://news.usni.org/wp-content/uploads/2015/04/2015_PLA_NAVY_PUB_Print.pdf

270. *The Tiananmen Papers*. Compiled by Zhang Liang. Edited by Andrew Nathan and Perry Link. New York. Public Affairs. 2001.

271. 'The World Needs a Proper Investigation into How Covid-19 Started.' *The Economist*. August 21. 2021. Accessed on August 24, 2021. https://www.economist.com/international/2021/08/21/the-world-needs-a-proper-investigation-into-how-covid-19-started

272. Thompson, William. *Great Power Rivalries*. Columbia, SC. University of South Carolina Press. 1999.

273. Thorne, Devin. Spevack, Ben. 'Harbored Ambitions.' *C4ADS*. 2018. 1–68. Accessed on September 2, 2019. https://static1.squarespace.com/static/566ef8b4d8af107232d5358a/t/5ad5e20ef950b777a94b55c3/1523966489456/Harbored+Ambitions.pdf

274. 'Tiananmen Square Protest Death Toll "Was 10,000".' *The BBC*. December 23, 2017. Accessed on May 25, 2018. http://www.bbc.com/news/world-asia-china-42465516

275. Till, Geoffrey. *Seapower*. Third Edition. New York. Routledge. 2013.

276. Todd, Daniel. Lindberg, Michael M. *Navies and Shipbuilding Industries: The strained symbiosis*. Wesport. Praeger. 1996.

277. Tunsjo, Oystein. 'U.S.-China Relations.' In the Robert Ross and Oystein Tunsjo eds. *Strategic Adjustment and the Rise of China*. Ithaca. Cornell University Press. 2017. 41–68.

278. Turner, Stansfield. 'A Former CIA Director Says Technology May Make Them "Superfluous".' *Proceedings Magazine*. Vol. 132. July, 2006. Accessed on August 26, 2021. https://www.usni.org/magazines/proceedings/2006/july/aircraft-carriers-are-their-way-out

279. U.S. Department of State. 'U.S. Bilateral Relations Fact Sheets.' Accessed on December 9, 2017. http://www.state.gov/r/pa/ei/bgn/index.htm

280. Vajpayee, A.B. 'Nuclear Anxiety; Indian's Letter to Clinton on the Nuclear Testing.' *The New York Times*. May 13, 1998. Accessed on June 4, 2017. http://www.nytimes.com/1998/05/13/world/nuclear-anxiety-indian-s-letter-to-clinton-on-the-nuclear-testing.html

281. Valencia, Mark J. 'Joining the Quad: Fear Versus Greed.' *The Diplomat*. December 15, 2017. Accessed on February 4, 2018. https://thediplomat.com/2017/12/joining-the-quad-fear-versus-greed/

282. Varshney, Ashutosh. *Ethnic Conflict and Civic Life: Hindus and Muslims in India*. New Haven. Yale University Press. 2003.

283. Wang, Xinhao. 'Interview with Zheng Yongnian: "Don't push India into the arms of the United States".' July 30, 2020. Accessed on February 18, 2021. 郑永年：不要把印度推向美国的怀抱，时代在线 http://www.time-weekly.com/post/271970

284. Wang Yifeng. Ye Jing. What the Nuclear Submarine Incident between China and Japan tells Us about the Ability of China's Nuclear Submarines to penetrate defenses, Part 2. *Shipborne Weapons*. February 2005. 33–41. 王逸峰，叶景。"从中日核潜艇事件看中国核潜艇的突防(中)."舰船武器. 2005. 34–41.

285. Wang, Zheng. *Never Forget National Humiliation*. New York. Columbia University Press. 2014.

286. Wee, Sui-Lee. Myers, Steven. 'As Chinese Vaccines Stumble, U.S. Finds New Opening in Asia.' *The New York Times.* August 20, 2021. Accessed on August 24, 2021. https://www.nytimes.com/2021/08/20/business/economy/china-vaccine-us-covid-diplomacy.html

287. Weiss, Jessica Chen. *Powerful Patriots.* New York. Oxford University Press. 2014.

288. Werner, Ben. 'Indo-Pacom Commander Says Only Half of Sub Requests Are Met.' *UNSI News.* March 27, 2019. Accessed on February 10, 2020. https://news.usni.org/2019/03/27/42212

289. 'Why China's Submarine Deal with Bangladesh Matters.' *The Diplomat.* January 20, 2017. Accessed on February 6, 2020. https://thediplomat.com/2017/01/why-chinas-submarine-deal-with-bangladesh-matters/

290. Wojczewski, Thorsten. 'China's Rise as a Strategic Challenge and Opportunity: India's China Discourse and Strategy.' *India Review.* Vol. 15. No. 1. February 2016. 22–60.

291. Womack, Brantly. 'Asymmetric Rivals: China and Vietnam.' In the Sumit Ganguly and William Thompson eds. *Asian Rivalries.* Stanford. Stanford University Press. 2011. 176–194.

292. Wong, Audrye. 'More than Peripheral: How Provinces Influence China's Foreign Policy.' *The China Quarterly.* Vol. 235. September 2018. 735–757.

293. Woody, Christopher. 'India Is Beefing Up Its Navy to Counter China's Increasingly Powerful Fleet.' *Business Insider.* December 6, 2018. Accessed on February 4, 2020. https://www.businessinsider.my/india-is-beefing-up-its-navy-to-counter-chinas-powerful-fleet-2018-12/

294. World Bank. 'World Integrated Trade Solution.' Accessed on June 15, 2017. http://wits.worldbank.org/CountryProfile/en/IND

295. Xavier, Constantino. 'Across the Himalayas.' In the Kanti, Bajpai. Selina Ho, and Manjari Chatterjee Miller eds. *Routledge Handbook of China-India Relations.* Routledge. New York. 2020. 420–433.

296. Xiang, Lanxin. 'China and the Pivot.' *Survival.* Vol. 54. No. 5. October 2012. 113–128.

297. *Xinhua.* 'Full Text of Hu Jintao's Report to the 18th Party Congress.' Published on November 27, 2012. Accessed on December 2, 2017. http://www.china-embassy.org/eng/zt/18th_CPC_National_Congress_Eng/t992917.htm

298. Yan, Zhongxin. Wang, Gang. Yang, ZuKuai. 'Analysis of antiship missile saturation attack capability of "Arlehigh-Burke"—class destroyer.' *Modern Defense Technology.* 2002. 10–13. Accessed on February 6, 2020. http://www.defence.org.cn/aspnet/vip-usa/uploadfiles/2006-1/20061313144410.pdf 颜仲新. 王 刚. 杨祖快. "伯克"级驱逐舰抗反舰导弹饱和攻击能力分析."现代防御技术. 2002年第3期. 10–13.

299. Ye, Jing. 'What the Nuclear Submarine Incident between China and Japan Tells Us about the Ability of China's Nuclear Submarines to Penetrate Defenses.' *Shipborne Weapons.* March, 2005. 27–31. 叶景. "从中日核潜艇事件看中国核潜艇的突防." 舰载武器. 3. 2005. 27–31.

300. Ye, Hailin. 'The Impact of Identity Perception Bias on the Prospects of Sino-Indian Relations.' *Indian Ocean Economy Studies.* July 30, 2020. 叶海林. 身份认知偏差对中印关系前景的影响，印度洋经济体研究. 2020年07月30日.

Accessed on August 24, 2021. http://www.cssn.cn/gjgxx/gj_ytqy/202007/
t20200730_5163496.html

301. Yoshihara, Toshi. 'Chinese Maritime Geography.' In the Thomas Mahnken and Dan Blumenthal eds. *Strategy in Asia*. Stanford. Stanford University Press. 2014. 43–60.

302. Yoshihara, Toshi. Holmes, James R. *Red Star Over the Pacific*. Annapolis. Naval Institute Press. 2010.

303. Yoshihara, Toshi. Holmes, James. *Red Star Over the Pacific*. Second Edition. Annapolis. Naval Institute Press. 2018.

304. Yoshihara, Toshi. 'U.S. Ballistic-Missile Defense and China's Undersea Nuclear Deterrent.' In the Andrew S. Erickson, Lyle J. Goldstein, William S. Murray, and Andrew R. Wilson eds. *China's Future Nuclear Submarine Force*. Annapolis. Naval Institute Press. 2007. 330–358.

305. You, Ji. 'China's Emerging Indo-Pacific Naval Strategy.' *Asia Policy*. No. 22. July 2016. 11–19.

306. You, Ji. 'The Indian Ocean: A Grand Sino-Indian Game of "Go."' In David Brewster ed. *India and China at Sea*. New Delhi. Oxford University Press. 2018. 90–110.

307. Yung, Christopher D. 'The PLA Navy Lobby and Its Influence over China's Maritime Sovereignty.' In Philip C Saunders and Andrew Scobell eds. *PLA Influence on China's National Security Policymaking*. Stanford. Stanford University Press. 2015. 274–299.

308. Zastrow, Mark. 'Four Chinese Scientists Were Killed in Sri Lanka Attack.' *Nature*. May 10, 2019. Accessed on February 5, 2020. https://www.nature.com/articles/d41586-019-01478-y

309. Zhang, Jiadong. 'Are the US and India Already a Paramilitary Alliance?' *Source: South Asian Studies Communication Time*. 2020-11-02 张家栋：美印已是准军事同盟了吗？南亚研究通讯2020-11-02 https://www.essra.org.cn/view-1000-1396.aspx

310. Zhang, Jie. 'The Security of Maritime Channels and the Construction of China's Strategic Fulcrum—Concurrently Discuss the Security Considerations for the Construction of the Maritime Silk Road in the 21st Century.' *Security Strategy*. November 2, 2015. 100–118.. 张洁，海上通道安全与中国战略支点的构建—兼谈21世纪海上丝绸之路建设的安全考量，国际安全研究，2015年第2期. 100-118. Accessed on August 17, 2021. http://gjaqyj.cnjournals.com/gjaqyj/ch/reader/view_abstract.aspx?file_no=20150206&flag=

311. Zhang, Li. 'A Preliminary Study of the US-India-Japan-Australia Quadrilateral Mechanism from the Perspective of Indo-Pacific Tension.' *South Asian Studies Quarterly*. No. 4. 2015. 1–8. 张力，"印太"视域中的美印日澳四边机制初探，南亚研究季刊，2018年第4期 1-8. http://kns.cnki.net/kcms/detail/detail.aspx?DBCode=CJFD&DBName=CJFDLAST2019&fileName=NYYZ201804001

312. Zhang Wenmu. 'China's Energy Security and Policy Choices.' *Global Economics and Politics*. No. 5 2003. 11–16. 张文木. "中国能源安全与政策选择." 世界经济与政治. 2003年第5期. 11-16.

313. Zhao, Suisheng. A Nation State by Construction. Stanford University Press. Stanford California. 2004.

314. Zhao, Suisheng. 'Beijing's Japan Dilemma.' In Thomas Fingar ed. *Uneasy Partnership*. Stanford. Stanford University Press. 2017. 70–96.
315. Zeng, Xinkai. 'The American Factor in China's "Indian Ocean Dilemma."' No. 2. 2012. 曾信凯，中国"印度洋困境"中的美国因素，南亚研究，2012年第2期 http://kns.cnki.net/kcms/detail/detail.aspx?filename=LAYA201202007&dbcode= CJFQ&dbname=CJFD2012&v=

Interviews

India Specialists

1. Maritime security expert bases at a New Delhi think tank. Summer 2016.
2. Economist based at a New Delhi think tank. Summer 2016.
3. International Security expert based at top New Delhi university. Summer 2016 and Fall 2017.
4. International security expert based at top New Delhi university. Summer 2016 and Fall 2017.
5. Former Indian Ambassador to East Asian countries. Summer 2016.
6. Indian maritime security expert based at New Delhi think tank. Summer 2016 and Summer 2017.
7. Indian politics expert based at New Delhi think tank. Summer 2016.
8. Indian naval expert based at Indian government think tank. Summer 2016.
9. Indian China expert based at New Delhi think tank. Summer 2016.
10. Indian maritime security expert based at New Delhi think tank. Summer 2016 and summer 2017.
11. Indian security expert based at international think tank in New Delhi. Summer 2016 and Winter 2017.
12. Indian security and international relations expert based at a think tank in New Delhi. Summer 2016.
13. Indian maritime security expert based at government think tank in New Delhi. Summer 2016 and Fall 2017.
14. Indian maritime security experts based at a government think tank in New Delhi. Summer 2016.
15. Indian foreign and security policy expert based at a government think tank in New Delhi. Summer 2016 and Winter 2017.
16. Foreign Defense Attachés based in Foreign Embassies in New Delhi. Summer 2016.

17. Expert on Asian maritime security working for American government. Shanghai. Fall 2016.
18. Expert on Asian security based in European security think tank. Beijing Spring 2017.
19. American think tank expert on Indian security. Phone interview. Beijing Fall 2017.
20. Expert on the Indian Military. New Delhi. 2018..
21. Expert on Indian Security based at a government think tank in New Delhi. New Delhi, 2018.
22. Expert on South Asian connectivity based at a New Delhi think tank. New Delhi, 2018.
23. Expert on the Indian Navy based at a New Delhi think tank. New Delhi. 2018.

Chinese Security Experts

24. Chinese professor of international security at leading Beijing university. Beijing 2016–2017 academic year.
25. Chinese professor of international security at leading Beijing university. Beijing 2016–2017 academic year.
26. Chinese professor of international security at leading Beijing university. Beijing 2016–2017 academic year.
27. Chinese professor of international political economy at leading Beijing university. Beijing 2016–2017 academic year.
28. Professor of Chinese studies at American university. Shanghai 2016–2017 academic year.
29. Chinese professor of international political economy at leading Beijing university. Beijing 2016–2017 academic year.
30. Chinese maritime security specialist based at Chinese government think tank. Beijing 2016–2017 academic year.
31. Chinese professor of international security at leading Beijing university. Beijing 2016–2017 academic year.
32. Chinese professor of international security at leading Beijing university. Beijing 2016–2017 academic year.
33. Chinese maritime security specialist based at Chinese government think tank. Beijing 2016–2017 academic year.

34. Chinese maritime security specialist based at Chinese government think tank. Beijing 2016–2017 academic year.
35. American think tank expert on Chinese security. Phone interview. Beijing 2016–2017 academic year.
36. Independent American security expert on China. Phone interview. Beijing 2016–2017 academic year.
37. American Department of Defense Political Military Advisor. Phone interview. Beijing 2016–2017 academic year.
38. Former American Defense Attaché Beijing. 2016–2017 and Phone interview. Beijing 2017–2018 Academic years.
39. Retired American General. Beijing and phone interview. 2016–2017 and 2017–2018 academic years.
40. Influential American security expert. Phone interview. Beijing 2016–2017 academic year.
41. Professor of Chinese maritime security. Phone interview. Beijing 2016–2017 academic year.
42. Professor of Chinese maritime security. Phone interview. Beijing 2016–2017 academic year.
43. American military official in China. Beijing. 2016–2017 academic year.
44. Chinese professor of international security at leading Beijing university. Beijing 2016–2017 academic year.
45. Chinese professor of international security at leading Beijing university. Beijing 2016–2017 academic year.
46. Chinese professor of international security at leading Beijing university. Beijing 2016–2017 academic year.
47. Chinese maritime security specialist based at Chinese government think tank. Beijing 2016–2017 academic year.
48. American professor of international relations with expertise on China. Beijing. 2016–2017 academic year.
49. Chinese security scholar based in top Beijing university. 2016–2017 academic year.
50. Chinese maritime security scholar based at top Beijing university. 2018.
51. Chinese security scholar based at top Beijing university. 2018.
52. Chinese security scholar based at top Beijing university. 2018.

53. Australian maritime security expert based at top Australian university. Sydney Australia. Summer 2017.
54. Australian China security expert based at top Australian university. Canberra Australia. Summer 2017.
55. Australian Asian security expert based at top Australian university. Canberra Australia. Summer 2017.
56. American Chinese security scholar based in Washington D.C. Winter 2017.
57. American analyst of Chinese maritime security. Washington D.C. Winter 2017.
58. Chinese maritime security expert based in a top Beijing university. Beijing. 2018.
59. Chinese security expert based in a top Beijing University. Beijing. 2018.
60. Chinese maritime security expert based in a top Beijing university. Beijing. 2018.
61. Chinese security expert based in a top Beijing university. 2018.

Index

For the benefit of digital users, indexed terms that span two pages (e.g., 52–53) may, on occasion, appear on only one of those pages.

Note: Graphs, Models, Diagrams, Maps and Charts have been specified as "*f*" preceded by the locator; Tables, boxes and notes are indicated by *t*, *b*, and n following the page number

Printed in the USA
CPSIA information can be obtained
at www.ICGtesting.com
CBHW061644201223
2787CB00009B/7

9 780192 865595